The Hopeless, Hapless and Helpless Manager

Further explorations in the psychology of managerial incompetence

Adrian Furnham is the author of:

The Economic Mind
The Protestant Work Ethic
Personality at Work
Consumer Profiles
Biodata
Corporate Assessment
Business Watching
Why Psychology?
The New Economic Mind
The Myths of Management
The Psychology of Behaviour at Work
The Psychology of Managerial Incompetence
Children as Consumers
The Psychology of Money
All in the Mind, The Essence of Psychology
The Psychology of Managerial Incompetence
Personality and Social Behaviour
Body Language at Work
Lay Theories
Assessing Potential

The Hopeless, Hapless and Helpless Manager

Further explorations in the psychology
of managerial incompetence

ADRIAN FURNHAM
Professor of Psychology, University College London

with the assistance of
SURGEON CAPTAIN RICK JOLLY RN(RTD)

W
WHURR PUBLISHERS
LONDON AND PHILADELPHIA

© 2000 Whurr Publishers Ltd
First published 2000
by Whurr Publishers Ltd
19b Compton Terrace
London N1 2UN England and
325 Chestnut Street, Philadelphia PA 19106 USA

British Library Cataloguing in Publication Data

A catalogue record for this book
is available from the British Library.

ISBN 1 86156 161 X

Printed and bound in the UK by Athenaeum Press Ltd,
Gateshead, Tyne & Wear.

Contents

Preface   ix
Introduction   xiii

Millennium management myopia   1
  Accident proneness   1
  Alternative management   7
  Amateurism and credentialism: two wrongs don't make a right   9
  Apostles and terrorists: the anatomy of customer loyalty   12
  The basic requirements of management   14
  Biting the bullet: what to do with a poor performer   18
  Body language at work   21
  Business babble and political correctness   26
  Business travel   29
  The career: a typology of careers   35
  Charging like a wounded bull: how to become a consultant   40
  Charity as revenge   43
  Cleanliness, godliness and shareholder returns   45
  Continuing management education   47
  Compromising at work: the art of the trade-off   50
  Cowardice: the pusillanimous manager   53
  Creating the right impression   55
  The detrimental effects of rewards   57
  Electronic mail   60
  Emotional intelligence   62
  Evaluating others: see, speak and hear no evil   65
  Evidence-based management   69
  Exceeding with excess   71
  Growing managers: sowing the seeds of success   74

Hooked on the Web   75
Just do it!   79
Knowing customer needs; what the public really wants   82
Laughter is the best medicine   84
Male hubris or female humility?   86
Management trainers   88
Managing call centres   91
Motivating the workforce   95
Organobabble   98
Outsourcing in HR   100
Pile them high and sell them cheap   102
The primacy and recency effect   105
Professional types: the four worlds of the professional   106
The psychology of absenteeism   109
Queuing at airports   113
Rating companies   115
Reactions to training   117
Revenue up and cost down: two management styles   119
Seminal experiences: a really good seminar   121
Sour feedback   123
Span of control   125
The sweet smell of success: ambient scent and   129
    consumer reactions
Time-filling strategies of the underemployed   132
TIPS: a form of performance-related pay?   135
Trainability: what you see is what you get   137
Unacceptable behaviour   140
What to do when the consultants come in   141
Working for monsters   143

Testimonial truths   147
Adaptability   147
Alcohol   148
Common sense   149
Courage and stamina   151
Effectiveness   151
Integrity   154
Intelligence   157
Leadership   159

Organization/management ability   161
Personal qualities   163
Power of expression   171
Professional knowledge   173
Reliability   175
Tact and cooperation   177
Zeal and initiative   180

Quizzes, questionnaires and quandaries   183
The bogus quiz   183
Brainstorms   187
Common sense in management   189
Decision-making styles   193
Ethics at work   196
EQ   200
The impostor syndrome   203
Money madness   205
Music while you work   209
Personality and being pissed off at work   212
Schadenfreude   214
Teleworking   218

For Benedict: Without whose help this book would have been finished
in half the time

Preface

A couple of years ago I wrote a book entitled *The Psychology of Managerial Incompetence*. I, and my publisher, were rather taken by surprise by the immediate success and almost rave reviews of the book. It was quoted on national radio and received positive reviews in all the broadsheets.

The Times review began 'A book certain to commend itself to whingeing workforces everywhere is headed for the bestseller lists'. The *Independent* took a similar line: 'A new book will gladden the heart of every downtrodden employee ... it seeks to explain why so many managers mess things up.' Specialist magazines such as *People Management* noted: 'Personnel and training professionals of a nervous disposition should avoid the temptation to look up their sections without a stiff drink to hand.'

And *Accountancy* commented: 'The lunacies that pass for normal management behaviour are pinned down with enormous accuracy and insight. This book should be every middle manager's *vade-mecum*. And as it is clad in a suitably academic cover it will pass as a serious book in any board meeting. But inside it is Dilbert. It is a dictionary of Dilbert's world.'

But my aim was not to belittle managers who frequently do a difficult and poorly rewarded job for which they are rarely properly trained. My aim was to provide something of an antidote to all the hype written about management and even, in a small way, proffer a little advice.

At the end of an interview on the BBC about the book, a quick-witted and sceptical interviewer bowled the inevitable googly. 'All right,' he said in a 'let-him-have-it-way', 'in the remaining 12 seconds can you say what you need to do to prevent incompetence?' In a flash I gave the standard answer about assessment, selection and training, and said: 'Managers are like all employees, for they need two things: challenge and support. They need to be set clear, explicit, attainable, realistic targets so that they are challenged to give of their best and get the most out of their people. They also need support in all its forms: informational, technical, social and emotional. They need regular feedback, a forum to hear their concerns and the tools to finish the job. Too much challenge and no support leads to stress; too much support and no challenge means neither manager nor his/her staff achieve their potential; and absence of both means he or she is effectively unmanaged. So, if one does nothing else, provide optimal challenge and support.'

That was enough for my 12 seconds but I believe what I said. I believe managers, management gurus and management writers all need challenging in two senses. They need to be confronted and required to explain both their actions and odd ideas. Management gurus in particular are prone to daft notions that need to be examined seriously before they are taken on board. But they also need challenging in the sense that they need to be given goals, objectives and targets that will help develop them and their staff. Too many managers languish in an odd world of little or no feedback, mainly because of poor appraisal.

Their strengths, weaknesses and potential need careful and continual appraisal to make sure that what they are asked to do is well within their capabilities. They need to be nurtured, not forgotten.

This book, like the first one, is aimed primarily at managers. It is not meant to celebrate *schadenfreude* at their expense. It takes a critical and sideways look at management issues and practices. One can learn from mistakes – particularly those of others – and much can be said through the medium of humour.

This book is divided into three sections:

1. *Millennium management myopia*: The first section of the book somewhat pretentiously talks of millennium management issues. This section is not unlike the entries in the previous book, *The Psychology of Managerial Incompetence*. There are around 50 entries of varying depth, length and style which attempt an analysis of contemporary issues.

2. *Testimonial truths*: The second section is a series of extracts from testimonials and references on incompetent managers. Although pithy and funny, what is most alarming about these is that they are not fabrications. Each was obtained by Surgeon Captain Rick Jolly of the Royal Marines who scoured naval reports for evidence of incompetence. The only changes made have been to rephrase them slightly in management- rather than military-speak to protect the innocent.

3. *Quizzes, questionnaires and quandaries*: The third section is designed to help in the process of self-assessment. Tests, in this section, cannot boast careful psychometric validation work. The tests are clearly much more appropriate for personal development and reflection than for actuarial predictions.

This book is meant to be dipped into. It may help those who are drifting into incompetence to climb out of the mire; it may even assist those managed by the helpless, hopeless and hapless to deal with their plight slightly better. But the primary aim is to entertain and, if possible, educate ... what those who deal in infomercials call edutainment.

   Enjoy!

Adrian Furnham
London
Autumn 1999

Introduction

Just as the psychological sections of libraries have 200–300 times as many books on depression as they do on happiness, so the business literature has the opposite problem. Shelves of business books boast successful techniques and remedies to intractable problems. Business biographies are all about swash-buckling heroes, brilliant investors and hard-working 'little people' whose sheer ability and technique lead to success. Business history is indeed written by victors.

Just as the tiniest part of the clinical psychology section of the well-stocked library is dedicated to happiness and adjustment, so cowering in the corner of the business section are those few books on management failure, derailments and incompetence. If it's true that one learns most from one's mistakes, then not a lot is to be learnt from popular business books.

Part of the problem lies in the books themselves. On my shelves next to the *Ten Day MBA* is *The One-Minute Manager*. Acquiring management knowledge and developing skills is portrayed as effortlessly simple – indeed, fun. It inappropriately raises the expectations of managers themselves and those who appoint them.

This book is about the dark side of management – it is about incompetence rather than competence. It is about undereducated, misinformed, pusillanimous, egocentric and fundamentally deluded human beings that end up being managers. They cause misery and poverty to thousands.

The world is replete with curious behavioural paradoxes – the dieters who get fat; the gamblers who want to lose; the successful who seemingly deliberately cause their own downfall.

One of the most common paradoxes is managerial incompetence. The paradox is that incompetence is held up as a model of excellence. Incompetence, not its opposite, leads to success in certain organizations.

Stifling, inefficient, constipated bureaucracy is still modelled in certain companies and sectors. The bureaucratically competent (and, by definition, incompetent) manager can rise up the greasy pole precisely because their management style is approved of and culturally sanctioned.

So, what are the signs of paradoxical incompetence? How does one achieve this status? Consider the following dozen traits of this dubious style of management.

1. *Diffuse responsibility*: It is essential to ensure that should anything go wrong you personally cannot be held responsible. So, form a committee of those with little else to do – namely, aspirant incompetent managers. Send e-mails and memos requiring that ideas and proposals are received and therefore accepted. It is better to prepare for cock-ups than ensure you can take unique credit for success.

2. *Delegate but don't empower*. Duties and responsibilities, particularly for dreary or risky activities, should be seen to fall clearly on others ... other departments, rival agencies, outside suppliers, even ambitious colleagues, and particularly one's own staff. The secret is to give them responsibility but without the actual power to do a good job.

3. *Expand your empire*: Grow your own department. There are many good reasons for this wasteful, self-aggrandizing strategy. First, the more people you have in your department (under you), the more elevated your title has to be according to the span-of-control principle. Second, in lean times, you can easily afford to cut a few out, so getting selfless hero-points but without any significant loss. Big is beautiful, powerful, successful.

4. *Never underspend your budget*, but pretend to be lean and mean. The essential principle here is to be modestly profligate while seeming to be the precise opposite. Remember that sending yourself on interesting conferences abroad is in the training budget, and buying an expensive computer for the home comes under innova-

tive IT solutions. Spend highly but secretively while talking a good game about underfunded, shoestring activities.

5. *Shun measurement around targets*: Never, ever, set clear, measurable targets or risk being objectively caught out by agreeing to have any 'objective' criteria of success measure. The favourite criteria are time, money, and customer response, and they could include many things such as measures of quantity and quality. Remember that useful phrase: 'What can be measured isn't important ... what is important can't be measured.' But do not hesitate to impose measurement on others. Remember that what you do is utterly unique and beyond simple and misleading measurement systems.

6. *Make a virtue out of stability*: Praise continuity and tradition; avoid change and innovation. Remember the concept of precedent, the phrase 'an interesting but alas premature idea' and 'we tried that before and it failed miserably'. Devise and practise ways to humiliate young, bright, innovators. Change is anxiety-provoking and threatens the status quo ... reason enough to oppose it.

7. *Pace yourself*: Eschew freneticism and any sense of urgency. As all good actors know, timing is everything. Although it is crucial to look busy, even stressed, don't accept deadlines, although you may quite happily impose them on others. Never concede to the obsessive desire to do things in a shorter and shorter time, and of necessity have a string of stories about how impulsivity is a recipe for disaster. The hare and the tortoise, after all, is an excellent fable to recount on occasions when you are asked to 'speak up'.

8. *Never, ever, take risks*: Bureaucracy is not about celebrating success but about avoiding failure. The steady-as-you-go philosophy means never being first with an idea. Let someone else be the guinea-pig. The risk-taking type might have occasional star-bursts of success but may fizzle out, whereas the cautious, one-foot-at-a-time type rises slowly and inexorably up the organization. Learn a vocabulary of derogatory terms for the risk-seeker, such as puerile sensation-seekers, dangerously deluded. Be cautious and guarded in all things.

9. *Put everything on paper, carefully and legalistically*: Cover your arse with good records. Remember to phrase delicate or difficult points very sensitively so that at a later time uncomfortable truths are not revealed. Records are power. If you keep better track of things than

your peers, you win arguments and vindicate actions. This does not mean establishing smart IT tracking systems – God forbid – but rather taking minutes of all meetings, documenting sign-offs, and so on. Never agree anything without it being put on paper. And have a legal mind and turn of phrase on everything. Beware multiple meanings and serious commitments recorded on paper.

10. *Establish protocol, procedures, rules and systems*: Of course, this is at the heart of all bureaucracy, but don't use words such as rules and procedures as they merely come back to bite you. You must, however, ensure that everybody follows your systems and guidelines, which are designed for quite specific purposes, such as to put off enquirers, scare off critics and baffle outsiders. It is true that people like an orderly, stable and predictable world, and that is what systems are there for. For every new technology and activity, we need a system and a protocol to ensure that it is used uniformly and correctly throughout the organization.

11. *Communicate nothing of real importance*: Knowledge is power; secrets are a resource. Never explain, never apologize, but communicate constantly. There is an art to constantly saying little of importance and letting out important facts in ways that render them unrecognizable. Open communication is the deadly enemy of all Sir Humphreys because it opens the path to powerlessness and exposure. Remember all sorts of talk about official secrets, the importance of confidentiality and the power of secret societies. Talking of which, consider joining the most famous for extra influence in certain circles.

12. *Consult through and with committees*: Committees are wonderful devices to find out things. They may even be used as private focus groups. They can diffuse responsibility (see point 1), and create the illusion of industry (see point 7). They are deeply conservative and nearly always inefficient. They are ideal for social loafing while appearing moderately democratic.

The above dozen behaviours are the hallmark of paradoxical incompetence; the stuff of all that is wrong with slow, backward-looking, public-sector, bureaucratic management. But don't kid yourself that it is dead. Indeed, the now-dated joke comes to mind:

Question: 'What is the difference between *Jurassic Park* and incompetent managers?'

Answer. 'Incompetent managers live in a theme-park of dinosaurs; *Jurassic Park* is a film made by Stephen Spielberg.'

The 'theory of incompetence'

Managerial incompetence is, alas, self-fulfilling. Managerial skills are not much different from social skills in general. And the academic literature on the aetiology and 'cure' of social inadequacy can tell us much about managerial incompetence.

People with social difficulties – like incompetent managers – tend to be sad, bad or mad. To consider these one at a time:

Sad: The sad, inadequate manager is often one who is prone to depression and self-pity. Many have a fine future behind them and probably will never reach their potential. Colleagues and schoolmates poring over photographs often remark of the sad, incompetent managers that, although they clearly had some promise, it was never reached. They may turn to pharmacological or psychological solutions to their sorry state, but with little success.

Bad: Some inadequate and incompetent managers are bad in the moral sense. The bully, the selfish, egotistical bastard and the psychopath are all well known in the managerial dungeons of notoriety. These managers often succeed in the short run. Indeed, it is a sad fact that some also succeed in the long run, threatening the happy myth that good wins out in the end. They can succeed in some companies in particular sectors during specific phases of the economic cycle. But they rarely last.

Mad: Some incompetent managers simply become deranged over time. They live in a fantasy world where they think they are successful, adaptive, healthy individuals. They start by believing their own press statements and strictly censoring negative feedback. They may develop a whole range of neurotic and psychotic symptoms before anyone seriously thinks of men in white coats.

Figure 1 shows how the pattern develops, and its consequences.

The 'theory' goes like this. Parenthetically, it should be explicitly stated that in management science a theory is really nothing more than a set of boxes loosely and even randomly connected by arrows.

The vicious circle starts with the poor soul low in managerial ability who finds him- or herself in the role of the manager. How, one legitimately and reasonably asks, can that occur? People with little or no

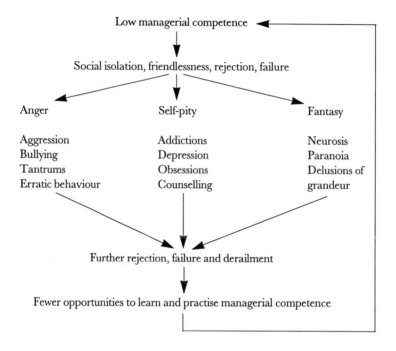

Figure 1: The cause and consequence of managerial incompetence (MI). So the cycle spirals down. The helpless, hapless and hopeless manager simply becomes more so.

talent are often appointed to managerial positions for a number of reasons:

- *Buggin's turn*: people who have done their time at lower levels deserve to be promoted, irrespective of their training, ability or motivation.
- *Peter principle*: people will be promoted until extreme incompetence is manifest.
- *Poor selection*: little or no serious data have been gathered on the individual; any data are of low quality, or simply ignored.
- *The triumph of hope over experience*: the admission that the candidate has little ability but it is hoped that it will be 'picked up' as he or she progresses (to wreck the department).
- *Reverse discrimination*: the appointment of individuals on criteria unrelated to their ability or potential.

There are probably many other reasons for this state of affairs. The situation, then, is that the hopeless, hapless and helpless manager is appointed. Soon the incompetence is manifest – to immediate reporting staff and customers, if not to senior management – and the manager tends to become socially isolated. They experience rejection and may get a (deserved) reputation as a failure. They experience friendlessness as no one wants to be associated with them.

How does the incompetent manager cope with failure or rejection? Coping skills are a good index of managerial quality. A good manager enlists help; attempts some self-study; and elicits and acts on feedback. But the incompetent manager seems to choose one of three paths. The first route is *to blame everybody else*. The incompetent takes out his or her rage on anyone at hand, in or out of the workplace. They may bully others where charm would work better. Certainly, moodiness, unpredictable rages and child-like tantrums are in part evidence of the frustrated incompetent manager. This is not the manifestation of occasional severe work stress but a chronic condition resulting from not having the appropriate skills and abilities to do the job well ... and knowing it.

The second reaction to rejection and failure lies in *self-pity*. It is amazing what a bottle of Chardonnay at lunch-time does to one's sense of failure. Prozac is even better. The self-pitying manager seeks solace in drugs, comfort foods and possibly counselling. They rarely confront their problems directly or make concerted serious efforts to acquire the necessary skills or abilities, but sink into a helpless state of requiring comfort.

The third response is clearly the most pathological. Faced with consistent evidence of failure, some become *paranoid*, which is the first phase of this disorder; the second phase is delusions of grandeur. Why is everyone against you? Why, because you have a secret they want, or because they are secretly jealous of you. Some managers can live in a state of serious delusion for long periods of time.

The trouble with these three inappropriate coping strategies is that they exacerbate the problem rather than solve it. They lead to further rejection and estrangement and inevitably fewer opportunities to learn and practise managerial skills. It is a stereotypical vicious, as opposed to virtuous, cycle.

Managers as fashion victims

The stereotypical fashion victim is an insecure, teenage groupie desperate to show that they are part of the in-group. Prepared to forgo all particular personal comfort, a sense of decency and decorum and, most of all, individuality – they pay considerable sums of money for items of clothing with little intrinsic value and massive in-built disposability.

The middle-aged, middle manager is often in the same boat. Although management issues change little, like the clothing industry, managers are encouraged to pay attention to the latest fashions, which they are assured solve all problems. They come and go, get rediscovered, forgotten, repackaged. Most offer quick-fix answers to pressing problems. They offer the magic bullet key solutions to insoluble and intractable problems.

- *Fads in planning.* One of the fashionable ideas is strategic alliance, which means that companies co-operate, as in forming a joint venture, often across national boundaries. Airlines, telecommunications companies and car manufacturers do this, and the trend is growing. Strategic planning is a little out of fashion now, but crystal gazing is still popular.
- *Fads in organizing. Corporate culture* refers to the values and beliefs shared by employees and the general patterns of their behaviour. Some believe that if this is planned, designed and controlled correctly then all the ills of the organization will be solved. An 'in-idea' remains restructuring, which is often no more than an excuse to remove layers of expensive middle managers. Another current popular idea is demassing, or down- or right-sizing, which is a euphemism for laying off employees or demoting managers, usually middle managers.
- *Fads in staffing.* Organizations have to be staffed by people who are not only competent but also healthy. This requires wellness or fitness programmes and the management of stress. It has also to do with selection for diversity and other unsubstantiated ideas.
- *Paying for performance.* Paying for performance is also currently fashionable. This means measuring the contributions of individuals and rewarding them accordingly, although the problems of measuring performance are often overlooked.

- *Fads in leading.* An *intrapreneur* is a person who acts like an entrepreneur but does so within the organizational environment. Intrapreneurs have been described as 'those who take hands-on responsibility for creating innovation of any kind within an organization'. Organizations are meant to chase and foster these people.
- *Fads in controlling. Quality circles,* widely used in Japan, are seen as a way of improving quality and making US products more competitive by finding better ways of working.

I have listed some of these fads (see Table 1) that have appeared over the years. In themselves fads are not particularly harmful; they may even be helpful. The problem lies in their over-application to the point of exclusionary fanaticism.

What do managers do?

Unless they have attended business school, there is a fair chance that the exasperated and frustrated, newly appointed manager has been heard to exclaim 'but they never trained me to be a manager'. Most managers are appointed to managerial rank after 'doing time' among the troops. They may or may not show any management potential and are equally unlikely to be given any formal induction or training. Some may have been fortunate because they themselves were well managed and had therefore at least the opportunity to see a good model.

Very few organizations take management and leadership seriously. The military and the civil service may be exceptions, but they tend to be rather constipated both in their training and in the conception of management duties and requirements.

One very obvious but not always clearly answered question is what do managers do? The Canadian expert in this area, Henry Mintzberg, made some simple but crucial observations nearly 25 years ago. He distinguished between folklore and fact concerning management work:

- *Folklore:* Managers are reflective systematic planners.
  Fact: Managers work at an unrelenting pace; their activities are characterized by brevity, variety and discontinuity, and most of them dislike reflection.
- *Folklore:* Effective managers have no regular duties to perform.

Table 1: Five decades of management fads

Decade	Buzzword	Fad
1950s	Computerization	Installing corporate mainframe computers
	Theory Z	Giving people more say in their work so they will produce more
	Quantitative management	Running an organization by numbers
	Diversification	Countering ups and downs in the business cycle by buying other businesses
	Management by objectives	Setting managerial goals through negotiation
1960s	T-groups	Teaching managers interpersonal sensitivity by putting them in encounter seminars
	Centralization/ decentralization	Letting headquarters make the decisions/ letting middle managers make the decisions
	Matrix management	Assigning managers to different groups according to the task
	Conglomeration	Putting various types of business under a single corporate umbrella
		Determining whether a manager's chief concern is people or production
1970s	Zero-based budgeting	Budgeting without reference to the previous year's numbers
	Experience curve	Generating profit by cutting prices, gaining market share and efficiency
	Portfolio management	Ranking businesses as 'cash cows', 'stars', or 'dogs'
1980s	Theory Z	Adopting such techniques as quality circles and job enrichment
	Intrapreneuring	Encouraging managers to create and control entrepreneurial projects within the corporation
	Demassing	Trimming the workforce and demoting managers
	Restructuring	Getting rid of lines of business that aren't performing, often while taking on considerable debt
	Corporate culture	Defining an organization's style in terms of its values, goals, rituals and heroes
	One-minute manager	Balancing praise and criticism of workers in 60-second conferences
	Management by walking around	Leaving the office to visit workstations instead of relying on written reports for information
1990s	TQM (total quality management)	Concentrating on producing high-quality (no reject) products and services
	Re-engineering	Restructuring the organization from scratch, based on an understanding of function
	De-layering/'rightsizing'	Cutting out layers of middle management to produce flatter organizations
	Empowerment	Pushing down responsibility to lower levels in the organization

Fact: Managers have many ritualistic, ceremonial and negotiation duties.

- *Folklore*: Managers need and use management information system aggregated data.
  Fact: Managers favour the oral medium.
- *Folklore*: Management is (becoming) a science and a profession.
  Fact: Much still depends on intuition and the personal judgement of managers.

Mintzberg observed that managerial work encompasses 10 roles. Almost all roles include activities that could be construed as leadership – influencing others towards a particular goal. In addition, most of these roles can apply to non-managerial positions as well as managerial ones. However, the role approach is more compatible with the situation approach and has been shown to be more valid than either the behavioural or trait perspective.

- *Figurehead*: The manager, acting as a symbolic representative of the organization, performs diverse ceremonial duties. By attending Chamber of Commerce meetings, heading the local charity drive or representing the chairman of the firm at an awards banquet, a manager performs the figurehead role. Inadequate managers either don't do this or do it badly. Further, being a figurehead means that one is in the limelight and inadequacies and incompetences may be very easily exposed.
- *Leader*: The manager interacting with subordinates performs this role. This role emphasizes the socioemotional and people-oriented side of leadership. Managers need EQ and IQ: people skills and task-related skills. Having a dearth of both – as is the case with some incompetent managers – is, alas, a situation of no hope.
- *Liaison*: The manager establishes a network of contacts to gather information for the organization. Belonging to professional associations or meeting over lunch with peers in other organizations helps the manager perform the liaison role. Alas, the incompetent manager is soon spotted by others in the professional association and quickly shunned.
- *Monitor*: The manager gathers information from the environment inside and outside the organization. The manager may attend

meetings with his or her subordinates, scan company publications or participate in company-wide committees as a way of performing this role. Many incompetent managers talk too much in meetings. Others don't understand technical reports. Some are just plain lazy so they are quickly seriously out of date. The really bad ones did not even do the work of the blackboard monitor well in third form.

- *Disseminator.* The manager transmits both factual and attitudinal information to subordinates. Managers may conduct staff meetings, send memoranda to their staff or meet informally with them on a one-to-one basis to discuss current and future projects. Incompetent managers can communicate. They need to be succinct, clear and inspirational. In fact, they are often the precise opposite – long-winded, incoherent and deadly dull. And some are as likely to be a dissimulator of the truth as a disseminator.

- *Spokesperson*: The manager gives information to people outside the organization about its performance and policies. The manager who oversees preparation of the annual report, prepares advertising copy, or speaks at community and professional meetings fulfils this role. Spokespeople are carefully chosen. They have to look and sound good. They need to appreciate the strength of each of the media and the agenda of each audience they are talking to. Often the incompetent manager understands neither.

- *Entrepreneur.* The manager designs and initiates change in the organization. The supervisor who redesigns the job of subordinates, introduces flexible working hours or brings new technology to the job performs this role. Incompetents are often change-averse. They are threatened by change and innovation. Entrepreneurs or intrapreneurs are also talented people. Being unable or unwilling to spot or use opportunities to innovate is certainly the hallmark of the incompetent manager.

- *Disturbance handler.* The manager deals with problems that arise when organizational operations break down. A person who finds a new supplier for an out-of-stock part at short notice, who replaces unexpectedly absent employees, or who deals with machine breakdowns, performs this role. Incompetent managers are not so much disturbance handlers as disturbance creators; not 'Mr Fix-it' so much as 'Mr Cause-it'.

- *Resource allocator.* The manager controls the allocation of people, money, materials and time by scheduling his or her own time, programming subordinates' work efforts, and authorizing all significant decisions. Preparation of the budget is a major aspect of this role. Balancing the budget is more than a money issue. A good manager is really a resource creator and allocator. An incompetent manager is unaware of the resources he or she has or needs.

● *Negotiator.* The manager participates in negotiation activities. A manager who hires a new employee may negotiate work assignments or compensation with that person. The incompetent manager is more likely to be a bully and an intransigent nay-sayer than a good negotiator.

Millennium management myopia

Accident proneness

British statistics in the early 1990s showed that around 500 people are killed each year in accidents at work, compared with 5000 or more fatal accidents on the road and another 5000 in the home. These figures suggest that work is relatively safe. Work is more organized and better regulated than domestic activities or driving.

But less than 40% of the population are exposed to the risks of work, and the working population does not include those people who are most at risk – the very young, the very old and the infirm. Most people work during the relatively safe daylight hours and when they are more or less fully alert; and people are more likely to be at risk because of the influence of drink and drugs away from the working environment. Taking these factors into account, work is surprisingly dangerous.

Recent facts, published by the Health and Safety Executive (1997), are enlightening:

- In 1995 British trade unions secured £304m for workplace injuries.
- One hospital worker recently received £235 000 for back injuries suffered while at work.
- Recent careful case studies in pretty typical organizations showed that one spent 37% of annualized profits on accident compensation; while another lost 5% of its running costs directly to accidents.
- In all, 8% of accidents at work were judged to have the potential for serious consequences such as fatalities, multiple injury or catastrophic loss.

- While accident insurance covers injury, ill-health and damage, there are many important, accountable costs such as legal costs, production delays, overtime working, fines, use of temporary labour and so on.
- Figures from the 1990s show that 1.1 million people per year in Britain sustained a workplace injury.
- 30 million days were lost annually on average, costing about £700m.
- The overall cost of work accidents and work-related ill-health is estimated to be between £4000 and £9000 per event.
- It is even suggested that 1.75–2.75% of the country's gross domestic product is spent on issues relating to accidents.

Although some employers seem to believe that complying with health and safety legislation is a cost and a drain on their budget, there is evidence that the reverse is true. *Accident costs exceed prevention costs.* Prevention costs include: safety materials and hardware, clothing and equipment, guards, communication and publicity campaigns, training time and maintenance, ongoing inspection and auditing effort, coordination and decision-making time, and support staff costs. But it remains difficult to persuade some employers to adopt safety procedures.

There are two principal ways of looking at the accident problem:

- *Theory A*: Accidents are caused by unsafe behaviour (and some people are more prone to behave unsafely than others). Accidents may therefore be prevented by changing the ways in which people behave. This is the concern primarily of personality and social psychology. This focuses on individuals.
- *Theory B*: Accidents are caused by unsafe systems of work. Accidents can therefore be prevented by redesigning the working system. This is the approach taken by cognitive psychologists and ergonomists. This focuses on systems.

As may be expected, older people have fewer accidents. Job-related experience seems to be most relevant to accident rate, although the effects of number of years in industry and of number of hours worked on a specific task (where the job involves a number of tasks) can also be demonstrated.

The relationship of physical and anthropometric differences to accident susceptibility has also been shown in many specific tasks. For example, the following physical attributes will tend to increase accident-proneness:

- Colour blindness – where colour distinction is important in the task. There are certain jobs, for example being a pilot, from which colour-blind individuals are excluded.
- Extremes of height and reach. Very tall people bump into things, whereas very short people may not have the required reach. Size is also related to strength.
- Slimness of arms, wrists or fingers (which could slip through safety gates, and so on). Hence, there are issues regarding the use of certain equipment by children.
- Epilepsy, where fits may be unpredictable and uncontrollable.

Some people do have a lot of accidents: the clumsy child; the forgetful adult; the poorly co-ordinated teenager. This concept of the accident-prone person originated when it was discovered that a small percentage of the population had a high percentage of accidents. Obviously, it is not true that some individuals are more prone than others to all types of accidents, nor, of course, are *all* (or even most) accidents sustained by a small, fixed group of people. But *people drive as they live* – that is, there are consistencies of behaviour (in response to particular stimuli) which suggest that they may be related to accidents. For instance, one researcher observed bus driver habits and by using behavioural measures such as unusual manoeuvres, near misses, ratios of rear-mirror usage to manoeuvres, of being overtaken to overtaking and so on, he found that definite classes of drivers could be identified.

Studies from First World War munitions factories showed that a small number of people had a disproportionately large share of accidents. Researchers asked why. Was this due to physical or psychological characteristics; specific to a job or more general; a permanent or transient effect; due to greater risk exposure; because having one accident may increase the likelihood of another; due to biases in reporting?

First, there is little evidence of the relationship between accidents and intelligence. People with defective vision are found to be accident prone in some (but not all) working situations. Accident-prone people perform significantly less well in a complex experimental task involving divided attention. Interestingly, accident-free steelworkers tended to be more popular than accident repeaters (that is, more extrovert and outgoing). Those *actively* involved in accidents have higher absenteeism rates than those *passively* involved or not involved. Not surprisingly, accident-prone individuals also take more risks and think the work is less dangerous.

By chance alone, a small number of individuals would be involved in many accidents. The theory of accident proneness is based on identifying *individuals* who have certain characteristics. The theory would have validity if the same individuals *repeatedly* had large numbers of accidents. Some people do fall into this category, but we do not need a theory of accident proneness to identify them.

For instance, alcoholism and drug addiction are valid predictors of accidents, and so we can reduce accidents by identifying and treating these conditions. However, on the basis of *group* data, it is fruitless to attempt to identify high-accident *individuals* without any other information.

Are accident-prone people more likely to have particular types of accidents rather than others? It is important to distinguish between personality *traits* and mood *states*. The former are stable over time (for example, neuroticism, extroversion) whereas the latter are transient. We know that psychological *states* (not personality traits) do affect accidents. For instance:

- *Influenza* can result in a *50% impairment* in a reaction-time test.
- Being over the UK alcohol limit by 5% means slower reactions and bad judgement.
- A typical worker feels 'low and miserable' for 20% of the time: 50% of accidents occur during these periods of negative mood.
- Drivers and pilots have more accidents when going through major life events (for example, divorce).
- Women are more accident prone before and during menstruation, both for active and passive accident involvement.

There are a number of studies examining the relationship between personality (particularly extroversion and neuroticism) and accidents (particularly car accidents). Despite various methodological difficulties and differences, the results are fairly consistent.

Extroverts seek excitement and stimulation whereas introverts try to avoid it. The former put the car radio *on* to improve concentration; the latter turn it *off*. Extroverts like variety, novelty and change more than introverts. They take more risks because they need stimulation. The long, straight road is tedium for the extrovert; a joy for the introvert. Being a quality controller, a security guard, or a lighthouse keeper is hell for the extrovert. So, when they are bored they do things to liven up their world ... and this leads to accidents.

The problem is even worse if the extrovert is rather emotionally unstable and prone to moodiness. And, finally, if they are young men with a lot of testosterone the combination can be lethal, as anyone observing the stereotypical 'white van driver' knows. Extroverts take risks, act impulsively and drive badly to increase excitement; neurotics react badly and erratically under stress and can easily have their attention distracted. This is why pilots are deliberately selected to be stable introverts not unstable extroverts.

Since extroverts are assumed to be less socialized than introverts, it is reasonable to assume that they should be less bound by the prescribed rules of society regarding motor vehicle operation. Therefore, they have more traffic accidents and violations than introverts. In short, they are more likely to ignore warning signals and legal requirements.

Not surprisingly, it is those types who love thrills and hate boredom that have accidents and get speeding fines. They can be found – young or old – queuing for dangerous rides at amusement centres and playing fast, aggressive video games. The need for constant new sensation is the factor that makes them so susceptible to accidents. They take needless risks, partake in dangerous sports, and are, quite simply, an insurance nightmare. In fact, not only do sensation seekers find it more difficult to get life insurance, given their hobbies and history, but they also choose not to buy it!

Thus, it seems that there is sufficient evidence that personality variables do relate to all sorts of accidents in all sorts of populations. Aggressive, impulsive, neurotic and fatalistic traits seem particularly associated with accidents. They seem to account for about 10% of the variance, which is certainly not to be dismissed. The *two independent, unrelated factors* that seem to be the *best predictors of accidents* are clearly extroversion/sensation-seeking/A-type behaviour and neuroticism/anxiety/instability.

Thus, if personality traits do relate to accidents and make people accident prone, they are these:

- *Stimulus seeking*: The more people like variety and change, prefer people to things, get bored easily, and trade speed for accuracy, the more they are likely to do things (drive fast, ignore warnings, try untried new activities) that lead to accidents.
- *Emotional instability*: The more moody, pessimistic and unhappy people are, the more likely they are to become self-absorbed or jittery and 'take their eye off the ball', which may lead to accidents.
- If they are *young, male* and *not very well educated*, as well as stimulus seeking and emotionally unstable, these people really do seem likely to be accident prone.

However, there are a great number of methodological shortcomings of research in this area which prevent the questions of the relationship between personality and accidents being fairly reviewed. These include the following:

- Accident reporting is erratic, biased, inconsistent and done for legal purposes only. Any investigation of industrial (or domestic) accidents is crucially dependent on the quality (and quantity) of accident reporting. Reporting systems might fulfil organizational, medical and legal needs but frequently not those of the ergono- mist or the industrial psychologist. Hence, they are investigated as events rather than as processes, as most measures do not provide measures of exposure.
- Retrospective studies cannot discriminate between the stress that caused the accident and the stress produced by its occurrence. There is a tremendous shortage of good longitudinal studies in the area.
- Confounding of dependent and independent variables by such practices as explaining causality by post hoc discrimination between accident and non-accident groups.
- The 'lumping' together of all sorts of accidents as if all accidents were the same. Clearly, one needs a good taxonomy of accidents in order to make prediction more clear. Thus, driving accidents may be seen to be quite different from household accidents; and accidents at work different from accidents at leisure.

● Although there is a welcome agreement over what personality variables are important in accident research, there does seem to be rather less agreement about which measures to use. Alas, this means that because different measures are used, exact comparisons cannot be made; hence, the corpus of knowledge arising is only at the rather vague conceptual stage.

Alternative management

Just as potential consumers and patients are constantly bombarded with 'new and miraculous' alternative (or complementary) therapies, potions and techniques, so the poor stressed manager is frequently offered novel management methods.

Many are encouraged to adopt 'liberation management', to do 'organizational re-engineering' or even embrace 'the Zulu principles' as the new way to corporate nirvana. Older, more established management practices must, it seems, be dispensed with. That old favourite, 'mushroom management', where workers are kept in the dark and have corporate manure shovelled on them, must go. An acceptance of the new seems to demand a complete rejection of the old.

It may be that people take up 'alternative' management precisely for the same reason that people choose complementary medicine. It is such things as lower back pain that drive the general practitioner's patient into the arms (literally) of the complementary practitioner. There is nothing like a *chronic* condition, incurable by general practitioners or specialists and their rocket-science technology, to drive the helpless, hapless and hopeless patient to seek an alternative to conventional medicine.

Moreover, complementary or alternative practitioners are warm, calming, therapeutic people who give you plenty of time because they are 'interested in the whole person'. Because there is nothing quite as interesting as ourselves, most of us are easily seduced into talking and disclosing various well-guarded secrets.

Most people are not pulled by the attraction of complementary medicine – they are *pushed* by the failure of orthodox medicine. They are hooked by the soothing balm and personal touch of the alternative practitioner, which stands in strong contrast to the cold, technical and all-too-brief interview with the GP.

Consider now the harassed, battered, CEO of a small British company desperately trying to keep afloat against strong competition. He or she knows that it is only through good management of the committed employees that survival, let alone success, depends. And yet traditional management techniques of carrot and stick, even of performance management, don't seem to be working.

Like back pain, managerial and employee incompetence seem to be chronic. And nothing much seems to change this – the disciplinary interview, a freeze on wage increases, seminars on the Nipponic, Teutonic even Franconic threat – all seem unable to do the trick. The high technology of management, such as the spreadsheet, the appraisal form, and the performance-related pay calculations, do not cure the chronic problem.

So, when the guru of alternative management comes along, the desperate manager pays attention. No longer smelling of snake-oil, alternative management gurus, like complementary medical practitioners, are polished, well dressed and sophisticated. In fact, they ape many of the practices and have similar tools to their orthodox and traditional colleagues. They may have the newest laptop computer, telephone and fax. They probably have impressive-looking certificates of less well-known qualifications from the University of the Watford Gap and – most importantly – they exude confidence.

Like complementary medical practitioners, the gurus or consultants of alternative management are interested in the *whole* business. They encourage the 'chronic sufferer', in this case the exasperated manager, to pour out his or her woes about all, and every, aspect of the business. They welcome the opportunity to counsel and it may be some time before they reveal their particular solution.

The tarot cards, crystals and essential oils of alternative management take various forms. They may involve complete restructuring of the organization, 'commitment workshops' or the pairing of mentors to subordinates.

The placebo effect works well for alternative management advocates, but like all placebos, its effects wear off and the chronic problem returns. It is a sad fact that most alternative management, like complementary medicine, is bogus, fraudulent and wrong. The principles on which it is based simply don't work in the long run.

One American consultancy called itself Lazarus because it

attempted to bring back companies from the dead. Some consultants and gurus certainly provide wacky ideas. Tom Peters told us to 'celebrate heroes and forget zeros'. Others demanded Japanese-style military PT before work. Curiously, some of the ideas and recommendations of the alternatives stick in the management lexicon, but others are soon jettisoned.

Yesterday's heresy can become today's orthodoxy. But a lot of the bird-seed of alternative management falls by the wayside. What did happen to T-groups? Management must hope that the Darwinian principle of the survival of the fittest means that what is good in alternative management gets picked up, and what is not good gets appropriately junked.

Amateurism and credentialism: two wrongs don't make a right

There are, particularly in the UK, two opposite and equally misleading theories about how to learn to become a manager. One celebrates commonsensical, experiential *amateurism*; the other training-course *credentialism*. The former believes in a paucity of formal training, the latter a plethora. Both extremes in the end make for bad managers.

The British in particular admire amateurs. Patrick Moore, the astronomer, who has no formal education, is a prototype. Some people believe that because anything can be taught, natural genius can be detected only in the untrained amateur. It is said that the 4-minute miler Roger Bannister trained at night so that nobody could see him and thus had to attribute his success to ability rather than effort. It is also a received myth that before one's final exams at Oxbridge, one should be seen drunk at parties. The idea is that any fool can get a first, if they are library swots, but only really clever people can exhibit their true genius by not working at all.

There are, however, two sides to the concept of amateur. On the one hand, the word suggests an admirer, a devotee, an enthusiast who engages in a (non-paid) pursuit for the pure intrinsic joy of the activity. The word amateur has a French etymology and is linked to the concept of love. Amateur choirs or theatrical groups can 'get away' with their less than perfect production by being simply very enthusiastic. The love of the activity is enough.

On the other hand, the word amateur can suggest unskilful, inexpert dabbling. To be described as amateurish is clearly an insult: it means crude, unsophisticated, even ignorant.

The school of management amateurism believes that with a modicum of intelligence and common sense anyone can become a manager. There is no need for further expensive education, which is seen as a waste of time and money. What needs to be learnt, this approach asserts, to become a manager is unteachable anyway. If one is able enough – that is, appropriately selected – one should be able to pick up and then refine the rudiments of management quite easily. Enthusiasm and some people skills are all one needs.

There are various examples of amateurs in the UK, particularly among the more famous entrepreneurs. Alan Sugar almost portrays himself as an oxymoronic professional barrow-boy and everyone knows that Richard Branson did not go to university.

Amateur managers and those organizations that believe in this approach can, of course, be very good. If they have been exposed to good models and have good systems to follow, the 'uneducated' manager can do quite well. However, the chances are likely to be against them. Companies and individuals who don't believe in management training are often poorly and erratically managed, don't have people management systems and are prone to the idiosyncrasies of individual managers who believe their home-spun methods and theories are best.

Precisely opposed to the amateur model is the *credentialist* approach. Technically, a credential is a title or letter that gives evidence of status or authority to the bearer. It is a sort of paper proof of competence. Credentialists are compensatory collectors of certificates. It is not uncommon to find on a manager's card five to eight sets of letters that one has never heard of. They are members, fellows and companions of all sorts of strange management organizations which seem to dish out awards on flimsy evidence of competence but good evidence of cash. They nearly always do not have degrees and certainly never an MBA, but believe that they can 'sort of' compensate for this with a raft of other credentials.

Another sign of credentialism are course-work book-trophies. These are great binders that collect dust on office shelves but are in some sense not only proof of course attendance but of skill competence. They are never referred to after the course and may not have been examined much on it, but they somehow remain evidence of know-how in the eyes of the credentialist attendee.

The credentialist company is training obsessed. It may produce catalogues of approved in-house or specialist outside courses on everything from negotiation skills to letter writing. The assumption is that no aspect of management, however mundane or trivial, can be acquired through observation or self-learning. Everything is course-worthy and there is a course for everything. Curiously, this approach believes that course attendance is sufficient in and of itself, and companies may even have elaborate charts that check off the milestones on the long and winding road of acquiring the skills.

Rarely, if ever, is it considered important by credentialists to show evidence of course efficacy, let alone relevance or cost-effectiveness. Credentialists are, however, eager to collect certificates, books and other flimflam associated with courses. And now the new universities pander to these bizarre needs by running advanced diplomas in everything from estate agency to sports management. It is easy money in the 'pile them high and sell them cheap' world of credential collection.

Some courses may be extremely useful. But it is unwise to presume that any set of letters after a person's name is indicative of any particular quality. A simple MBA and PhD is worth a dozen sets of letters, but even that may be more evidence of the ability to pass particular tests and assignments than of good management.

Neither the amateur nor the credentialist is a professional. The hallmark of professionalism is conscientious workmanship. It means that people conform to the technical and ethical standard of a vocation. The army offers a good model of professional management training. Officers go through a series of courses and exercises to learn simple but important skills. There are clear systems developed to encourage good management, including appraisal systems, skills and practices; because systems are followed, there is consistency in management over time and across different branches. The army is also less prone to following gurus' wild mood swings as they find new magic bullets in old ideas dressed up for the modern *Zeitgeist*. People have not fundamentally changed much over the past 500 years and if a management style and socialization process has been found that is efficient, there seems little reason to change it.

Indeed, the way in which people join professions through a lengthy and fairly arduous apprenticeship may be a good model for how to acquire management skills. An apprentice studies with, observes and learns from a master. This rather old-fashioned approach to learning seems to have been revived of late, with the very popular 'master-class concept' where people literally sit at the feet of a master and learn from him or her. It suggests a great hunger for a forgotten educational method. One goes to professionals because they are well trained to deliver exacting standards. Amateurs cannot do this, however enthusiastic they may be. Nor do credentialists, who are after the certificate not the learning experience. Too much or too little of a good thing (the education of managers), leads to equally unhappy consequences.

Apostles and terrorists: the anatomy of customer loyalty

What makes for a loyal and happy customer? The business world is extremely eager to ensure customer loyalty. Loyalty means repeat purchases and ensures a predictable revenue stream. Some people have calculated the lifetime value of the loyal customer, which can be astronomical. Some American pizza firms have estimated that loyalty to their brand over the adult lifetime may be worth more than £5000. Loyalty also increases referrals to other people, as well as repeat purchases of related products. The cost of attracting a new customer may be 10 times that of ensuring the customer stays loyal to the brand or service.

But what determines loyalty and how can one understand different types? Airline stories are probably the best means of understanding the true nature of customer loyalty. Everyone has the 'nightmare from hell' story: the 10-hour delay, the luggage to another continent, the breakdown in the in-flight entertainment, and the cabin crew who were rejected as traffic wardens because of their 'low charm level'.

Others tell the opposite story: the upgrade to first class, the limitless champagne, the limousine to their hotel, the major give-aways, and the free ticket for future travel. Are people in the 'nightmare from hell' irrecoverable and those relishing first-class treatment bound to give loyalty for all time?

The academic gurus have attempted to describe a taxonomy of customer types and understand the loyalty process. The real enthusiasts are sometimes called apostles or *champions*. They can be 'product bores'. One might think that they actually work for the company as they seem to remain illogically loyal to products (and services) that they really can't even differentiate from other brands. Thus, certain blended whiskies, through clever and sustained marketing, have ensured a loyal following who, under all circumstances, will insist on ordering only one blend, although in blind tastings they are quite unable to find it. They are what all companies want – the die hard enthusiasts who would, it seems, never consider changing brands.

Next are the *satisfied*. They are affectionate towards a product or service in the same way as one is affectionate towards an old car or familiar building. They are comfortable with the product. It is predictable and consistent and, quite simply, satisfies. This customer probably correctly believes that he or she could probably do better elsewhere, but the effort is not worth the gain. Rather than proselytes, these are the quietly faithful.

However, most consumers are quite rightly categorized as *indifferent*. They are the sort of people who circle 'moderately satisfied' on satisfaction measures and are not easy to please. Their indifference may result from many causes. They may be infrequent and therefore undiscriminating users of the product or service. Or it may be that the only thing that really motivates them is the price. Value-for-money people know the price of everything and the value of nothing. They seek out special offers; changing brand or service provider with little thought.

Indifference may also occur because some people feel it rather odd to be 'committed to' or 'loyal to' commercial brands. Seeing advertisements with housewives hugging soap-powder packets or roughnecks committing acts of folly for their favourite beer seems particularly odd. Watch a middle-aged man shopping from a list in a supermarket. The list says washing-up liquid and the poor innocent is confronted with myriad shapes, sizes and colours, some boasting their lemon scent, others their thickness, and still others detergent qualities. The indifferent husband simply reaches for the size container he believes is required and that is the end of it. Shop-phobics are usually the most indifferent, and many men hate shopping.

After the indifferent come the *defectors*. These are often the once faithful – the affectionate customer who received unexpected and very unwelcome poor treatment. They may be heard complaining loudly in stores and can be found practising their assertiveness techniques with bewildered staff. Defectors can be recovered slowly. They can be placated and nurtured into affectionate, even loyal, customers. But it is uncertain whether the game is worth the candle. Defectors become neurotically hypersensitive to inattentive or poor service once they have received it. Retaining the defector is a costly business.

But there is a final type characterized by nil retention and nil satisfaction – the service *terrorist*. These people are not happy with simply walking away from, or rejecting a particular brand, they want to tell the world how bad it is. They are, in a sense, apostles of the opposition; dedicated atheists not indifferent agnostics. They write to magazines documenting their 'appalling experiences'. They appear on television shows berating the top management companies, trying to intimidate shareholders. Hell, it seems, hath no fury like a customer's scorn. The 'terrorist' wants more than recompense, and once started on their mission can be difficult to stop. They can reach, and put off, hundreds of potential customers and can be a nightmare for any organization.

Fortunately, only the most dissatisfied become terrorists; but unfortunately, the opposite is also true of apostles, who are thin on the ground. What this means is that for nearly every service provider, you are, quite simply, as good as your last performance. Good reputation takes a long time to acquire and a terrifyingly short time to lose. The customer is coy and capricious ... but one does need loyalty.

Those who can remember the service profit chain idea may recall that the most direct and proximal predictor of company revenue growth and profitability was customer loyalty. Loyalty meant the three magical Rs: retention, referral and repeat business. The satisfied customer is loyal, but loyalty is always to be measured at the very upper levels of satisfaction. It is so easy to slide down the slippery slope from apostle to terrorist; from champion to destroyer of a company's reputation. No wonder there is all the hype about caring for customers.

The basic requirements of management

There have been many fashions in writing and thinking about leaders. For a very long time, it was thought that leaders had particular personality *traits* such as persuasiveness, persistence or dependability. But the list of essential features has grown over time, leading to confusion, dispute and precious little insight into how the factors work.

After the war, it became fashionable to think about *what leaders do* – their precise behaviour pattern – as opposed to what they are like. So, people thought in terms of authoritarian or democratic leaders. Others talked of country club managers who seemed concerned neither for people nor for bottom-line figures. This approach ran into problems because leaders' styles refused to fall into the neat categories that researchers had invented.

The next approach was the *situation* approach to leadership. It was argued that the abilities, qualities and skills required to be a good leader are determined primarily by the demands of each specific management situation. Naturally, the focus of this approach was to identify and categorize leadership situation characteristics, but this became rather complex.

More recent thinkers have distinguished between transformational and transactional leaders. Transactional leaders assume that they can achieve leadership and get subordinates to follow them only by offering some sort of exchange. Subordinates will follow a leader if he or she is able to offer them something that they value or need. Leadership is therefore a transaction whereby subordinates submit to the requests of the leader and follow his/her demands in return for something. Transformational leaders, on the other hand, supposedly use charisma to energize and motivate people to perform beyond their normal expectations. They do this by:

- raising their awareness about certain key outcomes or processes
- getting them to place team or organizational goals and interests above their own
- having them adjust their need levels so that they have a stronger drive for responsibility, challenge and personal growth.

One trick of understanding successful leadership is to look at failed leadership – flawed, derailed managers. Paranoid, narcissistic, dependent personalities seem poor at team building. They retaliate in subtle ways, and succeed in alienating everyone. Knowing what factors predict failure can give an insight into which factors are related to success.

To understand the real nature of leadership, however, one needs to understand the *psychological purpose* of leaders. They need both to reduce uncertainty and project a vision. They need to give people a sense of purpose and vitality – to energize and enthuse. And they need to help bring meaning to people's lives at work. In a sense, they are at once counsellor, educator, facilitator and often *in loco parentis*.

There are three central characteristics or skills that any leader needs:

Reading the signals

Leaders have to be perceptive. They need to understand their people and the business. They must read the mood, the expectations and the worries of all their stakeholders, particularly employees and customers. They must, of course, also read the markets, the budget sheets and the foibles of customers. There is a lot to be sensitive to, and different leaders rely on different data sources to read the signals.

People and markets are capricious and unstable. But there is such a thing as a *Zeitgeist*, which does endure over time. Good leaders are in tune with their times – they know how to package their vision, speak the language of their followers, and when to change what. Really good leaders are able to change the company culture and morale to fit their own needs. Some leaders are people-sensitive but market-ignorant, or vice versa. A good leader needs the intellect, the training and the insight to be both.

Engaging people

Leaders need to build teams. They need to develop and sustain a healthy corporate climate and culture. And they do this primarily by engaging people with their views, predictions and insights. It is no accident that most good leaders are, or seem to be, charming extroverts.

Good leaders know the power of praise and the need for open and regular communication. All leaders have to articulate a compelling vision of the current and future state of affairs that engages the desires and values of their immediate team and the organization as a whole. They need also to create a sense of community, belonging and identity. People need to feel not only part of, but proud to work for, the organization.

Through engaging people, leaders need to create trust and openness in work-related relationships. They must create a positive environment in which people can learn, experiment and even risk failure. Social skills, self-confidence, empathy and ambition go a long way towards helping potential leaders really engage their people.

Getting things done

The 'warm and fuzzy' or the 'analysis paralysis' leader does not get things done. One needs to push, demand action, call for progress reports, set deadlines and so on. Just do it! With a sense of urgency and purpose, it is easier to achieve co-ordinated action. Getting things done can be achieved through articulacy, and clear expectations, goals and standards. It needs to be most frequently done by judicious delegating, coaching and supporting others. Leaders need to push people to perform and give them feedback on their performance.

Being a good leader requires three out of three. One needs to be able to practise all the skills – reading the signals, engaging the people, getting things done. Not all celebrated leaders have had all three skills.

	Reading the signals	Engaging people	Getting things done
Gates	Yes	No	Yes
Roddick	Yes	No	No
Churchill	Yes	No	No
Harvey-Jones/ Tebbitt/Benn	No	Yes	No
Kennedy	No	Yes	Yes
'Just do it' CEOs	Yes	No	Yes

The real problem, of course, is all those CEOs who score No, No, No to these questions. In the short term, in times of extreme, one may get away with being a one-third, or even a two-thirds, leader. But over time, the deficits show.

The good news is that most people can be trained to acquire these skills. Equally, many leaders can appoint others around them to help with this three-pronged quest should they feel unable to do it alone.

Biting the bullet: what to do with a poor performer

Every organization has its share of employees from hell: the lazy, deluded, hypochondriac underperformer. They are difficult to manage and miserable to work with. Their productivity is low and ability to poison morale extremely high. They are, alas, always 'well entrenched' and 'management resistant'. Interestingly, their numbers in any organization have more to do with managerial pusillanimity than poor selection. That is, their existence in the organization is nearly always a result of a long line of weak managers who declined to 'bite the bullet'.

An important question for any consultant or indeed potential shareholder in any organization is how the organization deals with poor performers. Perhaps it could be asked at shareholder meetings and some evidence requested. Traditionally, HR specialists are long on reward talk and short on punishment talk. They invest more time and effort in selection than they do on sacking procedures.

Traditionally, there are three classic ineffective ways of dealing with the incompetent subordinate. The first is to *ignore the problem*, hoping that it will go away. It is clear why this occurs. Managers become exasperated and often frightened by the neurotic and demanding subordinate who responds to negative feedback with a mixture of tears, sulks, litigation and unionized threats. Rather than confront laziness or chronic absenteeism, the frustrated manager tends to give the problem employee less work to do. This inevitably leads to anger and frustration from the good, hardworking staff, who see the problem employee getting away with it. Paradoxically, the good are punished and the bad rewarded, and very soon the non-confronting manager has a serious problem on their hands – the good leave or reduce their performance, the bad stay on.

Indeed, it is the workers, more than the bosses, who know about actual contribution, and most of them are deeply sensitive to equitable comparison. That is, if people are rewarded much the same and one notices that their attendance, productivity, customer-response rate and so on is higher than that of others, then they will reduce their performance accordingly. And this process may occur until the lowest common denominator is reached. Imagine the organization that models itself on the most unpleasant and incompetent worker!

The second approach has traditionally been the most favoured: *pass them on*. Every organization has its place for the poor performer. For many it was personnel; for others it was stores. There is often a part of the organization where people believe that the poor performer can do no damage. The logic goes something like this: 'Because personnel does not really matter much, putting problem people there won't upset the apple-cart.' It may be an expensive strategy but some think that it is worth it. Smarter organizations have recently learnt to herd all the poor performers into one part of the organization (training, catering) and then sell off or privatize that part of the organization. A clever plan if possible. But most often, this pass the 'pissed off' parcel does not solve the problem at all. Unless, of course, there are tough managers willing to bite the bullet somewhere in the organization.

There are numerous variants of the pass-the-buck approach. They could be moved to another branch in the dreariest part of town, or another town, or even another country. Just as the empire was terribly useful for the third sons of talentless noblemen, perhaps we can still find distant outposts to send problematic employees. In Asia they are called FILTH (Failed in London Try Honkers) ... but these characters go of their own accord.

There is a third strategy and that is to *promote* the incompetent. It sounds bizarre and uniquely stupid, but is frequently done. If the person who is Manager: the North-east is clearly incompetent, then just make him or her Manager: North of England. Fail at that strategic role and one might try General Manager: England and then Director of Europe. The idea is that these are quite senior, well paid but pointless jobs where incompetent people can hide without being dangerous. The deluded employee is thus confirmed in his or her delusions of competence. This strategy is seriously dangerous as it means the Peter principle is alive and well.

There are a few give-away titles in some organizations that use this strategy. 'Manager: Special Projects' is a nice acronym of 'hopeless and past their sell-by date'. This strategy is most commonly used on those near retirement, those who are likely to cause a fuss or those who are prone to delusions of grandeur.

Ignoring, moving or promoting the incompetent employee is the result of not biting the bullet early on: that is, giving people negative feedback, followed where necessary by a formal warning. Many managers find dealing with incompetence very difficult, even if they talk in PC jargon about developmental opportunities. They do so because they believe the exercise is finger-pointing, blame-storming, and rationalizing – not problem-solving.

The scenario that all managers hate is this: show a subordinate a low mark on the appraisal form. First they want the behaviour defined; then they want an example of when this behaviour did or did not occur; then they argue about how this incident occurred and how typical it was. The net result is a row about the past, and frustration on the part of both individuals.

Instead, the problem-solving approach insists that one still shows the subordinate the low score, but rather than attempt to explain it describe what needs to be done differently to achieve a higher score. The emphasis is thus on the future not the past; on a clear description of the desirable behaviour not the incompetent behaviour.

Interestingly, the same principle applies to fairly good feedback. To be told that one's customer contact style is excellent does not describe precisely which of the many possible behaviours one did correctly so that they can be repeated.

Adopting a problem-solving approach to poor performance means helping the employee define a different behavioural style and giving the support to achieve it. The touchy, sensible or bolshy employee responds to this reasonably well. And it is a much better solution than sending him or her to stores or promoting them to head of customer relations.

But there are those who cannot, and will not, respond to good management. They may be unable to do the job because they do not have the ability to learn ever-changing tasks fast enough. They maybe distracted by problems at home or are more likely to have been managed very poorly in the past.

There is really only a limited number of things that can be done to the real incompetent. Buy them out, which may be the best solution for all concerned; raise the game by making sure they get ever higher, but reachable targets. A final strategy is to insist that they have not an annual medical but an annual 'psychological' where a perceptive and disinterested outside consultant does a motivation analysis and has the power to recommend that they be let go – not encouraged to go to another part of the organization but into the bracing waters of the job market.

Body language at work

Nearly all HR-type courses in the business world deal with non-verbal communication or body language. In *negotiation skills* courses trainers emphasize how to 'read' one's opponent; in *selection skills* courses instructors emphasize how one may detect dissimulation in applicants; in *appraisal workshops* consultants point out how video feedback indicates how pleased or disappointed appraisees are with particular feedback. And, of course, no *sales course* is without advice on how and what to watch in customers to maximize sales.

Curiously, research in the United States has shown that the size of a waiter's tip is partly related to non-verbal behaviour. Three behaviours were shown to be related to tip size: whether the server touched the diner; whether the server initially squatted in their interaction with the diner, as opposed to stood; and the size and 'authenticity' of their initial smile. The fact that in Britain these very same behaviours might lead to a total withdrawal of tip highlights an important issue.

There are different dialects of body language. Just as American English with its love of turning nouns into verbs is different from British English, so body language is often culturally distinct. Like Bulgarian wine, some winks, gestures and postures do not travel well. Japanese inscrutability is partly a function of very different rules associated with body language.

Body language may be coded in verbal language. Consider the following examples taken from the different areas of non-verbal communication:

Body state expression: Emotions are often expressed in terms of body language. We 'shoulder a burden', 'face up to issues', try to 'keep our chin up', 'grit our teeth', in the face of pain we have a 'stiff upper lip', 'bare our teeth', on occasion 'catch the eye' of another, and 'shrug off' misfortune.

Eye contact: 'I see what you mean.' 'Seeing is believing.' 'I can't see any other solution.' 'He has an eye for colour.'

Gesture: 'He gave me the cold shoulder.'

Posture: We have 'well balanced', 'take a firm stand', 'know where you stand on this'. When uncomfortable people shift their weight from one foot to the other they can be seen to be 'shifty characters'.

Odour. 'I like the sweet smell of success.' 'He has a nose for where the money is.' 'Yet she still came up smelling of roses.' 'He is always sticking his nose in other people's business.' 'She always sticks her nose in the air.' 'I will ensure that I rub his nose in it.'

Orientation: 'I dislike people who are always taking sides.' 'I feel diametrically opposed to everything he does.'

Territory/distance: 'I feel close to him.' 'She is very stand-offish'. 'Back off from me, buster!' 'I prefer to keep her at arm's length.'

Touch: 'I touched her for a fiver.' 'I felt touched by his concern.' 'Her plight touched me.'

Verbal and non-verbal communication are pretty intertwined.

Enthusiasts and advocates of body language are eager to see symbolism in small gestures. Playing with hair, fluff removing and fiddling with cufflinks can all be interpreted with crypto-Freudian glee. They often say that body language is much more powerful than spoken language, but fail to point out why charades is both an amusing and difficult game. What trainers like to point out is that a knowledge of body language makes one more insightful, even intuitive, which helps one to read others like a book. But books are passive objects, and people are not. In most business scenarios both interlocutors are simultaneously trying to read the other while concealing certain information about the self.

As adults, we are all skilled dissimulators. Many people are shocked to discover that weeping parents seen on television calling for the return of their children in fact murdered them the day before. Kim Philby lied blatantly on the BBC soon before his flight to Russia as a quisling. And the current US president, Bill Clinton, has provided excellent data for body-language watchers.

There are a few extremely important points to bear in mind with respect to body language. First, it is not random but follows certain rules. In short, it is law-like behaviour. Take eye contact – or mutual gaze – for example. This is in part determined by physical distance (stand too close in lifts and mutual eye gaze drops), topic of conversation (shame and embarrassment are signalled by reduced eye contact), interpersonal relationships (we look more at those we like), co-operative tasks (we look more at co-operators than competitors), and personality (extroverts look more than introverts).

The following are reasonably good cues for lying, given that the people involved are from the same culture and speak the same language.

Verbal cues

Response latency – the time elapsing between the end of a question and the beginning of the response. Liars take longer and hesitate more than when not lying. They have to think through the lie more.

Linguistic distancy – not saying 'I', 'he' or 'she' but talking in the abstract even when recalling incidents in which he or she was involved. The incidence of personal pronouns drops.

Slow and uneven speech – the individual tries to think while speaking but gets caught out. He or she might suddenly speak fast, implying something less significant or more exciting. It is the sudden change in pace in response to a particular question that gives a clue that something is not right.

Over-eagerness to fill silences – to keep talking when it is unnecessary. Liars overcompensate and seem uncomfortable with what are often quite short pauses. Good investigators learn this trick and hold silences longer, watching for what their interlocutor does.

Too many 'pitch raises' – that is, instead of the pitch dropping at the end of a reply, it rises like a question. It may sound like 'Do you believe me now?'

Non-verbal cues

Squirming/shifting around too much in the chair, indicating that they would rather not be there.

Having too much eye contact – liars tend to overcompensate. They know that liars avoid mutual gaze so they 'prove they are not lying' through a lot of looking. But this may let them down as it occurs simply abnormally too much.

Flickers of expressions – of surprise, hurt, anger. These are difficult to see unless the frames of the video are frozen, but occasionally they can be spotted by observant onlookers.

An increase in comfort gestures – touching his or her own face and upper body. Often fiddling with the hair or, more often, folded arms.

An increase in stuttering, slurring and, of course, *'Freudian slips'*, where people say exactly what they mean quite inadvertently. Generally, an increase in speech errors and clumsy phrases.

A loss of resonance in the voice – it becomes flatter, less deep and more monotonous because of the anxiety.

Second, body language is primarily learnt. With few exceptions (such as facial expression), many specific non-verbal features such as gesture and posture are learnt as part of growing up. In Naples, gesture capital of the world, five to six times as much routine, interpretable gestures are used to communicate ideas than in London.

Third, gesture, posture, touch and dress send clearly interpretable messages. Body language can complement and contradict verbal language. It can be used to restate and hence reinforce messages (the size of the fish caught). It can substitute for language (the slightly raised eyebrow at the dinner party). But often it functions to regulate and co-ordinate all communication. Body language helps to let people know when it is their time to talk, when yes means no (and vice versa), when things are getting rather embarrassing, and so on.

Fourth, neither sender nor receiver may necessarily be aware of messages sent. When people are angry, frightened or sexually aroused their pupils dilate. Women knew that when they put bella donna in their eyes, it dilated their pupils and men found them more attractive ... although the men did not know which signal theory they were responding to. Work on odour and pheromones has shown equally surprising results. In one study, a female applicant for a job was judged more technically competent simply as a function of the perfume she was wearing.

Fifth, and related to the above, non-verbal cues give a reasonably good indicator of the emotional state, particularly at extremes. Sweating, trembling and fidgeting are all known signs of anxiety which 'break out' whether the person wants them to or not. And it is this guide to the emotional state of the sender of body language messages that renders it most interesting.

But all this fascinating research by anthropologists, psychologists, physiologists and zoologists should not lead one automatically to conclude that communicating with body language (that is, face-to-face, video-linked) is necessarily better than using a more restricted medium such as the phone, e-mail or old-fashioned snail mail.

Take two examples. Imagine dividing a large group of people randomly into three smaller groups. One reads a message from the CEO; another hears a broadcast of exactly the same message; a third group watches a video presentation, again with the same message. They all have exactly the same amount of time in which to receive exactly the same message but through different media: print; audio-only; audiovisual. Afterwards you test their memory. Who remembers most? The print group remembers most, the audiovisual group least. Why? First, reading requires more mental effort and processing of the material, which results in better memory. Second, readers go at their own pace, not that of a possibly idiosyncratic CEO. Third, the picture of the CEO – that terrible tie, the awful glasses, that orthodontic treatment required – can interfere with concentration on the story line. In this sense, the two things – picture and sound –are not synchronized. Forget the power of television if you want to remember facts.

The second example is that, rather surprisingly, it seems that it is easier to detect people lying through verbal cues only (that is, on the telephone) than in face-to-face communication. Verbal cues include response latency (taking longer to reply to questions because of having to think through the answer); verbal distancing (saying 'one cannot be said to' rather than 'I'); slow but uneven speech; an over-eagerness to fill silences (because liars overcompensate for silences); and too many pitch rises instead of pitch drops at the end of a sentence (which sounds like 'Do you believe me now?').

Of course, there are good body language cues about lying: increased squirming/shifting around in the chair; a decrease in hand gestures; a loss of resonance in the voice; and an increase in face (particularly nose) touching. The last occurs supposedly because the hand is brought up to cover the mouth (unconsciously) to prevent the lies escaping, but also because increased nervous system arousal often leads to the nasal cavity tickling.

Liars get caught because it is difficult to lie about feelings rather than facts. It is difficult to fake powerful emotions even about long past events. Also, old-fashioned guilt means that some people still feel bad about telling serious (as opposed to white) lies. There is also the old problem of fear about getting caught, called detection apprehension. And, finally, liars get caught with 'duping delight' – the relief shown after the lie, believing they have got away with it.

But beware your new-found ability to catch liars. If one is speaking in a second language all the verbal cues may look like lying when they are nothing of the sort. And anxiety – often found in the job interview, or appraisal, or even public performance – can make a person seem to be lying when they are not. This is the whole problem with lie-detector machines, which are more likely to judge the innocent guilty than vice versa.

Certainly, an understanding of body language helps people in business to be better communicators – both senders and receivers. If this were not the case it is doubtful whether politicians, diplomats and spin-doctors would spend so much time and money on communication skills and body language courses.

Business babble and political correctness

Business babble is a growth industry. To be fluent in corporate speak may be a requirement for advancement. Being an inventor of business jargon terms, and having them exclusively identified as one's own, is practically a necessity for being called a business guru. No wonder, then, that journalists supposedly favoured the word 'guru' because they could not spell 'charlatan'.

Most people know about the systematized buzzword generator. This was actually no more than a list of three columns of words with a dozen or so in each column. The joke was that you could combine the three into an utterly meaningless, but serious-sounding, buzzword. For instance a 'responsive transitional contingency'; 'synchronized third-generation capability'; or a 'systematized incremental programme'. This gives one impressive obscurantist semantic possibilities whose terminologically inexact options can seriously inhibit documentary clarity! In short, one could easily invent meaningless buzzwords.

Reports and presentations are littered with this nonsense. Indeed, some companies appropriate, even rejoice in, this in-house, semi-secret language precisely because it is a marker of being 'one of us'. Knowing, or at least thinking that one knows, the meaning of this gobbledegook, and using it frequently, show loyalty, corporateness and the ability to speak more than one language. Because there are few English–Business Babble dictionaries, the tongue remains obscure except to anthropologists and missionaries who stumble on these tribes and have the time, patience and motivation to try to understand them.

The rise of corporate-speak and guru-nu-speak is attributable to many factors. Being fluent in business babble can help distinguish *them* from *us*; insiders and outsiders; top management and junior management; those with and those without an MBA. It can similarly give the impression of sophistication while obfuscating. Speaking an obscure tongue means one can have a secret language or at least a marker of education and group allegiance. Some gurus strive to invent, change or colonize words to make them their own so that whenever they are used they themselves are thought of. They are the catchword of comics, the sound of big success; the writing of mission statements added to business babble in a big way.

But perhaps the major reason for the increase in imaginative business babble is an attempt to present the unpalatable in an acceptable way. Corporate language is used as a balm, a bandage or at worst a blanket, not to solve problems but to hide them.

A second sort of corporate speak is the precise opposite of the above. The buzzword generator makes up obscure concepts that sometimes have a simple meaning ... that is, if they have one at all. The opposite is to use simple, everyday phrases that have a special meaning within the organization. Thus, to 'adopt an attitude of watchful waiting' means, of course, to do nothing. 'Taking a long hard look at', 'under active consideration', 'in a holding position' and 'evaluating the possible prematureness of this idea' are other synonyms for the same thing. 'Channels of communication' are trails of inter-office memos or interpersonal e-mails.

Then there are new management techniques, all of which are a form of impression, as opposed to real management. Managing by 'post-its' is to use these little pads to shower offices. Then there is management by reorganization. BUA management is popular – management *by using a*bbreviations.

Jargon can also be found in job titles. In the old days you were 'clerk of works' or 'technical supervisor'. Now the latter are 'laboratory stewards' and the former 'managers of infrastructural support'. The idea of a job title is to inflate the ego of the holder – often in exchange for a reasonable income – while baffling, but possibly impressing, a client. As the title 'manager' becomes overused, so everyone is then a director. Soon we shall reach the US standard where the first job in the company, like the last (bar one), is executive vice-president.

In the old days one had 'strengths and weaknesses'. Now we all still have strengths but we have 'developmental opportunities'. Those who can't calculate are 'mathematically challenged'. You don't sack people any more, but offer 'outplacement counselling'.

Business babble now surpasses psychobabble in its imaginativeness and impenetrability. This is based on all sorts of things. The airline industry contributed phrases such as 'I am in a holding position', 'Can I be upgraded', 'Old Curruthers is in the departure lounge of life'. Computers have helped or hindered the business babble industry depending on your view. 'To download a preformed intuition' is to have an idea.

Companies develop and enjoy their own in-house terms and jargon particularly for grades and customers. Sensitivity to being a 'level 4 manager' or 'grade 5 supervisor' means little to the outsider but everything to those in the organization. And some customer-facing groups develop a funny, telling, but deeply derogatory set of epithets to describe customers. Some are unprintable; most unattributable.

Those who support political correctness, although ironically it is not PC to describe it as such, proffer a simple explanation for their support. They argue that PC places emphasis on protecting the rights of minorities, 'respect for diversity' or accepting (even celebrating) differences. The philosophy is clear in the point that the right to free speech or airing unpopular opinions must be subordinated to the right of guaranteeing equal protection under the law, where comments may be seen as degrading, disrespectful or hostile.

PC philosophy argues that linguistic titles and labels used to describe others, usually minorities, convey a substantive political message. It is philosophy about the power of language. Hence the fascination with Eurocentrism and male bias – hence all the changes in words such as manpower, chairman and so on. Words don't judge, they involve meaning: they carry, enshrine and enforce attitudes both positive and negative. The 'gender' of words thus implies the gender of the occupant of the title. Even the etymology is suspect. Hence an academic wanted 'seminars' changed to 'ovulars' because of etymology. But that is feminism, not neutral PC-ness where one de-genders (as opposed to emasculates) words.

Is there proof for the PC position? Does changing words change attitudes? Does proscribing and prescribing acceptable and unacceptable words have a long- or short-term beneficial effect? Or is it nothing but time-wasting flimflam, a pleasant alternative to dealing with business problems? Alas, the jury is out ... the evidence is missing.

Critics of PC see it as a repressive orthodoxy that paradoxically attempts to achieve tolerance and harmony by tyrannical censorship and ideological coercion. They contend that by ensuring the veneer of polite language, the underlying problems, if there are any, are ignored. The anti-PC lobby sees PC as empty rhetoric and a hollow attempt to quiet the discontent and appease the complaints of certain bodies.

Whatever the motivation or the theory of the pro- or anti-PC camp, the business world is alive with people constructing buzzword generators or subtly censoring the language. Some terms have passed into history. 'The captain in the cockpit could not take tea from the stewardess, as he had both hands on the joystick' is something you would no longer hear.

Business travel

It is only the naïve and gullible who envy the business traveller. All those advertisements depicting cosily snoozing businessmen in luxurious aeroplane seats, or in plush hotels, seem to have done the trick. A trip to Barbados for a business meeting, Korea for a conference, Samarkand for a seminar, or the Philippines for a factory inspection hardly seem like work at all – to those who have never done it.

It is no accident that the words travel and travail are etymologically linked. Travel, at least the modern form of it, is just as likely to broaden the behind as it is the mind. But it need not be so. Preparation reduces problems; realistic expectations prevent disappointment; and a little psychological insight might alleviate some of the major stresses and pitfalls of the frequent flyer.

A lot of travel-induced frustration comes from waiting around. Even if the absurdly detailed timetable is running smoothly, there is inevitably much hanging about: for transport to the airport, the check-in queue, the compulsory two-hour margin. The shops may well be interesting, the business lounge comfortable, and the range of periodicals splendid, but still the businessman is adrift in an unfamiliar environment. Knowing when to travel can help: mid-week is better than the weekend; and on, rather than before, public holidays. Astute business travellers must learn the layouts of all long-haul jets, and ask for a specific seat. Others know quiet spots in airports.

For the 'little people', who travel 'at the back of the bus', the journey is not unlike a spell in prison. Airlines, like prisons, deprive the traveller of most of their belongings, reduce them to a number (64D, non-smoking); feed them bland fare when it suits the crew; and require undignified queuing for the lavatories. The hapless traveller is moved from one room to another for no apparent reason, and their papers are checked and rechecked by strict, no-nonsense members of staff. One is physically constrained in many senses, encouraged to remain strapped in, and required to share personal space with complete strangers. Ah yes, corralled, processed, drugged and dismissed: the four stages of the economy flight.

Business and first-class passengers are, by appropriate degree and according to the price of the seat, spared many of these indignities. They are addressed by name (sometimes their own), allowed to keep some of their personal belongings and given more space and flexibility for eating and ablutions.

But flying is tiring and stressful at the best of times. Everyone gets jet-lag; many people become dehydrated; and most lose sleep. A size-able proportion of travellers actually have mild to serious bouts of flying anxiety. This can be acute, brought on by turbulence, or more debilitatingly chronic, which is difficult to cure. And yes, there are business travellers who suffer from fear of flying.

Yet there is the excitement of anticipation, which accounts for why one is less tired or jet-lagged and jaded on the way out than on the way back. And you might meet interesting people with whom to exchange funny stories and frank confessions mid-Atlantic at midnight.

Experienced and psychologically astute frequent travellers are easy to spot. They travel light and pace themselves. They give clear signals about privacy or desired sociability to their fellow travellers. They know how to amuse themselves, and how and when to relax versus exercise. In short, they attempt to maximize control and personal preference and get the best out of ground staff and cabin crew.

New and unfamiliar airports are a joy to the extrovert seeking kicks, but yet another source of terror to the unstable introvert. There are many anxieties in store for the recently 'displaced' traveller. Getting through customs, dealing with the reception committee, find-ing the hotel, understanding the currency and working out the language are just some of the hurdles which await the business trav-eller abroad.

Having accomplished what frank Americans call the 'shit, shower and shave' routine, most people feel invigorated and ready to do business. The novelty of everything is at once exciting and frustrating. Even the most inexperienced traveller is usually prepared for climate change, but may not realize that nearly all climates are seasonal and variable.

Doing business abroad is tiring because one needs to concentrate more. Foreigners, whatever their native tongue, do speak another language. Even first-language English speakers in other countries can have almost impenetrable accents, and use unknown acronyms and metaphors. The smattering of the language one learnt at school is often useless. 'Where is the hotel?', 'That is too expensive.' and 'I need to check that with my colleagues' are far more useful phrases than those concerning the ubiquitous 'pen of my aunt'.

Foreign countries present problems: they do things differently. And it is probably at the most trivial level that these differences cause headaches. The electrical appliances are different. The tipping system is impenetrable. They don't take all your credit cards. All the concentration and adaptation lead quickly to fatigue. Bereft of the familiar comforts of home, overfed, overwatered and overstimulated, one can soon be tempted to behave like a fractious child. Capricious, irascible moods do not lead to fruitful or beneficial business. But they can be guarded against by a little preparation and quite reasonable demands for 'time out' from the frantic socializing and business activities. Sleep, exercise and cultural homework are better ways to use down time than in-house movies or a bender at the mini-bar.

Paradoxically, it is the after, rather than during, work activities with the natives that prove most difficult because of all the subtle cultural differences. Many behavioural norms and niceties are passed on by 'old hands', and can be found in books. The importance of gifts in the Far East is well known, as is the idea that whereas Americans like to socialize (casually) after a deal, the Japanese do so before. Many social traditions are bewildering: it is easy to be bored or boring, vulgar and rude, insensitive or garish, by misreading the signals or assuming that everyone is a PLU (person like us).

One can feel powerless abroad. The helpless, hopeless, hapless traveller is not an uncommon sight at airports, shopping arcades and business conferences. There is a powerlessness about fear of loss of influence, and about the speed and outcome of one's business.

There is, too, the powerlessness of not knowing what is happening at home. The phone, fax and e-mail trilogy won't do. It becomes impossible to be fully functional in two places at once. And the more powerless one feels abroad, the more the fear of being left out at home grows. The astute traveller, therefore, details what information is to be passed on, when, and by whom, and pre-plans the mechanism to deal with incoming calls.

Doing business abroad enables one to empathize with Napoleon on St Helena. Hence the cynicism about trips and all that 'win–win' hype. If one is less successful than (unrealistically) hoped, the trip nearly always has the 'lose–lose' feel, particularly given the number of people dying to 'push something through the committee' in one's absence.

The longer one stays, and the more frequently one travels, the more the honeymoon feeling subsides. Following an initial fascination with travel, frustration, bewilderment and depression take over. It takes time and effort to be bicultural. And for many, the game is not worth the candle – it is easier to go to the club and have a few pink gins with expats. This, in the long term, is a highly unadapative strategy.

It is amazing how orderly the house, how beautiful the spouse, and angelic the child seem, when one is stuck in an overcrowded airport lounge on the other side of the world. Even one's colleagues and boss assume a caring and benign halo after the fourth bottle of beer. Just as there are more suicides, divorces and physical abuse around Christmas and holidays because reality conflicts with fantasy, so the homecoming can be a big let-down.

The 'coming down' period can often be an unexpectedly difficult aspect of a business trip. The spouse may simply be used to frequent absences, and the children disappointed with carefully selected gifts. The office support staff still greet one with a pile of urgent tasks to be done and decisions to be made. Some colleagues show their jealousy by being conspicuously uninterested in the stories you return with. Others punish one for it, particularly if one looks tanned and relaxed, or has been especially successful.

On the other hand, family, friends and colleagues may be too inquisitive, interrogating you about the most trivial of travel experiences – almost as if they don't believe you.

Airlines sell their product either by emphasizing the wonder of the destination or the comfort of the trip. Both are highly select portrayals of the truth. As more people travel and become more demanding, the travel business becomes increasingly innovative about product packaging.

Stuck in an overcrowded metal tube in the sky, eating foreign food, sleeping in a foreign bed, and conducting intense and frenzied business is often the lot of the curiously envied business traveller. It does not have to be. Doing one's homework on the culture of the destination, the preferences and social etiquette of one's host, the travel facilities and the arrangements made for one's absence is a good start. Listening to bodily needs for R&R, water and exercise is a must.

Successful travel is as much about attitude as it is about following rigid codes of behaviour. It can be an enormously exciting, beneficial privilege which one's friends rightly envy. But all too often, it results in confusion, exhaustion and little success.

There are two main ways of dealing with the stress of a business journey, and people vary in the technique they find more useful.

Withdrawal/avoidance

This technique involves taking your mind away from the immediate situation:

- immerse yourself in a book or newspaper, which you can really 'get into'
- go to sleep
- daydream, fantasize
- make plans, lists, think about future projects at work or leisure
- take tranquillizers
- gain access to the quiet, other-worldly atmosphere of the airline lounges.

Distraction

By providing additional stimuli, the source of stress becomes less significant:

- shop at the airport/station. Not for nothing have shopping arcades sprung up at airport terminals
- eat and drink
- play games, watch TV
- strike up a conversation. Self-disclosure to a stranger can be very therapeutic
- take disinhibitors (for example, alcohol).

Almost everyone finds the following useful for reducing travel stress:

- take an 'adult comfort blanket' along – anything from a favourite type of sweet to a hot water bottle
- have your own amusements to hand – the crossword, a laptop, books
- mark out your own space with coat/jacket/briefcase. Adopt defensive seating to create security – a corner, the end of a row.

Finally, ensure that you don't inflict your own stress on the journey, in addition to stress from external sources:

> Allow adequate time. A certain machismo attaches to business travellers who habitually cut it fine and arrive at the airport as the gate is closing, necessitating a return of the steps to the aircraft; or who stand on the runway pleading with the pilot to open the door. It is far less stressful to know you will catch the flight, even if time is 'wasted' in the departure lounge. Check the details. Frequent business travellers can become blasé about this most elementary of stress reducers. A business team read an 18.00 flight as 8pm (a common mistake). The Lear jet which had to be chartered cost the entire project budget. Consultants have been known to fly halfway round the world, leaving the presentation behind in the office. It is not a relaxing start to a business trip if you arrive in a strange country without passport, credit cards or underpants. The Chinese definition of XXL creates an uncomfortable undercarriage for a Westerner.

How does one get an upgrade? The following may help:

> Dress the part. Most airlines try to keep up appearances in first and business class, even if the policy is not explicitly stated.
> Draw attention to your status by proffering passport/business card and exaggerate a little.
> Pull strings. Use any relevant authority you can muster – the name of a friend in the airline executive, for example.
> Stress the long-term relationship with the airline. State how long you have been in the frequent flyer club, how long your company

has had a special deal and so on. Emphasize mutual commitment. Be charming. Ground staff resent bullies and will punish, rather than reward, aggression.

Negotiate carefully. Be in possession of the facts (is the aircraft overbooked? In which class?) and be prepared to play a long game. Take the 'role of the other' and empathize.

Remember, many airlines will have 'occasion upgrades' for honeymoon, birthday and so on.

The British are poor complainers, moving between passive and aggressive without mastering the intermediary skills of assertiveness.

Whether one is protesting about airline personnel, fellow passengers or unreasonable demands, there are a few simple, but effective rules:

First *describe* the problem. Describe specifically and unemotionally the time, place and frequency of the action. Don't be vague or emotional and, initially, don't attribute motives. Literally describe the problem, calmly and coolly.

Next, *express* your feelings. State your feelings calmly, relating them to the goal you want achieved. If you express negative feelings to a person, do so only in terms of the offending behaviour, not their whole personality. No passive-aggressive sulking or sarcasm.

Then *specify* what you want. Request small, reasonable changes, one at a time. Specify the concrete actions you want stopped and those you want to see performed. Take account of whether the person/organization you are addressing can do this without major significant loss of time, money or 'face'. And say what behaviour you are willing to change to make the agreement.

Finally, make the *consequences* explicit. Reward people for any attempts to change in the desired direction. Emphasize the positive consequences for all concerned.

The career: a typology of careers

Once upon a time, or so it seemed, ability and long service were rewarded by a steady climb up the corporate ladder. The speed and end-point in the career were defined only by ability and service (and perhaps a bit of politics).

Today, the idea of a 'job for life' is, for many people, neither possible nor desirable. In many European countries, about one-third to one-half of the workforce are in temporary or self-employment. There is now a cohort of young people, aged 30 years and under, who expect and look forward to building up a portfolio of jobs in different companies. They are content to give 5 to 8 years' loyal and enthusiastic service to a variety of possibly widely different companies so as to increase their experience and competence.

For many people, this new approach to a working life is exciting rather than worrying. It has been estimated that people used to have about 100 000 working hours over a 47-year working period to pursue a career. Now 47 years has shrunk to 30, with many retiring at 50 and thinking of a 'second career'. Whereas some older people perceive this as a threat, many younger people interpret it as a major opportunity – with change comes growth and opportunity, in their opinion.

Employment has changed and so have careers. The way people approached a career was characterized by many different strategies:

Drifters seemed rather directionless and unambitious. Some seemed not to be able to hold down a job for any period of time, but they had to be flexible and adaptable as they took on new jobs every so often. Drifters could be seen by some people to be capricious, fickle, or even reckless. More positively, they are adventurous and experimental.

Lifers are the opposite of drifters – the lifer's first job is their last. Although they might not have chosen their first job judiciously, or with foresight, they settled down for life. Although this may be an excellent strategy if one is in a company on the move, it is more likely to be a trade-off of high risk/gain over security. Further, downsizing and restructuring has left them not very employable. Lifers are loyal, but they are risk-averse, and liable to be alienated as performance management systems replace seniority-based or service ideologies.

Hoppers look like snakes and ladders experts. They seem to go up short ladders quite fast, perhaps in small companies or departments, but slide down slippery snakes as they change jobs in the search for betterment. They lack the long-term vision of the planner, who has the whole journey mapped out. They may have made job move decisions too quickly, based on too little data.

Planners have clear targets, sometimes over-ambitiously fantasized. They can articulate where they want to be at the big milestones of life (aged 40, 55 or 60). They may even cultivate head-hunters, apply (whimsically) for jobs on a regular basis, and update their CVs quarterly. Planners are committed to their career development. They understand the modern world of portfolio management.

Hobbyists are masters of this final strategy. Some are SOBOs – Shoved Out, but Better Off – but many, often in their 40s, become concerned with self-development. They echo the observation of a priest, who for years counselled the dying, heard their confessions and their regrets; no one said that they wished they had spent more time in the office. The hobbyist may take early retirement, turn to consultancy, or simply define quality of life as more important than the rat race. This makes them interesting people, but not always deeply committed to the company's interest. Work is a hobby for these people.

Those who have studied jobs, careers and the world of work have long argued that it is misleading to believe that permanent jobs are good and temporary jobs are bad, or vice versa. It has been suggested that good jobs are characterized by quite specific factors that include:

1. *Control*: some opportunity to decide and act in one's chosen way, and the potential to predict the consequences of one's actions. Being given limited control, such as the offer of flexi-time, is very desirable.
2. *Skill use*: jobs that allow people to practise learnt skills and acquire new ones are desirable. Job change often involves the necessity of skill acquisition, which, in the long run, is very desirable.
3. *Clear goals and feedback on performance*: being given or, better still, helping to decide clear goals is always desirable. More attractive still is being given regular, honest feedback on one's performance. Increasingly, portfolio jobs are being set up, which have the requirement that employees give and get regular and explicit feedback on their performance.
4. *Variety*: tedious, monotonous tasks are a thing of the past. Indeed, many temporary jobs are characterized by novelty, both of task and location. Of course, too much variety can be stressful, and

    lead to burn-out, but too little leads to 'rust-out', which is prob-
    ably worse.

5.   *Contact*: all jobs provide the opportunity for interpersonal contact
    with others, be they fellow employees, customers or even share-
    holders. Contact provides the opportunity to make friends and
    reduce loneliness. It allows people to provide emotional, informa-
    tional and financial support to each other. And it allows for social
    comparisons, an opportunity to compare themselves with others,
    to interpret and appraise themselves.

6.   *Valued social position*: this is not only about job title but the value
    attached by society at large to the role and the contribution made.
    Jobs can boost self- and social esteem – and undermine it. Jobs
    provide public evidence that a person has certain abilities,
    conforms to particular norms and meets social obligations.

7.   *Security*: there are many types of security, the most basic of which is
    physical security. Temporary jobs frequently supply security of
    tenure over a specified period. Indeed, paradoxically, the nature
    of the legal contract of many temporary jobs actually makes
    employees more secure (for a specified period) than those on
    longer and vaguer contracts.

8.   *Money and reward*: some permanent jobs are very badly paid, as are
    temporary jobs. Money is a powerful short-term reward only, and
    is more likely to be a source of dissatisfaction than satisfaction.
    Some temporary jobs are, in fact, well paid because of the expect-
    ation of unemployment (for example, pilots).

Who exactly is responsible for one's career or, more likely, careers?
Three groups have specific responsibilities for an individual's career
development. First, the organization itself should provide training and
developmental opportunities where possible. Courses, sabbaticals, job
shares and shadowing experiences, for instance, all help. They need to
provide realistic and up-to-date career information and, where necessary, outplacement services. Indeed, these may become more and
more important reasons why people would choose to work for any
particular organization.

    Managers, too, have responsibilities. They need to provide high-
quality and timely feedback on performance so that staff get to
appraise themselves realistically. They need to have regular, expect-
ation-managing discussions and support their reports in their action

plans. Again, where possible, they need to offer developmental assignments where they can acquire new skills. Honest feedback and opportunities to develop new skills are the best things any manager can do for his/her employees, permanent or temporary.

Of course, individuals must accept responsibility for their own career. They cannot expect to remain passive. Individuals must seek out information on careers within and without the organization; they must initiate talks with their managers about careers and be prepared to invest in assessing their strengths and weaknesses. They need to be prepared to take up development opportunities even if they are outside their particular comfort zone.

We all make our beds and then we lie in them. Fatalists believe that the success of their working life is dependent on powerful forces – the international economy, politicians, God, the lottery and pure chance. But instrumentalists know that we can all be captain of our ship and master of our fate. The fact that we may all now have nine (working) lives, rather than one, presents much greater opportunities for growth, development and upward mobility.

The career is dead – long live the career! Certainly, the long-service-in-one-organization career is on the decline. The old career contract with the organization is less relevant, the new contract is with oneself. The ability to have multiple careers, probably a better way of working than the temporary career, means that people will have to learn new skills and reinvent themselves. We shall all need to be more feedback-seeking and more eager to learn from others. If you don't know where you want to go, you will certainly end up somewhere you don't want to be. Chosen jobs need to fit ability and values, and a sense of identity. The use of support and affinity groups, networks and adult learning centres, is one of the best sources of help in personal career development. We shall all need to learn how to plan and develop our working careers in the future.

Paradoxically, learning from experience seems to be more critical than ever, yet past experience has less relevance to current experience, because of the speed of change. In the new world of self-reliant careers, it will be essential for individuals to take an active role in steering their own ship and plotting their own course. Compared with the past, there will need to be a higher degree of learning by oneself, of communicating with others, interdisciplinary work, working in groups and solving personal problems.

Personal initiative is more and more rewarded. Self-starters, the proactive and the persistent will inherit the earth.

All the shock headlines about 'The end of the job', 'The age of downsizing', 'The outsourced manager' do not mean that people are not interested in their careers. Organizational factors are becoming less important in determining individual career outcomes – personal identity and values, and interpersonal factors are becoming more important in shaping career directions and rewards.

Non-traditional careers will soon become traditional. The flexibility of opportunity structures and labour markets is growing. Organizations are preparing for the new and different needs of the new careerists. Both the formal employment contract drawn up by companies and the psychological contract that temporary employees have with the organization are being rethought and redrawn. There is no going back. We are all careering in a new direction.

Charging like a wounded bull: how to become a consultant

Top barristers, business gurus and management consultants can easily command £5000 a day, and very often twice that figure. Although people seem to accept the legal fee structure and the opportunity to listen to and quiz a captain of industry, politician or academic, they are genuinely surprised and shocked by what the average management consultant charges.

Consultants learn various tricks when disclosing their fee. Some say they charge 'around 3 a day', hoping that the client understands £3000 not £300. The 'problem of fees' has to be dealt with through the straightforward, but all-important, process called contracting. This may be a simple agreement of a daily billing rate plus specified expenses. This is usually termed the fixed-fee plus expenses, but others such as an incentive-fixed price, retainer contract, and performance category contract often exist. Because contracting often goes wrong, it can cause a lot of frustration for both parties.

The average daily rate for a management consultant is probably about £1000. There seem to be different cost categories, broken down into four bands: under £500, £501–1000, £1001–2000, and more than £2000. These charges seem excessive to many new clients and almost preposterously unbelievable to the average Brit on about

£16 000 a year. So why are they so expensive? Is it greed, avarice, materialism, market forces, or even cost effectiveness? If they are in some senses not cost effective, why do so many companies employ them? The answer is really threefold.

First, £500 a day may be very cost effective. Take the senior manager on £65 000, who works 250 days a year (excluding weekends, holidays and public holidays). This works out to about £300 a day. But added to these costs are considerable overheads of offices, and all the necessary support systems: secretaries, telephones, electricity, water, personnel administration, car parking space, security. Indeed, some organizations are actively trying to convert certain, specifically full-time employees into consultants because of the money it saves. These new, and often involuntary, consultants are paid much the same as before, but they are required to telework out of their spare bedrooms, saving considerably on overheads.

The sort of costs that many consultants have are:

Secretarial support: for report word processing, data input, reception, diary control and occasional administration.
Rent, telephone, postage, especially fax and Internet charges where they apply, although rent is often by far the highest.
A car and other transportation costs.
Insurance, pension, medical and personal benefit costs.
Equipment and supplies from modest stationery to ever-changing computer equipment.
Marketing through brochures, advertisements and so on.
Dues and subscriptions to professional bodies, magazines and technical publications.
Accounting and legal services: always the former, occasionally the latter.
Professional development: to keep abreast of all recent developments, even consultants have to attend courses to maintain or 'upskill' themselves.

Add these up and they can be quite excessive. Now assume that a consultant works 120 days a year @ £1000 a day. Once you start deducting the above, the salaries may not look so good. Despite this, many people secretly (or, indeed, openly) want to become management consultants. So, how to do it?

No area of knowledge, skill or expertise is too small, trivial or mundane to have consultants. The idea of working for oneself, charging large fees and being able to pick and choose from various jobs only the most interesting and lucrative, is indeed appealing. So why not 'go for it', as we New Britons from Cool Britannia say, and become a consultant. After all, success is just a matter of pluck.

But there are downsides – and not only the irregular income. Economically, consultants are a bit like lemmings: they breed like crazy in the good times and have a habit of casting themselves from cliffs in the bad. That is, when the economy is buoyant, there are swarms of eager, avaricious people who call themselves consultants, but when times get hard, the consultancy firms downsize at a phenomenal rate.

The problem for the one-man band, the affiliate rather than the member of a company, is often loneliness. Sitting in the spare bedroom playing with e-mail (or 'fiddling with the gerbil' as Australians have it) is no substitute for office gossip and the daily chat. Workmates are the source of stimulation, ideas and, above all, playmates.

But most important of all, it is difficult, if not impossible, to market while working. So, the pattern goes like this: the consultant spends much time and effort networming (another Australianism), putting themselves about a bit, directly marketing themselves. They then get work – often too much to handle. So they choose the best offer and get on with it. While working, however, they can't do the personal calling. So when the job ends, there is an extended fallow period while they cast about for business. The next round of marketing then occurs. This can be very frustrating, even if the target number of days charged a year is as low as 120.

But the number of consultants in all fields is still increasing. Some choose to leave organizational life, others are pushed. But there is a growing trend for organizations to have a 'teleworker'-style relationship with most of their employees. In a sense, people are becoming consultants in and to their organization, rather than employees. It is certainly a good deal for the organization, and perhaps for the individual. As long as one is talented, hard working and well connected, this arrangement is fine. But beware the organization whose restructuring is always a way of letting go the expensive, often loyal, employee from the past.

Consultancy is not a bed of roses. Most people work hard for their money. For those emerging from the warm and cosy environment of the head office, the baptism in the icy waters of economic reality is often a nasty shock. But the fittest survive, and it is very rare indeed for a consultant to yearn to return to his old life, being what the Japanese call a salaryman.

Charity as revenge

It is possible that charity – the voluntary giving of often large sums of money to a worthy cause – could be an aggressive, vengeful act. Might a donation to a university (the building of a library), a bequest to a museum or a large monetary gift to a hospital be motivated by aggression or revenge?

It is not only Freudians who have pointed out the paradoxes of human behaviour. Anthropologists have, for instance, long acknowledged that there can be a dark side to a gift. One can humiliate people by giving too small a tip, as any user of New York cabs will readily acknowledge. Similarly, because gifts are reciprocated one can render a person acutely uncomfortable if they are unable to give one a gift of equivalent worth.

Some gifts can also have a rather direct message: the gift of after-shave or soap to the person with unpleasant body-odour; the watch to those who are habitually late; the personal organizer to the conspicuously disorganized, are all examples of the dark side of the gift.

Others have pointed rather cynically to other motives of those giving money. For some people, donations are little more than a tax dodge. For others, they are a very good alternative to PR, being both cheaper and more effective. They can also be seen as a way to reduce guilt and clear the conscience. Hence donation to a hospice or hospital may be seen as a way of expunging the guilt of not having taken good care of a dying relative or having been neglectful of the health of a significant other.

To what or whom the money is given and with what particular provisions are seen as highly significant. The anonymous, no-strings-attached donations are the exception not the rule. Some benefactors are particularly specific in their requests.

Just as wills are often attempts to control affairs from the grave, so donors and benefactors may be particularly eager to set constraints on how their money is spent. Of course, the motives for this may be opaque or crystal clear, and they may be driven by concern and love or hate and revenge. Solicitors will tell of amazing wills where it seems that people have plotted for years how to get even with those who spurned them. Or they have found ways to humiliate specific others by getting them to do certain things before they can get hold of the money. The contemplation of the shame and degradation of others who will do anything for large sums of money has been the theme of novels, films and books, such as *Kind Hearts and Coronets* and Peter Sellers' *The Magic Christian.*

A surprising number of donators to educational institutions had only a modest education. They were drop-outs, failures, even expelled, and left secondary education with little or no qualifications. Some made an issue of their lack of education, seeing it a part cause of their success. Others tried to hide it. But many privately recalled the personal humiliation at the hands of supercilious and bullying teachers and the taunts of the more successful swots.

There are two ways to see the significant educational donation. The philanthropic, perhaps naïve but most accepted view, is that the educational donation is to prevent young talented people failing in the system, being misunderstood by it, or simply not entering it. Remembering their own story, the munificent benefactor gives as a prophylactic to ensure that history is not repeated, not so much for themselves but for others who did not thrive after failing.

The second interpretation is less generous. The donation is aimed at point scoring, even humiliation. Remembering the rejection at university by pompous, arrogant, snobbish dons, how sweet it is to have the self-same, rather greyer, individuals fawning over one years later as the chequebook is brought out. The roles become quite reversed: the power and the control in the opposite hands.

The entrepreneur knows that everyone has their price and that with the right amount of money they can get their way. They know the poorly paid, cash-strapped, academic will dance to their tune.

Take the example of Arthur Koestler, who endowed a chair in paranormal psychology at Edinburgh University. He knew that the academic psychologists were deeply cynical about extra-sensory perception and other paranormal phenomena which he believed in. How sweet to know that university administrators would lean heavily on psychology departments to fight for the endowed chair to be placed at that university. To see dons squabbling to do research in the area they despise is surely a fine example of revenge.

In one study on attitudes to charitable giving, the cynical British public agreed with the following statements:

- Many individuals and large organizations who donate money to charity have ulterior motives.
- For many people, charity donations are a tax dodge.
- Many people try to salve their conscience by small gifts to charity.

There is a language of gift giving and donation to charity. The legacy or donation is an expression of both giver and receiver. The motives of those who donate to charity may be entirely altruistic – but then again they may not.

Cleanliness, godliness and shareholder returns

A few years ago, a major brewery which owned a chain of hundreds of pubs tried to find out the best predictors of pub profitability. Before the research was done, there was a long list of hypotheses (and associated bets): the range of beers available, the price of the 'house pint', whether hot or cold food was available, the attractiveness of the bar staff, whether there was a car park, even the vague concept called 'ambience'. Much to the surprise of the executives, the best predictor was the cleanliness of the toilets. Some argued that cleanliness was particularly an issue with women, and that women brought in family groups who ate more food. Others thought that dirty toilets signalled to customers that there would be dirty kitchens, dirty cellars and thus unhygienic food and spoiled beer.

Data from airlines showed that travellers associated dirty cutlery and toilets with poorly maintained engines. Singapore Airlines thus ensure that in first class, the toilet is cleaned after *every* visit. The idea is that cleanliness is a simple index of care. It is a fundamental requirement; it is an index of good maintenance. Many managers also tumble to the insight that dissatisfied employees often complain about cleanliness in the kitchen and the canteen. The whole 'smoking in the building' debate is often couched in cleanliness terminology.

What is at issue here? Is this a manifestation of cultural fetishes or personality pathology? Some explanations cite our cultural obsession with freshness, newness, cleanliness, and concomitant bizarre rituals about wrapping. The Chinese obsession with really fresh fish has been linked to the hot climate, the absence of refrigeration and the resultant risk of illness. Psychologists have always seen concerns over cleanliness to be a personal pathology – and one related to money.

But how much should organizations be concerned with superficial and real cleanliness? Does it make a difference to customers and staff? The data suggest that it does – and not only for the anal obsessives. The problem, however, is getting companies not specifically dealing with foods and hygiene-related products to take cleanliness seriously. Shareholders hate conspicuous consumption. Bosses are embarrassed by large cleaning bills and feel it difficult to justify full-time cleaners who have to go behind all staff like nannies. So they hire cheaper cleaning companies who hire fewer and cheaper (read foreign) staff who are often shoddy and unreliable. They are also prone to throw away valuable papers but leave rubbish, partly because of cultural differences but more likely because they, quite simply, can't read the messages in English left for them.

But just as bosses and shareholders hate extravagance, so the workforce and customers hate meanness. Many resent blow-driers replacing towels; they resent a reduction in the number of times communal areas are vacuumed. Surprisingly, many people would even be prepared to pay a small amount for a visit to the 'washroom' if they thought it would be clean.

Scrimping on hygiene is often a false economy. And yet, curiously, it may be one of the few areas where the accountants and actuaries, and other grey men of the bottom line, are not zealous penny pinchers. And the answer lies in why they become accountants in the first place.

Freud identified three main traits associated with people who had fixated at the anal stage: orderliness, parsimony and obstinacy, with four linked qualities of cleanliness: conscientiousness, trustworthiness, defiance and revengefulness. If the child is traumatized by the experience of toilet training, he/she tends to retain ways of coping and behaving during this phase. The way in which a miser hoards money is seen as symbolic of the child's refusal to eliminate faeces in the face of parental demands. The spendthrift, on the other hand, recalls the approval and affection that resulted from submission to parental authority to defecate. Thus some people equate elimination/spending with receiving affection and hence feel more inclined to spend when feeling insecure, unloved or in need of affection.

Freudians have attempted to find evidence for their theory in idioms, myths, folklore and legends. There is also quite a lot of evidence from language, particularly from idiomatic expressions. Money is often called 'filthy lucre', and the wealthy are 'stinking rich'. Gambling for money is also associated with dirt and toilet training: a poker player puts money in a 'pot'; dice players 'shoot craps'; card players play 'Dirty Gertie'; a gambler who loses everything is 'cleaned out'. The rich are 'rolling in it', but the poor let it 'slip through their fingers'.

Families, groups and societies that demand early and rigid toilet training tend to produce 'anal characteristics' in people, which include orderliness, punctuality, compulsive cleanliness and obstinacy. Hence one can be as miserly about knowledge, time and emotions as much as about money. Anal people, if of course bright enough, are attracted to particular jobs such as accountancy. And, as we shall observe, nearly all companies are run by accountants these days. So, pity the poor accountant faced with an increasing cleaning bill. They are pulled by two equally powerful, but alas contradictory forces – to save money but to maintain hygiene.

Continuing management education

The world of medicine has long been interested and concerned about continuing management education (CME). The reason is obvious: although all doctors have experienced a long, difficult and demanding training, once it ends and they become qualified, licensed professionals they may lose touch with important developments. In a fast-changing world, they start becoming out of date the day they qualify.

The avuncular Dr Cameron image might be comforting and reassuring if all you want is Vick rubbed on your chest, but positively dangerous if you have a complicated and recently diagnosed virus. Important discoveries, new ways of treating illnesses and of being diagnostically sensitive to early signs of major diseases may pass by the hard-working doctor. So medics try hard to encourage continuing medical education to keep the profession up to date *and* to stress the point that education does not end on graduation.

Does the same happen to the MBA graduate? Is the Institute of Directors in favour of CME for managers? If so, what does this CME look like? What does a finance director or a marketing director need to know and how will he/she acquire that knowledge? Will reading the *FT* and *Marketing Week* suffice? Or is the in-house training course a good source of education?

Management, like medicine, changes and develops. Some of these changes are fashion based, others economically driven, and some reflect real developments in the discipline. Expensive, inefficient, unreliable and painful methods are discarded. Just as card files were replaced by computers, which took some mastering, so older methods of management are jettisoned in favour of better ways of doing things.

Most of us have at some time encountered a curious, neo-Dickensian world of management alive and well in a time capsule, insulated against the modern world. Curious, quaint and fascinating they may be; efficient they rarely are. Sir John Harvey-Jones's celebrated TV programmes were eloquent exposures of British companies that the world had passed by.

If one believes in CME in principle, there are inevitably what and how questions: What needs to be taught? How is one best educated? What does the hard-pressed, reactive, modern manager need to know through CME?

CME should be providing three things: knowledge, skills and attitudes. Business schools and universities prioritize them thus, but professionals stress skills first, the right attitude next and knowledge last. Despite the debate about priorities, most would agree that all three are important. Knowledge is essential. There is nothing as practical as good theory. Knowledge liberates – it teaches people to know how to ask questions, evaluate answers and solutions, and, more prosaically, where to look for an answer. Putting knowledge into practice by the use of skills is also crucial. Language skills, computer skills and people skills are the efficient application of a knowledge base. But skills training without a good knowledge background turns out operators and technicians, not professionals. Equally important is the socialization, which Americans call 'attitude'.

Many employers complain most about the attitude of young, thrusting, MBA-touting graduates: too much knowledge, too few skills, but worst of all, a bad attitude. They are perceived as being arrogant, selfish and unworldly. Equally, the middle-aged, middle-brow, middle manager may be seen as cynical, sceptical, conservative and against change. Neither naïve optimism nor cynical pessimism about education and change is appropriate. But one should not underestimate the socializing power of education. Business and medical schools know this. They are just as much about inculcating an attitude to work as knowledge and skills.

The next, just as relevant, CME question is not what to teach but how to teach it: seminars, lectures, videos, homework exercises, mini-MBAs, shadowing others? There are many different educational methods, but they can be categorized. For instance, one dimension is the *speed* at which they aim to work: fast versus slow. Second, the breadth of their *impact* can be broad or narrow. The traditional academic education via lectures and book reading is slow and narrow. It is ideal for an in-depth knowledge, carefully acquired, of a particular issue. A slow method aimed at a broad effect is group learning. In this method, groups meet on a regular basis, perhaps with specific rules, to explore issues together. Groups often learn more about the members of the group and group dynamics than anything else – but that, of course, may be the purpose.

A fast and narrow method may be expensive but often involves hiring a specialist to give an update. This means a careful and thorough review of the state of the art, and an analysis of recent trends, issues and debates. A fast method with a broad effect is the video-based skills development method. The short course can be highly effective for the quick acquisition of a broad perspective.

But beware the fast and broad. As the Bible says, the way to doom and destruction is broad and the way to enlightenment narrow. Different methods serve different purposes. They have different costs in every sense of the word. The traditional talk from a well-prepared and competent lecturer may serve the educational purpose best in one situation, and the slick video, copied to each member of the organization, may equally well serve a different purpose.

CME in knowledge, skills and attitudes is surely important. Equally, it is crucial to find the best method for the task. To some extent the medium is the message. Clearly, an astute fit between the two is crucial for CME.

People who advocate CME need to be closely questioned. Voltaire said that the Holy Roman Empire was neither Holy nor Roman nor Empire. Similarly, CME is rarely continual or continuous; it is not often for or about management; and it may be more like entertainment or punishment than education.

Compromising at work: the art of the trade-off

The British, it is said, are masters of compromise. The act of compromising can, of course, be seen as positive or negative, weak or strong, pusillanimous or practical. In a negative light, we talk of 'compromising our principles' or 'compromising the strategy'. It means that we settle for less than best; we give up on our original (explicit) plans and draw back to a weaker, less desirable position. But compromising can also be seen as skilful diplomacy – the finding of the *via media* (the middle way) and obtaining agreement from disparate, perhaps antagonistic, parties.

To compromise is to trade off one thing for another. So much of business is designing the optimal trade-off of different qualities or values. For all businesses, the three most quoted trade-off issues are *quality*, *speed* and *cost*. Imagine that you want to commission a piece of work. It may be the manufacturing of a product; a staff survey; the evaluation of a management process; or the purchase of a new IT system.

At the most mundane level, think of getting in an artisan (plumber, painter, decorator) to work on your house. What you want is for the work to be good, fast and cheap. Naturally, you want the quality of the craftsmanship to be high; you want the work done quickly so as to minimize the disruption to the house; and you certainly want the work to be cheap (affordable, value for money).

Alas, trading off means not getting the maximum amount of all three, but trading off one against another. You can usually have two of the three, but not all three together. Consider the organizations and managers who typically trade off one of the three.

Good and cheap, but not fast

This is where speed is traded off for quality and price. In this sense, quality can be cost-effective, but at the price of speed. If one is prepared to wait for people to work at their own speed, or when their erratic timetable allows, they may do the job well (even relatively cheaply), but it does drag on. Amateurs, part-timers and enthusiasts often perform tasks with total commitment and with relatively little reward, but they cannot be rushed.

Some organizations believe that quality is worth the wait. They may even argue that there is no alternative (the thing cannot be rushed), or indeed, that time spent is an index of quality. Research and development scientists, academics, writers and so on believe that they can come up with the goods only if they are not hurried. The 'folksy' family restaurant may provide uncommonly good food at very afford-able prices – but at their speed.

Good and fast, but not cheap

This is where price is traded off for speed and quality. If you want high-quality work with a very short lead time, you must be prepared to pay for it. In a sense, this is the concept of overtime. You can get sophisticated professionals (lawyers, doctors, engineers) to work through the night to provide excellent results, but you need to be prepared to pay for it. High flyers working to a tight delivery date command high salaries. There is always a cost, which is (pun intended) money.

Some businesses are used to frenetic output. They believe things have to be 'right first time' and on time – and they are prepared to pay for it. Looking back, it seems incredible to see what the rush was all about, but at the time, no one seems to question it. Money can buy hard work, commitment and quality.

Fast and cheap, but not good

This is where quality is traded off for speed and price. This is the cheap-and-cheerful, pile 'em high and sell 'em cheap end of the market. The fast-food industry does not pretend to offer fine dining. It provides cheap and tasty (semi, quasi, crypto) nutritious food served immediately. Naturally, organizations and individuals that trade off this way do not neglect quality; they merely set a lower standard.

One can buy products and hire people at highly competitive prices, but most people rightly suspect that just as there is no such thing as a free lunch, there are very rarely any real bargains. At the end of the day, one gets what one pays for. And if it is really cheap and quickly done, it is rarely very good.

The fast-good-cheap golden triangle applies well to services and products, but what about the hiring of people? Perhaps there is an equivalent set trade-off. Here it is between ability, effort and personal-ity. Every manager wants a person who is able, bright, quick to learn, sharp, talented, a high flyer or a person with the capacity to become one. Whatever politically correct term one chooses, we all know what this means: it is a correlate of intelligence.

All managers want the motivated individual: the self-starter, the committed hard worker, the conscientious employee willing to go the extra mile for the company. In most organizations, the most motivated people often complete two to three times the amount of work as the least motivated, irrespective of their talent.

There is a third factor, which the layman calls personality and the psychologist calls social skills. If you like, this is EQ. Your parents may have called it charm. It means warm, friendly, empathic, insightful, sensitive: a person, in other words, who is pleasant, helpful and agreeable.

As to the trade-off, consider the options:

1. *Clever, hard working, but not charming.* Some selectors believe that EQ is an added benefit and not essential. IT specialists, bankers and so on don't seem particularly eager to select for social skills. This may be because they believe that those who are selected are primarily backroom boys who don't face real clients. Whether this is true or not, the low-charm manager is often a poor manager.

2. *Clever, charming, but somewhat lazy.* The easy charm of the highly talented 'public schoolboy' type may easily be accompanied by a belief that their natural ability and polished social skills mean that they do not have to work too hard to achieve success in life. Occasionally they are right – their ability to master complex briefs and to persuade others to help them means that they never have to work too hard. But they can easily be caught out when there is no substitute for old-fashioned grind.

3. *Hard working, charming, but not too bright.* The successful sales person is usually dedicated and personable, but not overly clever. In many ways, they do not have to be: their task is repetitive rather than challenging, and what challenges there are are to the ego rather than the intellect. The urbane, avuncular, highly motivated middle manager is often the social glue of organizations. But without capacity they may not be able to adapt to change and to anticipate future developments. If their only response is to work harder, rather than smarter, they may be easily stressed.

But there is good news. Although the trade-off between speed, quality and cost is very real in products and services, it does not have to be made so often with people. The reason is that the three qualities are unrelated: intelligence, motivation and empathy are pretty well dissociated. You are just as likely to find all three together as all three absent.

But recruiters do have a difficult task: that is, deciding on the optimal amount of each quality. A highly intelligent person in a moderately demanding job may become bored. The only moderately motivated person in a job requiring total commitment may well fail. The EQ learning disabled may survive in certain environments, but not all. The trick for the selector is to be able to specify the optimum level of the three important characteristics mentioned above, and find them in one individual.

Two out of three won't do.

Cowardice: The Pusillanimous Manager

Be honest now, when was the last time your manager called you to his/her office and you spoke exclusively and consistently about your performance? In other words, when did you last get honest, accurate feedback on how your boss perceives your performance?

I have asked this question of well over a thousand middle to senior managers in more than a dozen countries. Sadly, about half say never; and this despite the fact that many may have been with the company for well over a decade. Another third distantly remember a boss, whom they admired, who maybe light years ago gave them an honest appraisal. And they remember this rare but highly beneficial event well. Lucky ones get it regularly, so to speak.

The question is why this fundamental process is so rare and, when it is done at all it is so frequently done badly. It is particularly important because feedback is necessary to all learning. All change and learning programmes – from Weight Watchers to computer skills – give regular, specific feedback on performance. The role of the sports coach is as much to give feedback as it is to encourage and give advice. Indeed, the video camera has replaced the coach for just this reason. And it accounts for why it is used so often in training.

These are the major reasons why managers do not carry out serious appraisals. The first is pusillanimity – they are too scared to give negative or corrective feedback. The more authoritarian the organization, the easier this is (consider the army for instance), but the rise of assertive, demanding, litigious staff means that managers always feel uncomfortable about negative feedback and simply duck the issue. Fearful of the tears, anger and sulking that may follow a negative performance review, most managers simply evade the task. Indeed, it's pleasant giving positive feedback, but it's rare that all feedback is exclusively good.

The second reason is related to the first. It is that managers have not been trained in the skill of appraisal. Many are offered courses but resist them, partly through fear of being shown up. The skills are relatively simple – managers need to structure the appraisal interviews and have an agenda; they should ask the appraisee to summarize at the end; they should move towards establishing agreed action points that form the basis of the next agenda, and so on.

The pusillanimous manager's most common excuse for not going on a course is that they 'appraise people all the time'. Their argument is that rather than having a couple of specific hour-long meetings over the year, they give subordinates constant feedback on a day-to-day basis. But what they fail to realize is that discussion about software, the strategic plan and sales figures is not an appraisal. There is an easy way to test this. Ask reluctant managers on the course if they believe they do regular, relevant appraisals. Then ask those whom they (supposedly) appraise. The difference is salutary and sobering.

The third reason is that the organization, despite much rhetoric to the contrary, clearly does not take the whole process seriously. It is usually not modelled from the top; there are no consequences of appraisal ratings; there are no punishments for managers who simply do not comply. Indeed, there is a collective cowardice in many organizations that talk about merit, promotion and people being our greatest asset and so on. The problem lies not so much in rewarding the good performer as in dealing with the poor performer.

A good appraisal system is one that is transparently fair and equitable, where there are checks and balances on ratings and clear consequences of them. What sanctions do HR directors apply to managers who don't play the game, either by ducking appraisal or attempting to 'fix the system'? Most of the time, none. HR directors are not usually selected for their courage. So the pusillanimity starts at the top. And that, rather than good appraisals, is what is modelled.

Sir Michael Edwardes, who faced the problems of British Leyland head on, said about British businessmen: 'We are tough and brave in war. We are soft and compromising in management.' The problem of pusillanimity is not that it leads to an unhealthy tolerance of poor performance, but rather its effect on the morale and maturation of good performers. Paradoxically, it is frequently the high-achieving, ambitious and hard-working who are most eager for feedback – good or bad – because they know it is helpful. And if the organization ducks the task, they feel deprived and poorly managed.

Good managers, like good teachers and good coaches, conduct 'appraisals' anyway, whatever the policy in vogue. They know the importance of feedback. And bad managers – the pusillanimous, the unskilled, the devious – do not give appraisals, whatever the HR hype.

If you are not prepared to give each direct report a minimum of two one-hour appraisals annually, you should not be a manager.

Creating the right impression

We all make disastrous selection decisions. The divorce statistics alone are, perhaps, the best testimony to self-admitted decision errors. Consider the sheer quality and quantity of data accumulated by both parties before they make the matrimonial decision. However, most of the data on potential marriage partners is derived in some sort of interview. As far as I know, no one yet has gathered assessment centre, personality/ability test, work-sample data, or even formal references and testimonials, before making 'the big decision'. But that day may not be far off.

What good data we have suggest that the interview is not a very valid way of selecting people. Too many false positives (selecting poor workers) and false negatives (rejecting good workers) occur. And yet very few people would select without the interview. They believe they somehow get a better impression of a person face to face than by any other method.

The selection interview is, alas, not a clinical surgery where salient personal information is gathered, evaluated and integrated. All too often, it is a parlour game, a hall of mirrors, and a charade of bluff and pretence. It is a stage for what psychologists call *impression management*. The interviewee is selling; the interviewer buying. Of course, the sales person presents their best possible view as they perceive the needs of the purchaser. And the purchaser prods, questions and negotiates to make sure they get what they want.

In short, whether you want to call it 'telling porkies', wrap it in psychobabble and say people are prone to 'occasional dissimulation and social desirability responding', or come clean and say 'lying', we all know that it happens in interviews. There are, of course, many kinds of lies – of omission (concealment) and commission (falsifying), white lies, even unconscious lies – but lies they all are. Psychologists have distinguished between self-deception (the tendency to overattribute desirable characteristics to the self) and denial (the tendency to deny undesirable characteristics). Inevitably, both lead interviewers to get highly selective data.

Concern about this issue has led to a profitable industry in the United States dedicated to honesty testing. Again, we have various synonyms such as conscientiousness, dependability, integrity, trustworthiness or reliability testing – but they are all aimed at measuring attitudes and propensity to, as well as history of, lying. Honesty is absolutely crucial in some jobs; and nearly always desirable from the perspective of the employer.

The trouble for the interviewer is that it is very difficult to detect lies. We are all adults and socially skilled, sophisticated people who, not wanting to hurt people's feelings, can obfuscate facts to make them more palatable. Most of us are accomplished liars!

All those Desmond Morris-esque TV programmes and conferences on non-verbal behaviour have convinced many people that they are not only good judges of character, but also good interview-based lie detectors. Most are sadly mistaken. Even acknowledged world experts in the area admit the difficulty of being able to tell when people are telling the truth. We do know that some non-verbal behaviours tend to be associated with lying: a decrease in hand gestures, an increase in hand-to-face (especially nose) contacts, as well as an increase in squirming body shifts and hand shrugs. The explanations for these observations are certainly interesting. Liars tweak their nose for two reasons: to block the lie subconsciously, even 'pull it back in', and also because it twitches more when people are physically tense (during lying).

The trouble with being too sensitive to all the non-verbal cues (gaze patterns, gestures, positive shifts) is that one can so easily 'overinterpret' what is going on. Thus the nervous person can easily be seen as guilty, and the confident, ever-lying, psychopath as honest. Indeed, the lie-detector more often errs on judging the truthful as liars than liars as truthful.

But we do know a few things about liars. They get caught for five main reasons. First, lack of preparation: some interviewees can be caught out because they have not fully prepared their story and get confused, contradictory, and hence embarrassed. Second, it is more difficult lying about feelings than about facts – there are often 'emotional escapes' where people cannot hide anger or shame about some past event. Third, feelings about lying let people down – that is, guilt about lying can be a give-away, except, of course, in the psychopath, who neither knows nor cares what a lie is. Fourth, there is, not unnaturally, fear about being caught – called detection apprehension in the jargon. This is why it is useful to cultivate a reputation as a tough and insightful interviewer.

Finally, many liars get caught after the event by duping delight – the obvious (and unexplained) relief that appears after the lie. In this sense, the Customs officers should video the 'over-the-limit' passengers as they come out of Customs, not as they queue to go in.

Of course, the vast majority of interviewers could hardly be accused of telling major lies in the selection interview. But it should never be forgotten than they are always presenting the truth in the way they believe best suits them.

The detrimental effects of rewards

For some time, a rather controversial and counterintuitive idea has been around that is simply described by the title of a popular book *Punished by Rewards* by A Kohn (Houghton Mifflin, 1993). The idea is that a reward (usually monetary) inherently reduces task interest and creativity.

Put simply, the thesis is this: people who have been given (explicit) rewards at work (such as performance-related pay) work harder and produce more *but* it is of lower quality, contains more errors and reduces creativity. Rewards may make people less willing to take risks, be less playful and experimental and more mechanical.

According to some psychologists, when people begin to evaluate our work and explicitly reward some measurable output, the creative juices dry up. The creative process is replaced by 'reward thinking', which distracts individuals from the activity, thereby reducing the spontaneity and flexibility of performance.

What many popular critics have asserted is that in various educational and workplace settings the introduction of reward systems does more harm than good whenever creative performance is a desirable outcome.

Take the case of the creative writer scribbling at home on a new novel. Local children had for three days played extremely noisily in a small park near his study. The sound of their playing was simultaneously loud, uncontrollable and unpredictable. What could he do: Ask (politely) that they quieten down or go away?; Call the police or the parents if he knew them; threaten them with force if they did not comply?; or pay them to go away?.

Play is fun and can be creative: it is intrinsically satisfying and can be extinguished by rewards. In the story the writer went to the children and said, somewhat insincerely, that he had very much enjoyed them being there, and the sound of their laughter, and he was so delighted with them that he was prepared to pay them to continue. He promised to pay them each £1.00 a day if they carried on as before. The youngsters were naturally surprised but delighted. For two days the writer, seemingly grateful, dispensed the cash. But on the third day he explained that because of a 'cash flow' problem he could only give them 50p each. The next day he claimed to be 'cash-light' and only handed out 10p. The following day they got nothing.

True to prediction the children would have none of this, complained and refused to continue. They left promising never to return to play in the park. Totally successful in his endeavour, the writer retired to his study luxuriating in the silence.

He had rewarded the children for their creative play and hence stopped it. But is this true? Does pay for performance in R&D people, in advertising agencies and in marketing circles lead to less inventiveness? A recent careful analysis of all the existing data, plus careful experimental work, suggests this is not true. In fact the data show that if a (creative or analytic) person receives a tangible reward (money) that depends on completing a task *to a particular quality standard* and then subsequently that reward is eliminated, the person spends as much time on the activity as he or she did before the reward was introduced.

Moreover, there are two reliable and robust effects of extrinsic reward on intrinsic interest. With verbal reward (praise), people spend more time on a task following the reward's removal than before its introduction. Further, most people state that they like the task better after verbal reward or monetary reward that depends on performance quality. Reward for high creativity in one task also enhances subsequent creativity in quite different tasks.

In fact the only time when rewards have detrimental effects is when rewards occur on a single occasion *without regard to the quality of performance* (actual creativity) or *the speed accuracy of task completion*. It is alas true in business that there are occasions where people are rewarded irrespective of their real performance. Some compensation and promotion systems are, quite frankly, pretty insensitive to performance so that employees can vary their performance (both ways) with little effect on tangible rewards. This definitely reduces effort *and* satisfaction *and* commitment.

For the old-fashioned behaviouralists the news is good. Rewards can be used either to enhance or diminish creative performance, depending on how they are used. Rewards presented occasionally and independent of performance may encourage individuals to believe that they have no control over the reward and they lessen their performance. However, rewards presented repeatedly in a non-salient fashion for genuinely original work increase creativity and positive attitude to entirely different creative problems. A tangible reward that people see for successful work is likely to enhance their feelings of self-confidence.

Explicit promise of reward for creativity does increase that creativity, unless, of course, people believe that level of creativity is beyond their capability. Also, the unattractive combination of a great prize with great time pressure to find a solution may cause such anxiety and passion that it disrupts the cognitive juices.

All this does not necessarily mean that intrinsic task interest – sheer personal love of the activity, whatever it is – has no effect on creativity or productivity. It is and will always be vital. But there is no such simple evidence that explicitly rewarding creative task performance interferes with that performance. The secret lies in *what* is rewarded, when and why.

Electronic mail

Many organizations have enthusiastically adopted e-mail in order to maintain competitiveness and contain rising costs. Its supporters argue that it accelerates and regularizes information flow: it's fast, cheap and, unlike the telephone, is asynchronous, which means parties do not have to be available simultaneously. It also offers a wider spread of contacts. It seems generally agreed that it may be less friendly, but more business-like and therefore useful for task-orientated communication. Or is it the ideal communication medium for the angry, the unassertive and the attention seeking?

We have all received e-mail from a person across the room or one next door. It has proved a wonderful mechanism for the 'disgusted of Tunbridge Wells' type or the underemployed secretary who wants to indicate how important or busy she is.

Studies in the late 1980s reported that the introduction of e-mail reduced telephone calls by 80%, and saved 36 minutes a day in communication and millions of pounds in associated costs. Most importantly, the number of meetings was reduced, because on e-mail everyone can 'talk' and 'listen' at their own convenience. However, recent British research suggests that people spent more than 45 minutes a day on e-mail activities, and that number may be rising steeply. They sent and received, on average, about 15 e-mails a day, and read their e-mails as many as 10 times a day!

E-mail is typically used *within* organizations for four purposes: *scheduling*, such as announcing time and place of an upcoming meeting, *task assignment*, *reporting accomplishment* and *general awareness*. E-mail is democratic once it is introduced company-wide. One can easily, comfortably and regularly communicate with important people higher up the pecking order, to whom one is unlikely ever to speak.

The CEO, guarded by PAs, was usually quite inaccessible. His or her post was opened and only a filtered version of what was going on ever reached him/her. But now the lowest can speak directly to the highest through e-mail. What some users report is that they like the rapid speed of message delivery; access to a wider spread of contacts; the savings coming from fewer non-work-related discussions, and the fact that the sender and receiver do not have to be present at the same time.

But the system clearly has drawbacks. There are three sorts of concerns or disadvantages with e-mail:

Work-related problems

● *Information overload:* because it is cheap and easy, too much trivial, irrelevant and redundant information is sent via e-mail. Many people are tempted to communicate before they reflect, and injudicious messages can be the result.
● *Security of information:* there is a small, but real chance that mail can be intercepted. Of more concern is the ease with which mail can be forwarded to a third party.

System-related concerns

● *Users require training:* certainly much more than telephone or fax users, though frankly this is a minor point.
● *Archiving:* the storage of outdated messages is commonplace, but expensive and pointless.

Social impact

● Social isolation: face-to-face contact is reduced. This can have very real consequences. Propinquity used to lead to social contact and thence liking and trust. One gets a sense of belongingness when meeting with other work colleagues. Some argue that one may as well work from home for all the actual contact you now get with the e-mail addict.
● Misinterpretation of messages occurs: this often leads to angry, uninhibited, less empathetic messages being sent, seemingly anonymously.
● The filtering out of social cues: this means less effective communication.

There are two types of people in this world: those who believe there are two types and those who don't. But there are, very clearly, two types of e-mailers. Some people want a system that manages their mail before they see it: a sort of cyber-secretary. Others are adamant about

reading all their incoming mail first, but want subsequent help to store
and later retrieve messages.

The first group can be classified as *prioritizers*. They are interested
in limiting the time they spend on e-mail and in maximizing efficiency.
They want help in selecting important messages to be read immediately, deleting finished ones, and organizing the rest for later reading.
They are willing to risk missing an important message for the sake of
increased efficiency in managing their mail. These people are not
necessarily more successful than others at managing their time. But
they are more likely to describe time management as a central function in their work.

The second group could be called *archivers*. These people want to
ensure that they read every message and are willing to spend extra
time on their mail so as to avoid missing a potentially important
message. They want help in categorizing and storing messages and
want better tools to aid in the later search and retrieval of messages.
Archivers are not necessarily just hoarders, afraid to discard anything.
Instead, they regard the gathering, digestion and distribution of information as critical in their work. These users are also not necessarily
very well organized. Some display very efficient strategies for the storage and retrieval of messages. Others are very disorganized and spend
a considerable amount of time searching for stored messages.

The psychological impact of e-mail lies in the effort required to
complete normally straightforward conversations. Whether or not
people send a message depends on the degree to which its relevance
and urgency exceeds the effort required to compose the message and
complete the transaction.

However, the main problem lies in the ability of people to write
clear, comprehensible English. The irony is that the non-literary,
monoglotic techies who are attracted to e-mail cannot write any better
than they can speak. Although they might feel more comfortable
communicating with the world electronically, there is little evidence
that the quality of the communication increases.

Emotional intelligence

To a psychologist, the term 'emotional intelligence' is an oxymoron:
the juxtapositioning of incompatible terms. For a psychometrician,
intelligence is measured by *maximal* performance, and emotionality is

judged by *typical* behaviour. Indeed, nearly all psychologists agree that intelligence and personality are unrelated, and have collected a quantity of data to prove it. Thus, one may be an intelligent neurotic or a dim extrovert just as easily as a dim neurotic (highly emotional) or an intelligent extrovert. Intelligence tests do not measure personality, emotionality, creativity or social skills, and nor do they intend to.

Many lay people know that this is intuitively true. However, when a popular book appeared with this title, it seemed interesting enough to read. In it, we are told that emotional literacy or intelligence is the key to everything in life – health, happiness and success at work. There is a chapter in Daniel Goleman's bestseller (*Emotional Intelligence*, Bloomsbury, 1996) called 'Managing with heart', which quite clearly says that interpersonal skills are more important than intellectual skills for getting on at work.

The idea is that stress makes people ineffective, and it is the job of managers to reduce stress by recognizing and dealing with feelings in themselves and others. The more you understand and 'get in touch with yourself' and those who work for you, the better a manager you will be. EQ is supposedly good for appraisals, negotiations, teamwork, networking, and practically all aspects of behaviour at work.

But what is EQ? The term 'emotional intelligence' was first used in 1990. At the time, it was defined as a type of social intelligence that involves the ability to monitor one's own and others' emotions, to discriminate among them, and use the information to guide one's thinking and actions. It is a new word for old concepts, such as social skills, interpersonal competence, psychological maturity and emotional awareness.

EI supposedly comprises different domains such as self-awareness, the ability to manage (that is, control) one's emotions, self-motivation and empathy. EI is the ability to perceive emotions (in oneself and others); to access and generate emotions so as to assist thinking; to understand emotions and the subtle expression of emotions in others; and to regulate emotions. Just as not being able to read or express emotions can be socially handicapping, it is possible to argue that this form of illiteracy leads to poor decision-making.

But is EQ any different from older concepts such as warmth, charm, empathy, insight or maturity? Probably not. Is the theme of this work any different from the ideas that Dale Carnegie published more than 50 years ago, which are still in print? Again, it is unlikely.

Few would disagree with the premiss that these factors are important at work. They are, in part, the characteristics of a good boss who can motivate both him/herself and others. Of course, EQ could be seen to be more relevant in certain jobs – the GP, the consultant, the social worker and the teacher all need EQ. Possibly those with lower EQs gravitate to jobs that require less of it – the anaesthetist, the shepherd, the accountant or the lighthouse keeper. But the argument goes that the more you have to manage people, be they customers, shareholders, subordinates or superiors, alone or in teams and groups, the more EQ becomes important.

Few would disagree. But it is surely a serious error to suggest that it is both necessary *and* sufficient. The good manager requires many skills, abilities and traits. They need to be bright (enough), conscientious, and aware of the complex issues in the business world. They need, above all, to be courageous. It is all very well understanding the needs of people, but it is equally important to understand the needs of the business. Empathy and emotional maturity will take people only so far.

Everybody wants an emotionally stable, perceptive and intelligent boss. To be successful at work, most people need to be able and motivated – and to cultivate a good reputation. The question really is the predictive power of IQ over EQ in job success. If you had to choose between high IQ and moderate EQ or the other way round, I have no doubt in whose company I would put my money. The bright, aloof boss versus the average, warm boss would, in the end, have a significant impact on the company, whatever sector it is in.

Of course, senior people can choose to have people around them who compensate for their deficits. So the low-EQ, high-IQ manager could have a deputy who is highly emotionally literate and who 'picks up the pieces', 'calms the water' and 'smooths down the feathers' of the hurt or ignored subordinates of the boss. Equally, the high-EQ, low-IQ manager may select a really bright, fast-tracked, high-flying whiz kid to do the 'hard stuff' in the world of management, while he warmly deals with all the emotional issues. It is possible and has been done – but rarely. Most managers select others in their own image. The seriously bright boss soon gets annoyed by the high-EQ, low-IQ colleague who can't grasp the facts fast enough. Equally, the empathic, high-EQ boss may quash the recommendations of high-IQ colleagues because they would 'rattle the cage' of too many others. To misquote the bard: 'Give me bright men around me Gates, young ... has a warm and fuzzy look.'

Perhaps the interest in EQ is a comment on our times. Perhaps it is a reflection of going against the tough, avaricious 1980s with all the pain of lay-offs, re-engineering, mergers and acquisitions. As Dilbert notes, the idea that 'people are our most valuable asset' is a deeply cynical comment when they are so obviously not treated as such. It may well be that the EQ has found a deep resonance with managers because of its 'corrective message' that empathy and social skills are important at work. But the trick is not to let the pendulum swing too far in the opposite direction and take one's eye off the reason why people are at work.

Evaluating others: see, speak and hear no evil

Hands up those who believe their organization has a good appraisal system. All right, hands up those who believe we need some sort of appraisal system. So, it's nought for the first question and a 100% for the second.

It remains true that performance appraisal systems are a constant source of employee (and employer) dissatisfaction. So, how does one get it right?

Some people believe that the problem with these systems lies in their design. Hence they attempt to design integrated, metricated and sophisticated systems that end up requiring literally dictionaries and 100-page handbooks/manuals to explain how to use them. Frequently, organizations swing from ultra-complex to ultra-simple systems to overcome apathy, discontent and bewilderment. Some organizations even give them up altogether after persistent but misinformed attempts to redesign them. This is a bad idea as they provide for most people their only structured, regular feedback on their performance. At the very least they can help build and cement employee commitment and satisfaction.

But perhaps the most common cause of problems associated with appraisal systems lies in the insensitive, inaccurate ratings of the managers. These occur not primarily because the managerial rater is ignorant or lazy but rather because he/she has a particular style which they believe will fulfil their aims. Three clearly discernible styles – all poor and non-differentiating – are apparent:

Manager Softy

Manager Softy likes to see the good in everyone and advocates win–win – or that's what his or her ratings show. This type of manager believes that as well as keeping him/her popular, rating all subordinates highly on all aspects of their work simultaneously avoids conflict and ensures maximum performance-related pay for each of their reports. They believe that this strategy motivates all concerned, and frankly wonder privately why everybody does not adopt it. But it fails badly for four good reasons:

- By rating everyone as excellent it lets down and demotivates the really good performers who clearly know about their performance relative to their peers. Why 'bust a gut' and achieve impressive output both qualitatively and quantitatively if the second-ratee you know gets the same score and bonus?
- Getting consistently good marks makes staff complacent. If your boss 'haloes' you as way-above-average on all performance measures all the time, it seems quite legitimate to relax as effort and output do not seem clearly related.
- Manager Softy looks a pushover, and assertive, demanding staff members may exploit his/her good nature to receive even greater ratings. Curiously, Manager Softy, like the lenient teachers we all had, is not particularly liked and certainly not well respected.
- But the greatest problem is when ratings relate to pay. If the appraisal system standardizes the data, or insists on within-group comparison as is often, and rightly, the case, staff with very good marks can receive very little bonus pay precisely because of mark overinflation. Given very high ratings, the employee naturally expects concomitant rewards, but if all subordinates of Manager Softy are at the top end of the scale only the very, very high marks yield rewards.

Manager Midway

For this manager everyone is mediocre. All staff are average – no high flyers, no poor performers... average on everything. Manager Midway, like Manager Softy, is really a coward. They adopt this rating strategy because they do not like to confront poor performers with their deserved and explicit poor ratings. They also do not like to raise expectations of good performers by high ratings for fear they cannot fulfil them. So, their strategy is to mark everyone average. And this too backfires for three very good reasons;

- Ratings give staff feedback on their performance but if, in effect, all ratings are on or around the mid-point, it is difficult to know what one's supervisor thinks. Staff get no pointers as to what they do well or badly.
- Similarly, as a consequence of mediocre ratings, it is common for the staff of Manager Midway to believe that their manager neither appreciates nor understands their strengths and weaknesses or those of their peers. Many raters believe they have both an imperceptive and non-caring manager. Further, this information is pretty useless if one wants to use it to underpin career, succession planning or other information.
- Finally, medium ratings mean median pay awards for all those under Manager Midway, irrespective of their performance. People at work are always very sensitive to equality-based rewards and if they see the incompetent slackers getting the same awards as dedicated and conscientious staff, their confidence in both their manager and the system suffers.

So rather than solve the problem of confronting the incompetent and excessively raising the expectations of the successful, Manager Midway demotivates all the staff, who believe he or she cannot possibly either understand or appreciate them.

Manager Nasty

We probably all had the Sergeant Major school teacher who perversely thought it was motivating and encouraging to be told that you were probably the worst class he/she had had in 30 years of teaching. Manager Nasty believes that people will take advantage of you if you encourage or endorse them – a give-them-an-inch philosophy. This manager believes that threat of punishment (sticks) is more effective than promise of reward (carrots), so gives all his or her staff low marks on appraisal forms. In turn they get minimum rewards and this leads to three obvious and predictable problems:

- All staff need encouragement or 'stroking' if you like feline California-speak. If staff believe, and see through low ratings, that their effort (and ability) is not rewarded or recognized, they are naturally likely to become less motivated.
- Managers who punish may be feared but are rarely considered fair. They tend to have high turnover in the department and acquire a reputation of not being good to work for.
- And low ratings can mean little or no performance-related pay year after year. Hardly a recipe for a hardworking and motivated workforce.

So Manager Nasty too finds that his or her strategy backfires. Although he/she can hardly be accused of pusillanimousness, they rarely succeed in getting the best out of people.

Appraisal systems stand or fall by the ratings generated. If the manager's rating is based on attempting to fix the system, or personal bias, or on a fear of negative reactions, they provide poor data for any system to interpret.

Managers' ratings need to be reliable and able to differentiate within and between employers. Years ago we used the word discriminating. Old advertisements talked about customers with taste and discrimination. To discriminate is to differentiate – to notice, remark on, and act on, subtle but important differences. Wine and tea tasters, dog and horse judges, all have to learn to differentiate on subtle cues. Managers need to notice the strengths and weaknesses (now called developmental opportunities) of their staff, give them clear feedback on those and rate them accordingly. Most employees have reasonable self-insight – they know what they are good at and what does not come naturally. And they like being praised for the former and helped with the latter. They need to be appropriately challenged and supported.

At the heart of all appraisal systems philosophy is the concept of equity – the idea that people should be rated and rewarded for their individual performance. It is the manager who supposedly notices individual differences and rates them appropriately. In the old-fashioned sense of the word, managers need to be more discriminating for appraisal systems to work well.

Evidence-based management

'Medicine is a science; but management is an art.' True or false? The vast majority of people say true. They believe that medicine deals with tangible phenomena, such as bone structure, blood pressure, micro-organisms, that can be, and have been, subjected to rigorous scientific testing. They also point to the numerous impressive discoveries in medicine this century, which have almost doubled the life expectancy of adults.

By contrast, managing people seems hopelessly unscientific. Work motivation, morale and corporate culture seem vague concepts that are not available to scientific observation and experience. Although there is a so-called academic discipline called management science, most people are pretty sceptical of it as they see guru after guru giving contradictory, impractical, bizarre advice. Management, it seems, is at the pre-scientific stage and is likely to remain there.

But the medical world has seen an enormous threat over the past 10 years. Critics claimed that much of medicine was based not on scientific evidence, but on superstition or simply custom. Hence the differences in treatment in different countries. Take, for instance, how to treat the newborn. Russian neonates are immediately swaddled, removed from their mothers and lined up like chess pawns to be cared for by nursing staff for the first weeks of their life. It was ever thus. And why? The argument goes that swaddling both ensures a more constant body temperature and prevents babies from injuring themselves. But in Britain the idea is to encourage maximum maternal (that is, naked) body contact between mother and child to help bonding – almost the opposite treatment.

Is either based on evidence? No – tradition, guesswork and custom seem to dictate practice. When science police of the medical world started asking their avuncular medical practitioners what evidence there was for this or that treatment, everyone was horrified to discover that the answer was often none or mixed. And it wasn't as if this was the case for exceptional or rare practices. Everyday surgical procedures, drug administration and hospital regimes all failed the 'What evidence is there for that' test.

It wasn't only doctors but also patients who were, and are, alarmed at this challenge. Doctors seemed to have the rug of profes-sional scientific respectability pulled out from under their consulting-room chairs. They seemed to many not very different from some of the obvious charlatans that one finds in complementary medicine. And, of course, the patients believing in the invincibility of modern medicine began to worry who to turn to for certainty in scientific medicine and *proven* cures.

But isn't it time one challenged the awesomely confident, self-proclaimed omniscient hubris in the management world with the challenge of evidence-basedness? What is the evidence that pay-related performance increases productivity? Is there any (let alone clear and unequivocal) evidence that brainstorming produces more and better-quality ideas than people working alone? What proof is there that people communicate more in open (versus closed) plan offices? Are 'electronic meetings' more effective than the old-fashioned type? The list is endless, but the question remains the same.

Gurus, consultants and trainers are often hard-pressed to mention any good recent study subject to the usual scrutiny of being published in a peer-reviewed scientific journal such as *Administrative Science Quarterly* or the *Journal of Applied Psychology*. Most simply don't know or care about evidence. They are a bit like religious believers confronted with evidence going against their beliefs. The simple truth as they see it (and proselytize it) is too important to be clouded by such trivial things as facts.

On the other hand, the business school professors use the words equivocal, pre-paradigmatic or heuristic, which are words that mean either the facts are mixed; there aren't any because we don't know what to test; or the model has no empirical support but looks pretty and seems useful.

But there is good, replicated, clear evidence in management science. We know how, why and when brainstorming groups are useful and when they are not. We know the validities of certain selection procedures such as assessment centres and graphology; we know why some forms of training are more successful than others. Yet the question is a really useful one. When somebody advocates the introduction of a new management system or the further flattening of the management hierarchy, simply ask the question, 'what evidence exists that it works?' And don't be put off by all that best-practice flim-flam that masquerades as evidence. Neither are sexy case studies in airline magazines real evidence.

Evidence is best established by having a theory that leads to a prediction that can be tested. Most management science can be as good as any other social science like economics or psychology. But it does take time and conscientious effort. More importantly, perhaps, it starts with good theory, which the whole management area is alarmingly without.

So, when you sit in the next seminar that advocates this or that magic bullet to solve all human resource management problems, ask politely the simple question. 'What evidence is there that this is true?' And be Paxman-like if you don't get a clear answer. The chances are that you won't.

Exceeding with excess

I am firm; he is stubborn; they are bloody-minded. Carruthers is 'too clever by half', while Stringfield is 'a sausage short of a fry-up'. These statements reflect the important but neglected idea that too much or too little of any human characteristic may be undesirable. It is the optimal amount that is crucial.

This idea, however, seems to be lost on selectors, many of whom see more as good. To misquote the Duchess of Windsor, 'one can never be too bright, or too motivated'. Many interviewers believe that when selecting others, the brighter the better; the higher the EQ the greater the likelihood of success; the more the motivation the greater the chance of being a high flyer. In their minds, the graph (ability versus success) is positive, linear and straight. But just like the classic cartoon of the sales-figure chart showing ever upward and onward growth, the idea is a myth.

Similarly, one needs to optimize, not maximize, competency. The HR world has been excited by the 'difficult-to-define' concept of competency. It is often referred to as a mix between a personality, a trait, know-how and ability. These terms are used to describe characteristics people want from their managers in organizations. Organizations, like people, think they are unique, and insist that they spend days of executive man hours coming up with their special list of competencies to use as an HR framework. Any cursory glance at those published competencies between companies, radically different in size, structure, product and workforce, soon reveal that the lists are almost identical. And so they should be. Management is fundamentally the same process, whatever the organization.

But once having got their competency requirements, the head-hunters and selectors go full out to find the candidates that seem to hit the minimum level on nearly all of the competencies. Although smarter organizations attempt to introduce rather different profiles of competence for different jobs (the Head of Sales versus the Head of Finance), they nevertheless nearly always conceive of this as setting the minimum cutoff points.

When did you last hear an 'expert' in selection saying that a candidate was too intelligent, too motivated or too committed? Indeed, they may talk of overeducated and overqualified, but the problem here is nearly always thought of as managing the expectations (and salary) of the applicant.

Over the past decade or so, business writers have been writing about the 'dark side' of derailed managers. It is a good analogy: dark is the opposite of light, it is hidden, it can also indicate gloominess or evil. The Jungians talk about the shadow. The idea is that there is a side to people that one may get to see only too late for good decisions or in particularly difficult circumstances. In the selection interview, both parties are concerned with putting their best foot forward, focusing the spotlight on their best features and accentuating the positive.

Most selectors are aware of negative traits: the pathological liar who comes across as extremely charming; the chronic absentee worker who looks the picture of health; the stress-carrier who seems to have not a care in the world; or the whingeing, negative, perpetually job-dissatisfied worker who talks happily about how much they enjoyed their previous job.

But few consider the dark side of talent; the consequences of too much of a good thing. Consider what most selectors look for: intelligence, motivation, social skills, ambition and, of course, a history of success. Intelligent people may intimidate others whose excellent ideas are self-censored. The highly motivated may expect everyone else to be workaholics, or treat others as a means to an end. The socially skilled may be interested only in using their charm to manipulate others. Ambitious people can easily break rules, laws, minds and bodies to achieve personal success. And track records may be deeply misleading, because it is unclear how people have achieved success (destructively, by luck and so on).

Consider the downside of being 'too high' on the common competencies specified by companies. The *team player* is much sought after, but people may have chosen to hide in teams because they are indecisive, dependent and rather eager for others to take the lead, the risk and possibly the blame for failure. Those *good with people*, with a high EQ, may be too soft on employees and unable to make tough people decisions. The highly empathic often put up with acutely and chronically underperforming staff for far too long, explaining away their ineffectual incompetence. Those too *customer-focused* may easily overrun budgets, not understanding financial implications, in their desire to please the customer. Paradoxically, they may also be rather too conservative, offering the customer only what they say they want, rather than what they might greatly appreciate, but can't articulate.

Those with a just do it *bias to action* may be impulsive and authoritarian; whereas those with *analytic skills* may be prone to analysis paralysis. The former tend to be too fast, the latter too slow to act. Equally, the *creative* may be daydreamers. Innovation can be as much associated with lack of realism and impractical money-wasting as genuinely being able to solve problems in a novel way.

Those with *global vision* may be so one-worldly that they miss local markets and become overextended and badly unfocused. Equally, the *culturally sensitive* may get so hung up with frankly trivial etiquette that they lose all sense of the greater customer base.

The one competency with which all struggle is *integrity*. It seems to be so hard to assess and yet so important that many companies agonize over ensuring that their managers are of the highest integrity. But those of proved integrity may too easily be thought of as rigid and zealous. They may enjoy the deeply alienating holier-than-thou, quasi-sanctimonious position of those who know they are right. Worse, they may impose their particular ethical codes and personal standards on to others hamfistedly, whole-heartedly and inflexibly. Beware the manager who wears his integrity on his sleeve.

Whatever the list of competencies one may wish to make, it is always important to consider the consequences of having these in excess. One can indeed be too thin and too rich. Rather, one needs an optimal amount – a cutoff point at each end of the spectrum; a window of opportunity; a desirable score. Nothing exceeds like excess. It is just as dangerous having too little or too much of a relevant competency.

Growing managers: sowing the seeds of success

There are plenty of books on *business high flyers*. Some are auto-hagiographies written by successful tycoons themselves (witness Richard Branson's latest opus). Others are based on interviews with nominated executives who have agreed to be interrogated by zealous MBAs or voyeuristic writers in the hope of good press.

Of late, a new and much more interesting genre of business book has appeared on our shelves – a diagnosis and description of the derailed manager. These are often business people with a history of success and an impeccable reputation, who have suddenly and spectacularly fallen from grace. And the derailed often take whole companies with them. In a frighteningly short period of time, the granite solidarity of a blue chip can fold like a house of cards.

The question for those interested in the lessons of experience is whether more is to be learnt from the study of success or the study of failure. In all biographies, memory is selective and explanation self-serving. Rarely do high-flyers mention luck or opportunity. Equally, the derailed seem more obsessed with running 'blame storming' groups than accepting personal responsibility for their sad demise.

What does emerge from a study of high-flyers and derailers is not that the latter were lacking or fatally flawed in their attributes, but rather that their developmental experiences were inappropriate or non-existent. The vast majority of British companies believe in the *Darwinian* model of executive selection and development. This nearly always involves the following steps. The organization tries to specify the abilities, traits and knowledge-base of those they want to select. Some organizations call these competencies and develop a short checklist (wish list) of the qualities they uniquely and specifically require. They may or may not expend a lot of money or effort in the selection procedure, but seem pretty clear on what they want. The issue is really what happens *after* the selection. The Darwinians believe that if one has the required competencies, not only can one cope with, but excel at, any job thrown at them. They argue that if one finds the individual with superior genes, they will deal best with any eventuality. The fittest survive: indeed, one way therefore to find which of those selected are the real stars is initially to give them rather difficult challenges.

There is, however, another perspective. We might call these the *agriculturalists*: those who grow managers. They certainly do not disagree with the Darwinians about quality seed or superior breeds. They are eager to seek out the best raw materials to work on. But they differ in one respect: the procedure once the potential high-flyers have been selected. The agriculturalists believe in the power of watering, fertilizing, weeding and spraying. They know about crop rotation, selective breeding and the consequences (cost-benefit analysis) of providing superior silage and nutrients.

In human terms, the agriculturalists believe that well-selected recruits need specific sequential experiences to develop to their full potential. Some companies deliberately move managers around. They are required to do a 'stint' in marketing, HR, accounts, and so on, to get a good understanding of the business. Some organizations believe that all young managers need a few 'developmental' challenges: launch a new product, spend some time with a subsidiary or work abroad, design and lead a training programme, lead a turnaround that requires re-engineering and organization, participate in a cross-functional working team, work for the best boss in the company and so on.

Agriculturalists believe that their farming practices cannot be opportunistic or haphazard. There is a time to sow and a time to reap. There is a plan and a strategy based on the climate, the soil and the crop. It is on this point that real and opportunistic agriculturists can be identified. Organizations that really believe that they are responsible for the development of their staff have a clear plan for development. They think through a 'developmental curriculum' designed to get the best from their potential managers to ensure they become high-flyers. Some organizations are filled with chaotic and opportunistic agriculturalists. They know the value of experience in developing the next generation of leaders but somehow can't or won't develop a programme for their acknowledged experiences.

Both Darwinians and agriculturalists agree that high-flyers have the ability to learn from their experiences. The challenge is providing those experiences that are the ultimate opportunity to learn and practise the executive status of the high-flyer.

Hooked on the Web

One can, it seems, get addicted to many things. We all know about alcohol, drug and tobacco addiction, which is chemically based, but people get seriously addicted to gambling, overeating, exercise – and sex. Perhaps the most interesting of the non-chemical, electronic add-itions are computer-game, amusement-arcade machine and one-arm-bandit addiction. But the tabloids and media-hungry psychiatrists have recently discovered another addiction – Internet addiction. For some people the net is the Prozac, for others the Viagra, of communi-cation.

These technology addictions all have things in common: sound and bright lights, fast-moving images and personal control of the tech-nology. Frequently there is the element of surprise or exploration, which adds to the excitement of the whole thing. The stereotyped addict is a young(ish) introverted, clever(ish) male. Computer addicts miss meals or eat while at the keyboard, have strange patterns of sleep, lose sense of time and quite quickly become very withdrawn. They like the puzzle features of Internet and computer use. Some like the idea of downloading software toys, so getting the feeling that they are getting something for nothing: the enhanced taste of stolen fruit.

Some of these addicts curiously find that their addiction boosts their self-esteem, partly because of their feelings of modernity and pioneeringness but also because others – technophobes – call on their expertise for help. The inadequate becomes the expert: a nice reversal of roles. Never before have they been taken seriously – now they are listened to. And best of all, the inadequate e-mailer can hide behind a fantasy name and persona: because of the technology nobody need discover they are short, spotty and cross-eyed. They can easily present themselves as suave, mysterious, quirky or whatever – and no one has the first idea what they are really like. The Internet offers another real-ity – a text-based relationship. There is anonymity – and limitless possibilities for voyeurism, protected self-disclosure, even shopping.

Witty, charming, middle-class professionals are amused by what they see as inadequate techies unable to communicate or amuse them-selves without the favoured electronic technology. Others believe that all this hype about technological addiction is nonsense and not compar-able to the chemical addictions that ravage the lungs and liver of one's closest friends.

As Mark Griffiths, a British expert in this area, has noted, to qual-ify as an addiction the behaviours of the addict need to conform to a number of quite specific criteria. Does the activity tend to dominate the waking hours of the person? Does it lead to total preoccupation, to cravings and most importantly to a reduction in social contacts? The addict needs to be at it, not with others, and able to think of little else while deprived of their electronic toys. Does the activity lead to a high? Just as music can quickly and easily help change mood, so a key feature of addiction is that getting a fix leads initially to a high, and later to feelings of 'flow' or a semi-tranquillized feeling of well-being. These mood changes can be seen in all addicts and play an important role in the addiction. Does the dosage have to be regularly increased? The story of the small glass of dry sherry before luncheon leading to a couple, half a bottle and then ever more until alcoholism sets in, is a familiar one. Addiction causes tolerance in the addict – and frequently intolerance in others. They need more of it – unreasonably large amounts of their favoured poison. Three hours surfing the Web becomes four – then one needs five – and so on. Is there clear evidence of withdrawal symptoms? What happens when the toy or drug is taken away, or even reduced. In short, how does the addict cope? If the person suffers both chronic and acute negative mood changes after withdrawal, this is clearly not a good sign. The Internet addict needs to be at the keyboard and the screen and, like the nico-tine-deprived quitting smoker, is ratty, moody and miserable until the dose is restored. Is there an increase in social conflict and rows? Does the addiction to whatever lead friends, family and employers to complain about the addict's single-minded, selfish devotion to this activity? Of course it must be borne in mind that it is quite possibly the conflict that leads to the addiction. That is, one could take to the Web to escape an argumentative spouse. Is there a tendency for sudden relapses and benders? After a period off the addiction, do people suddenly take it up with all the passion and intensity that they had before?

Usually, to be classified as an addict one needs to qualify for at least five of the above symptoms, preferably all. To some extent, quick, cheap communication on the Internet makes mild forms of addiction understandable. But now there is a new, additional component to the potential cocktail – the possibility, indeed the reality, of *shopping on the Web*. Some people already swear by book-buying on the Web, and there are increasing opportunities and, with them, increasing stories rather than evidence of tele-shopaholics who do their 'retail therapy' from the spare room.

There is a small but fascinating psychiatric literature on shop aholics called 'buying maniacs' by the celebrated German psychiatrist

Emil Kraepelin a hundred years ago. The current pathology is called 'compulsive buying' and has been described as 'a mood, obsessive compulsive, or impulse control disorder'. It has a number of diagnostic criteria:

> frequent preoccupations with buying
> impulses to buy that are experienced as irresistible, intrusive and senseless
> frequent buying of items that are not needed, unaffordable and shopping for longer periods of time than explicitly intended
> distressing consequences of those impulses marked by problematic social, marital and occupational functioning and financial and legal problems.

Most case studies show the victims to be women. And, to use the jargon, they often exhibit comorbidity, that is, they have other problems. Many have personality, mood or anxiety disorders and often a family history of some sort of addiction. Interestingly, these compulsive shoppers who preferred to shop alone said they felt 'happy' and 'powerful' while shopping. They often said they liked the colours, sounds, lighting and smell of stores – they even said it was sexually exciting. Favoured purchases were clothes, shoes, jewellery and make-up – and in serious bulk.

Shopaholics get better (or are stabilized) on antidepressant medication and psychotherapy. So we have the picture of two types of addict: the young, inadequate, Internet-addicted male and the depressed female shopaholic. What if we combine these addictions so that you can be a website shopaholic, with equal numbers of males and females.

There is a lot of hype about shopping on the Web and impressive numbers about the growth of this activity, particularly in the Untied States. But equally there is concern about whether this is indeed the best way to shop for any goods.

Whether novices, addicts or virgins to teleshopping, people point out three drawbacks or at least worries about shopping over the Web:

Credit card fraud: Many people are concerned with hackers getting hold of their credit card numbers and abusing them. Having one's wallet stolen is a ghastly business but we all know that credit cards can be quickly and easily cancelled to prevent thieves dipping into one's account. Usually the theft is discovered quickly. But because one waits for goods to arrive, the delay may allow the thieves to take their time in raiding your account.

Goods never arrive: The old days of COD (cash on delivery) have gone. You pay up front – and wait. You may never get what you ordered. The company may go bust, or may not even exist. They fob you off with the 'lost in the mail' story. Of course this is also true of mail-order catalogues but because advertising on the Web is easier and cheaper, there is the possibility of bogus firms taking your money and not delivering.

Shoddy goods: All of us have a flattering photograph of ourselves which somehow does not quite match reality. A 'trick of the light'; the skill of the photographer; the mood on the day all contribute to the effect. Buying on the Internet is, to use a very old metaphor, a bit like buying a pig in a poke. One needs to feel the quality of the width, and hold the potentially purchased product up to the light.

Shopping is also a social activity. People enjoy taking a friend for a second opinion; getting advice from a well-trained assistant; and 'trying on' the goods. The Web allows nothing of this. But these are early days: the naïve enthusiasts who predict the end of both the high street and the out-of-town mall, and the unbelieving sceptics who see teleshopping as a flash in the pan for the electronically addicted, are both wrong. Just as we have learnt to find the optimal way of using all technology, so the same will no doubt be true of shopping on the Web.

Just do it!

Heroes of modern management are nearly all portrayed as an *Action Man*. There is no ponderous deliberation or analysis paralysis of the 20th-century manager. The successful manager is encouraged by mission or vision statements or in-house models in the 'just do it' philosophy. To be is to do. Form a team and *get on with it*.

Hence, the finding in organizations that everyone is doing the job of one level below them: directors manage, managers supervise, supervisors work. They do this not because they don't know how to do the job they are appointed to – although this is sometimes the case – but rather because the higher you go, the more you think and the less you (physically) do. So, if you don't want to be seen as an idle, academic imitator you must do something one level down.

This frenetic philosophy 'just do it' has two central axioms. Managers have to be action-orientated because they have no choice (... in this fast, ever-changing, customer-demanding, competitive world ... blah, blah). Second, activity is good because its opposite, even reflective analysis, is undesirable.

Many gurus and senior managers believe that if you are not in a meeting, managing by walking about, or in negotiations with others then you are not working. Thinking is not a business activity. The argument goes: executives are meant to execute; if all they want to do is think, plan and study they should have become academics.

While the 'bias to action', 'get-on-with-it' philosophy is not necessarily bad, and often desirable, there are various misguided assumptions underlying it. First is the idea that management is not an intellectual, analytic activity and that planning, reflecting and studying data, problems and trends is time-wasting. Second, that management activity is anyway based on instinct, intuition and common sense. It is believed that mastering new technology and keeping close to the customer (alone) is as good as any MBA. Third, and this follows 'logically' from the above, most executives are overpaid compared with middle managers and engineers, who do the real work – because all they do is strategic planning and other essentially irrelevant activities.

Most managers feel pressured to do something rather than think. Some are genuinely so busy that they do not have the opportunity (or perhaps desire and skill) to step back and reflect on their actions. Many believe that staff and customers are capricious, the market unstable and competitors devious. Trying to analyse and predict the unpredictable is therefore a waste of time.

Was it ever thus? In a famous study examining what exactly managers do, it was found that their average day was characterized by activities that were brief, fragmented and varied. Most do a lot of talking – real activity; some listened – the lesser activity. But time spent planning and deciding was minimal. Compared with real professionals such as accountants, doctors and lawyers, whose job is the rigorous and judicious application of knowledge, managers seem not to value education and thinking. They all invest in ongoing education and training. Medics call it continuous medical education.

Professionals don't believe in intuition unless it is seen as the product of studying. It is about seeing patterns, integrating data and drawing on a bigger knowledge base. Management is intuitive only in the sense that experienced and educated managers can reach conclusions faster than lesser mortals.

A lot of the new 'magic bullets' for managerial success seem to imply there is little point to learning. But they are wrong. Consider two examples:

● *The wisdom and power of team*: Supposedly teams produce extra energy and dynamism and break through bureaucracy. But teams differ in resources and abilities. Further, people in the West are not natural team players. This is why they have to endure sadistic ex-corporals shouting at them on outward-bound-type training on wet hillsides to learn how to become (often very unwillingly) team members.

● *Trial and error is enough*: Medicine and science in general have long moved on from inspired guesswork to both theory building *and* measurement. Even sports psychology has moved beyond quasi-motivational therapy to careful observation and accurate recordings of movements and techniques of specific athletics. Management science and managers individually need to do this themselves.

The idea that management science is nothing more than common sense dressed up in jargon is half true. But countries that put a premium on technical education (IT, accountancy, engineering) also value professional management. These countries, such as Japan and Germany, also, paradoxically perhaps, neither spawn nor overuse management consultants.

The commonsensical, intuitive, action-man manager as model and hero is bad news. He or she undermines the work of real managers. Scientists, doctors, academics and engineers acquire their knowledge and skill by extensive research and study. Writers, craftsmen and entertainers acquire their skill by disciplined practice. Ideally, managers acquire theirs by both study and practice; not just the latter. So think about it before you just do it!

Knowing customer needs: what the public really wants

What makes one choose one airline over another? Being locked into an air miles straitjacket? The schedule (if you can understand it)? The price (even if the company is paying)? Yes – all of the above.

But deregulation and privatization of airlines has led to hyper-competition. There are more airlines, more routes, more bargains. Airlines have teamed up and even an air miles junkie still has choice between different carriers. So what are the primary determinants of airline choice? And are these different for the business versus leisure traveller?

Ask passengers, and all agree that there are some factors that they take for granted but which are *musts*. First, of course, is *safety*. Certain airlines have a dubious record regarding safety – Aeroflot, Garuda, and so on. As possible choices, these fall at the first hurdle and are never on the list. The reputation of a poor safety record is very difficult to change. The picture of the PanAm jet on its side was the final nail in the airline's coffin. It may be that being associated with a poor safety record spells long-term ruin for an airline.

Interestingly, *cleanliness* throughout the plane, but particularly in the holds, is expected as standard. This is not just the problem of the poorly potty-trained obsessives. One study showed that the single factor that best predicted pub popularity was the cleanliness of the toilets – not the range of beers, jukebox, car parking space or food. One experience of dirty seats, dirty blankets, dirty cutlery or crockery, or even hearsay evidence about lack of hygiene, is enough to make a clear choice to avoid the airline.

All passengers are deeply committed to *timeliness*. They want and expect good schedules. Most of all, they want to leave on time. Now transportation companies, from the buses to the trains, publish their on-timeness as an index of their success. The most common reason for being 'seriously browned off' is leaving late, irrespective of when they arrive. Passengers expect punctual delivery. Again, a reputation for being regularly late is a no-no.

Finally, there is the issue of *friendliness*. We live in a customer-focused era where most staff facing customers have been trained. Polite, flexible and personable is what travellers have been led to expect from airline staff. None of the grim *nyet* philosophy of the old Aeroflot, but rather 'can I help you?'

There are many airlines that are safe and clean with a reasonable time record and fairly friendly staff. Indeed, one should expect this from all carriers.

So, what do the public want from the total in-flight experience? While there are individual and demographic differences generally, very clear patterns do emerge. Five issues tend to be highlighted as *the* criteria on which choices are made:

Individual attention: Economy passengers value some individual attention. They like to have their name used – after all, it is on the boarding card examined by half a dozen airline employees in order to get on board. Passengers like to feel special even in 'cattle class'. And nearly all greatly appreciate, and have come to expect, little personal favours (a glass of water, an extra pillow) being provided.

Ease; hassle-free flight: All passengers want the airline to do the work, not them. The time-poor, cash-rich business customer is particularly eager to avoid the waiting around, the boredom and the sensory deprivation that go with so much airline travel. The little hassles mount up and tend to be very memorable. Equally, making the flight easy is a good criterion for recommendation.

Comfort: Many airlines have recognized the importance of comfort – seat width, pitch, foot-rests and so on. Twelve hours in a small seat can be hell, particularly for the large passenger. Get a reputation for comfortable seats, for pillows, head-rests and so on, and one is on to a winner. And the race is perpetually on to make seats more spacious and comfortable.

Control/choice: Albeit in small things, all passengers like choice – of reading material and films, what to eat and when. It is interesting to note that all airlines have experimented with 'personalized' items such as screens and so on to fulfil this wish. The amount of control may be minimal, but it certainly helps to make the corralled and dragooned economy-class passenger feel like a human being.

Information: How long does it take before an airline explains the cause of a delay and the approximate time of departure? All passengers would rather hear the unpleasant truth than silence. And they all appreciate information of relevance to them: not at what height one is flying, but when one lands; not the flight path so much as the films available. Providing thoroughly accurate information to satisfy a variety of customers is increasingly cheap and easy.

So why choose the world's favourite airline over the Singapore girl? Are the friendly skies preferable to the mid-class massage? At least we now know the criteria by which explicitly to compare and contrast.

Laughter is the best medicine

Very, very unusual people end up as 'warm-up artists'. Imagine what it is like: you have to get a cold, possibly indifferent, audience excited. You have to tease and titillate, beguile and bemuse, stimulate and satisfy. In short, you have to make them laugh so that when the stars come on they are even more appreciative.

Being a humour consultant can be pretty bleak. Consider the picture: you walk into a room full of middle-class, middle-brow middle managers on a Monday morning. They have other things to do: respond to their urgent e-mails, attend meetings, complete balance sheets. And most don't want to be there – almost by definition they have been sent. After all, the unassertive go to assertion workshops; the weak, naïve or failed negotiator to a negotiations workshop; the shy, diffident, low-EQ person to the interpersonal skills workshop. So your group may be humourless – selected for having a laughter bypass. And it is your job to make them laugh.

So, you begin, not with a funny story but with a rationale for all this caper: you tell the blank, expressionless faces that because of its proven effects, humour consultants are being employed by cancer clinics, by homes for elderly people, even by technology-based companies. Unfortunately, this fact causes laughter in a few – a hollow, cynical laugh, not the one you are after. But you continue with the 'scientific bit'. Laughter, you inform the humourless, not only has short-term benefits but it has been shown to help release endorphins that bolster resistance to illness and cause a feeling of well-being.

At this point you put on a slide showing how the number of jokes told in a work group predicts team satisfaction, productivity and commitment. Another hollow laugh from a bolshy member of the audience. A final slide – funny people live longer. Surely the idea that laughter and longevity are linked should inspire attention.

But the giggler puts up his hand. 'What sort of funny people live longer?' He asks; 'those who are funny ha ha, funny peculiar or funny pathetic'. Oh dear, you think – we have one of those in the audience. 'All three' you respond confidently – swiftly moving on.

There follows a well-prepared series of tapes and stories definitely known to make people laugh. A few tape recordings – one where Brian Johnson becomes uncontrollable over the concept of 'getting one's leg over' during a cricket commentary. Then a few well-chosen video clips combined with a 10-minute videotape. And of course a few good stories – fast, pithy and hopefully funny.

Any researcher knows that there are various types of jokes. There is sexual humour and aggressive humour. Some people like nonsense humour and others satire. Men like sex and aggressive jokes more than women. Extroverts are more keen on all jokes compared with introverts but less fond of nonsense and satire. But the good humour consultant, like Phineas T. Barnum, has 'a little something for everybody'.

Fortunately humour is infectious. We often say that the book was so funny we laughed out loud. Further, we have also probably had the embarrassing experience of being asked by somebody who 'missed the joke' to retell it, only to discover we did not really get it ourselves and simply laughed because others were laughing. For this reason it is good to plant a real belly-laugher in the audience. People laugh at the laughter of others and begin to feel they are having a good time. In the jargon, they infer their emotional state (happiness) from their observation of their own behaviour (laughter).

With enough good and varied material it is not too difficult to get even the most dour to laugh. They do so despite themselves.

But probably only the laughter consultant knows other important facts. First, a laughter workshop has to last an optimal period of time. People cannot go on and on laughing even if they are really enjoying themselves. And, alas, not only does the effect go away quickly, it can leave people temporarily feeling worse.

So the laughter consultant hands out the 'happy sheets' (the evaluation documents) at just the right time and flees.

Is this yet another form of corporate madness? Is the key idea laughable? Does it have a long- or short-term effect? Comparatively, it may be good value for money. That is, if other short courses are poorly received and little is learnt, laughter workshops may seem good value. They may have a short-term impact, even beneficial publicity, though that may backfire. But it is certainly unlikely to cause any damage and one might keep a few aspiring comics off the dole.

You've got to laugh, haven't you?

Male hubris or female humility?

Ask a large group of British young people to estimate their IQ and you may be surprised. Not by their arrogant high score, or self-effacing modesty, but by a consistent sex difference. Boys (males) think they are (or at least say they are) cleverer than girls. Thus, Scottish male students thought their IQ was 127 points, whereas equivalent females estimated 120. A London University-based group of male students thought it was around 118, whereas the females estimated about 112.

And asked to estimate their parents' and grandparents' IQs, the pattern continues. Males in particular think their fathers are brighter than their mothers (116 versus 109) and their grandfathers brighter than their grandmothers (106 versus 99). Notice how the further one goes back, the dimmer one's relations seem to be.

Most surprising, however, is a recent finding just published in the US psychology journal *Sex Roles*. When British parents are asked to estimate the IQ of their children, both parents rate their sons brighter than their daughters (109 versus 102). Clearly, this has important implications if there really is such a thing as a self-fulfilling prophecy. If a male child is believed to be more intelligent by his parents, and this is constantly reinforced through childhood, he may be more immune to negative (if accurate) feedback that is given later on in life. Thus there may be a very extensive Pygmalion effect working on behalf of males. It may be that people based predications about intelligence on beliefs that have been firmly entrenched since childhood, and that there are differences in the prototypes held by males and females that are the cause of adult sex differences in the perception of intelligence.

These sorts of results can easily polarize the social scientists. Feminists argue that these findings are the result of 'modesty training' in girls, and the beliefs in many families of 'inferior women and superior men'. Females are encouraged to hide their success and be humble about their own achievements. Equally, males are encouraged to brag about their successes. So, the truth about real IQ scores apparently lies in the mid-range between the two estimates.

The psychometricians and sociobiologists, on the other hand, claim that overall these estimates are a true(ish) reflection of the real state of affairs. When testing large populations, recent British studies have found males *do* do better than females. Further, some studies have looked at the relationship between self-estimated and actually measured IQ, and the correlation is modestly positive. Males score (a little) higher, but certainly believe they are (a lot) brighter than the average. Why males are more intelligent may be in dispute, but the psychometricians argue that the data speak for themselves – males have a slightly, but noticeably, higher score than females.

However, a clue to resolving the dispute lies in the idea of more populist notions of 'multiple intelligences'. Thus, different types of 'everyday', practical intelligences have been described thus:

Verbal or linguistic intelligence (the ability to use words)

Logical or *mathematical* intelligence (the ability to reason logically, solve number problems)

Spatial intelligence (the ability to find your way around the environment, and form mental images)

Musical intelligence (the ability to perceive and create pitch and rhythm patterns)

Body-kinetic intelligence (the ability to carry out motor movement; for example, being a surgeon or dancer)

Interpersonal intelligence (the ability to understand other people)

Intrapersonal intelligence (the ability to understand yourself and develop a sense of your own identity).

Ask young people to estimate IQs on all seven types and a different pattern emerges. Females actually give slightly higher self-estimates than males on interpersonal, intrapersonal and body-kinetic types. But where the big and significant differences lie is in mathematical and spatial intelligences. Males give an 8–10 point higher score on average for those related skills. And they tend to be right – in spatial intelligence tasks, males nearly always outperform females. Sociobiologists argue that the hunting males needed spatial skills in tracking animals and getting home, whereas females needed superior verbal and interpersonal skills for educating their young.

Management trainers

Corporate education and training bills are significant. Most organizations realize that you cannot promote people to supervisory or managerial levels without teaching them *how* to manage. Aspirant, potential or newly appointed managers are often required to go on expensive management training courses. These may last anything from three days to three weeks, and take place in plush hotels, old châteaux or bare polytechnic classrooms. The organization may look on training as a punishment or a benefit; a 'jolly' or a necessity; an educational or an experiential phenomenon; a cost or an investment.

Personnel, or human resource, departments, which usually take responsibility for education and training, have the choice of developing an in-house training department or hiring in consultants/trainers, or both. This decision is based partly on history, partly on the number of people who have to be trained (as a function of organizational size and staff turnover rates), partly on the money available, and partly on the experience of the HR director. They are nearly always the people who choose the course and the trainer, which may well reflect their own needs and preferences.

Course junkies who have attended a variety of programmes have seen various trainers at work. Naturally, they come in all shapes and sizes, have different styles and preferences, and different pet methods and fads. And it is also true that there is often a good fit between the content of programme and the style of the presenter. However, clear categories of trainer styles are in evidence. Check out each one, rating them out of 10 on three factors: (i) *preference* (how much you like the style of the trainer); (ii) *learning* (how much you think you would learn from the style of trainer); and (iii) *fun* (how much fun you believe you would have with each one).

The evangelist game show host

These trainers are often vacuously extroverted show-offs. They believe the course is about having fun, winning prizes and 'believing'. The programmes are all about the showing and sharing of emotions. The evangelist in them feels the need to convert the delegates to their way of thinking, their models and their methods. They are often exhausting to be around, and definitely not the choice of the quiet, serious-minded participant.

P   **L**   **F**

The academic, donnish guru

This is the talking head of the training business. Often, they have a touch of arrogance and let you feel that this is all slightly beneath them. Some patronize the audience, others drone on, ignoring the perplexed looks of the delegates. The guru in them is often the dangerous element because they may genuinely believe that they have found the Holy Grail of management.

P   **L**   **F**

The therapeutic doctor

Some trainers like to give the message: 'Trust me, I'm a doctor', or 'Put your faith in me, I'm experienced'. They affect the air of a wise Dr Cameron of the marketplace who has seen it all before and knows how people behave. This front can, of course, always serve as a way of diverting attention from the fact that there are no real data or research evidence on which to base the theories expounded. Training is really a form of group therapy.

P   **L**   **F**

The condescending assassin

Some trainers revel in their power to expose and humiliate the powerful, the great and the good, whatever their personal ability, skill or history. They belong to the Dame Edna Everage school of picking on hapless and helpless victims of the course. Sometimes put up to it by senior management, but often at random, these missiles in a course can do great psychological damage. Most of these types of trainers are short – in physique, intelligence, empathy and educationability.

P   L   F

The bullshitter/facilitator

For those who have precious little knowledge or skill, or simply those who have done no preparation, there is always the fall-back position of the facilitator. In essence, this means others (the course participants) do the work. The bullshitter simply encourages them, by a variety of methods, not only to diagnose their own problems, but to solve them on the course, and then takes the credit for the solution. Beware the break-out plenary sessions in the programme. What this means is that you, not the trainer, do the thinking.

P   L   F

The manual-dependent school-marm

Some trainers are rendered speechless if their slides and manuals are taken away from them. Theirs is the 'open your textbooks at page 1' approach. Participants are simply required to complete a series of preordained exercises that are supervised and inspected by the strict nanny-teacher. This is the serious, and rather boring world of skill acquisition. This type of trainer could easily be replaced by a video-tape, and probably will be in due course.

P   L   F

The creative mind-expander

Occasionally, one finds the trainer who has taken Edward de Bono too seriously. They are full of games, puzzles and other gadgets that have little or nothing to do with work. They believe it is their job to think 'laterally' on all occasions; to come up with radical, albeit impractical, alternatives. They may do this through brain-storming exercises or public free-associations, but the outcome is the same.

<u>P</u>   <u>L</u>   <u>F</u>

The world of the professional consultant and trainer is a strange and unreal one, and this, in part, helps generate the odd characters in the field. Often, because they are both well paid and well treated by their client organizations, they come to believe that what they say is profound, whereas those who adopt the seagull management style (fly in, defecate on everybody, fly out) never see the consequences of their advice and may delude themselves that it is inevitably useful. That said, there are serious, well-briefed, concerned trainers like the best teacher you ever had. Of course, they are the ideal choice, but they are so rare that we often have to trade off the pluses and minuses of the above seven deadly sinners.

Who should you choose? Add your three scores together (maximum 30, minimum 3). If none gets about 15, refuse to go on their management training course. If more than 15, choose the one with the highest score and explain to the training manager why precisely you like that style.

In training, for the cynic, it is always a case of 'Those who can, do; those who can't, train; those who can't train, train trainers; while those who can't train trainers become management consultants.'

Managing call centres

It was not until comparatively recently that recruiters and selectors began to look systematically for telephone-based customer skills in their staff. When goods were ordered and complaints made by letter, the skills of drafting sensitive, firm and clear documents were obviously valued. But the widespread use of telephone sales has changed that; as have customer expectations of how they should be dealt with.

People who know they can phone high street fashion shops until 11pm, as well as computer companies until 9pm, have come to expect that they can generally do business 'over the phone'. And they may become angry if they discover that they cannot use electronic media and have to resort to the pejoratively termed 'snail mail'. Companies that boast how quick, reliable and effective it is to order from them can easily be seriously handicapped either by not providing a full telephone answering service, or training frontline telestaff inadequately.

The spread of access to the telephone, and the comparative reduction in the cost of a call, as well as the huge improvements in technology, have meant a rapid growth in telemarketing and telesales. The boom in communication technology, mobile phones and free phone numbers has also contributed to the change in buying patterns.

The financial sector (banks, building societies, insurance companies), the transport sector (airlines, railways), the leisure industry (various holiday companies) and the ever-present mail-order companies (small and large, general and specialist), have responded to telephone trends by building more call centres. Call centres can be designed and staffed to handle every type of telephone business or enquiry. Customers now want and expect them to be open 24 hours a day, 7 days a week.

Telephoning allows call centres to be located anywhere: in areas where wages and related costs are lower. The Americans favour Ireland, with its well-educated, low-wage, English-speaking workforce, for establishing telemarketing centres. There is no doubt a substantial EU subsidy for locating there.

Managers of call centres try to make processing costs as cheap as possible. Most attempt to do this through technology such as the use of telephone management systems, workflow systems, profit/service data systems for the employee, and database management software. Conferences on these topics abound, but the emphasis is almost entirely on technological and engineering solutions.

The human factor in call centre staff remains neglected. The customer is interested in the price and quality of the service they receive from the person they speak to. They like clear, jolly, patient, understanding people on the other end of the line. Most don't like the 'hard sell', the undertrained novice, the incomprehensible and inarticulate person.

Defining customer service on the telephone, face-to-face, or even by letter, is difficult to do. Services are intangible because they are about performance rather than product. Also, most services cannot be counted, measured, inventoried or verified in advance of sale to ensure quality. Further, the product and the service are often inseparable because both are involved in the contact between customer and service provider.

Customers are becoming more demanding of what they want from service providers. They can, and do, specify all sorts of qualities, such as:

- reliability – consisting of performance and dependability
- responsiveness – obvious willingness and readiness to provide a service
- competence – having comprehensive knowledge and skills to deliver the service
- access – the approachability and the general ease of contact with staff
- courtesy – explicit politeness, respect, consideration and friendliness
- communication – keeping the customer informed in a language they can understand, and listening to them
- understanding – making an effort to understand the customer's needs.

Reading the increasing number of (printed) advertisements for telephone personnel, one could easily believe that it is the best job in the world. It's fun, exciting, easy, done from near home, working in and with a supportive team, and the potential for making a good living is high.

Yet, if you can get hold of them, it seems that the data on call centre personnel tell another story. Job turnover and absenteeism are high, as are customer complaints. Little attention has been paid to the recruitment, selection and training for this frankly unusual and specialized job. How can recruitment be done in line with business needs? What is the demographic and psychological profile of the ideal employee? What sort of training do call staff need initially and then later in the job? Are the incentives appropriate to the personality types employed?

The problem with recruitment and selection of call staff is that one has a conundrum on one's hands. One wants extroverts rather than introverts, because they are more sociable, lively and interpersonally skilled than introverts. But extroverts also like variety, and sitting all day answering the phone is tedious. Extroverts trade off speed for accuracy and may answer more calls, but take down incorrect information. Extroverts are certainly more sensitive to promise of reward rather than threat of punishment, but if these rewards are difficult to achieve because of the number and type of callers, they can become dispirited. They can also be erratic, particularly if a little unstable, and the last thing the customer wants is an irascible, capricious telesales person who, having been rattled by the previous customer, takes it out on you!

More importantly, what specific skills do managers need to get the best out of their staff, in the short, medium and long term? How can one create, maintain and manage a high-performing team over time? Technology is available to everyone; management and skills are not. It is the one area where real added value and higher return on investment can be made.

Tony Miller, ex-Training Director at Frizzell, has considerable experience in this area. He is responsible for the effectiveness of training and development of more than 700 call centre staff, and has been involved with high-results training for over eight years. He has researched the field and uses various psychological techniques to achieve improved performance.

Miller says:

> Selection is key: applying a standard battery of tests will not give the results of high-performing individuals. Often there is a misunderstanding of some of the basic requirements – whether to select the compliant introvert, or the perceived difficult-to-manage extrovert. Decisions are often made to suit the manager's style. Conventional training methods are not effective for creating high-performance personnel.

Managing call centre teams is equally complex. Call centres are unusual places to work. The open-plan office with dim light and hundreds of people speaking at once is not everyone's idea of a pleasant working environment. Visits to the toilet and the canteen may be the major form of exercise for some staff. And they can get, quite understandably, pretty rattled and snappy after dealing with dim, demanding, rude, inarticulate or naïve callers. But they need to be recruited and retained in larger numbers. Recruiting the wrong types and giving them little or inadequate training is likely to lead to poor sales and disgruntled customers.

The practice of buying products and services over the phone is on the increase. Shopping via the Internet will be next, but for the masses, this may be some years away. Until then, the special nature of the people suited to the job, and effective at doing it, not to mention those who manage them, remains less well understood.

Motivating the workforce

Managers, company owners and supervisors have always been frustrated and bewildered by the employee with little or no work motivation. We have all seen the 'quit-but-stay' employee who has severed their psychological contact with the organization, has little commitment and just goes through the motions. Nothing seems to fire them up, making firing them from work a real option.

The demotivated firmly park their brains and enthusiasm for life in the staff car park in the morning, re-engaging them with gusto 30 seconds past the official end of work time. They shrewdly avoid doing anything that warrants dismissal and seem content to keep their heads down, doing the minimum, volunteering nothing.

The downsized, right-sized, almost capsized 1990s has seriously damaged employee morale, and with it, their motivation. In the modern economy, many organizations have taught individuals that they work for themselves, because organizations won't or can't guarantee jobs five, even two years from now. Thus anybody who is not pondering his or her career is a fool. Company loyalty really only means not looking for your next job on company time. Some feel it is foolish to be loyal to a company that is not loyal to them. The relationship between employers and employees is increasingly exploitative on both sides. Hence many employees feel about their organization: 'If you use me, I'll use you.'

The challenge to motivate the worker of the 1990s is thus a major one. So how have the management gurus responded with new techniques to repair and rebolster motivation? The answer, it seems, is not a lot. Ideas in motivation get repackaged, renamed, rebranded, but fundamentally remain the same as ever. The fact that we know some of the key factors in motivation, however, has surprisingly not prevented many managers ignoring them.

As believers have found, the 'good news' has to be repeated and repeated because it seems to be ignored. The story is the same; the principles remain unchanged, but each generation seems to be in need of a retelling of the fundamentals in the sort of language they can understand.

So what's new? Some of the more popular motivational techniques currently employed are the following:

- *Give employees the information they need to do a good job.* Make sure they know their priorities and give them the appropriate tools and training for the job. For some, this can be expressed in the jargon of setting key objectives, or key result areas. Despite much talk, a high number of people still cannot articulate very clearly, if at all, what their key objectives are.
- *Give all employees as much meaningful work to do as possible.* The less intrinsically interesting the work, the more motivational is anything done to encourage job enrichment. This often means job rotations, job sharing or job enriching. Also, to enrich jobs may make employees less efficient – but more happy.
- *Pay people what they are worth.* Consider market forces, predatory competitors as well as individual contribution. Consider what insurers call replacement costs. Most people benchmark their salary more regularly than do their employers. Feeling inequitably paid – that is, paid less than the market rate – is sure to make them very unhappy and demotivated.
- *Offer employees a share of the profits.* Let them feel part of the organization as one of many stakeholders. Lots of companies talk about this, but few do more than token offers. There are many ways to ensure that employees feel part of the family – all on the same side – but these are rarely done at lower levels.
- *Demonstrate* as much as possible a *commitment to long-term employment,* career development and promotion from within.
- *Reward commitment* manifest by loyalty and continuous performance. Most companies now do the opposite, punishing loyalty. It is deeply alienating to believe that no one, apart from yourself, is doing anything about your career.
- *Provide regular, specific feedback to all staff.* If necessary, write notes to employees about their individual performance. Make sure each knows what their boss (and customers) feels and wants. Ask the average employee when they last had 30 minutes with their boss discussing just their performance and few will say this has

happened in the past five years. Giving progress reviews is cheap, easy, important and motivating.

- *Publicly recognize and personally congratulate employees regularly* for good work and, more specifically, after the good work occurs. Celebrate success: create heroes. The army does it, and so do politicians. Many British companies find the idea faintly embarrassing, or are scared that they may create jealousy.

- *Foster a sense of community or teamwork.* Include recognition as part of morale-building meetings that celebrate group success. Make it apparent that most people at work are interdependent. You don't have to do fire-walking or outward-bound courses. It is enough to provide opportunities for people to meet, talk and share together. Propinquity is a powerful predictor of joint liking and co-operation.

- *Be accessible to employees.* Establish easy-to-use channels of communication, both formal and informal. Make sure they are kept open and communicate real, salient information about the company and the department. Do the MBWA (Management By Walking About). This does not mean sending lots of e-mails. It means being physically and psychologically accessible, within reason. It means not punishing those who want to meet you.

- *Ask employees for their feedback and their ideas*, and involve them in decisions that affect their jobs. Reward them for good ideas that, when implemented, improve both individual and group efficiency. Genuinely listen to them – most of them are at the coal-face. Publicize the rewards given to those with good ideas.

- *Pay attention to individual differences and personal needs.* Ask each employee what motivates them and consider a cafeteria of well-equilibrated reward to choose from. Consider their free-time activities and create opportunities for them to use these skills in activities at work. Just as we have flexitime to suite individual preferences, consider other aspects of free choice.

- *Use performance appraisals and behavioural measures as major criteria for promotion.* Make it clear that rewards are contingent on progress, that the equity principles apply in the organization.

The astute reader may be tempted to ask: so what in the dozen points is really new? The answer is, nothing really. Motivational techniques get rediscovered and readvertised, but they have been known for hundreds of years. Fads and fashions in the management consultancy world seem to dictate which particular technique is seen to be the most powerful and popular. Old ideas get repackaged in the jargon of today. Some are more fashionable at one time than others.

But the puzzle remains why, if all of this is known, is it not done? Do a climate/employee survey in any organization and ask staff about their manager's motivating and demotivating behaviour. Ask them when, if ever, their boss actually uses any of the above techniques such as asking their opinion, offering specific job feedback, or attempting job enrichment. So well known, but so little done: and managers and supervisors still complain that staff cannot be motivated. It is possible to use all these various techniques simultaneously – none is mutually exclusive. However, the power of the technique may depend crucially on the age and stage (demography) of the majority of employees. Younger employees value intrinsic factors (having fun) and teamwork much more than middle-aged employees. The above techniques are taught to military officers and MBA students. If you have been fortunate enough to have a good boss, they may have modelled the above behaviours. But because few managers are trained or educated in the art and have themselves never been well managed, one gets the perpetuation of incompetence. This explains the paradox of why people seem to have heard about, but not seen, successful motivational management in practice.

Organobabble

About 30 years ago the term psychobabble was first coined. It was a derogatory and pejorative term to label the then enthusiasm for west-coast, Freudian, psychological jargon that was used to describe the obvious. Babble is a good word – it refers to meaningless, unintelligible, incoherent sounds. The word implied that in an attempt to be psychologically sophisticated these new jargon concepts actually obfuscated the obvious.

Although enthusiasm for psychology has not waned, it has a new competitor. This can be seen in the way self-help books (pop psychology) have been overtaken by management books in high-street bookshops. Management consultants are now more plentiful than media

Table 1: How to translate into Psychobabble and Organobabble

Idiom	Psychobabble	Organobabble
Clothes make the man	Interpersonal attraction and trust are largely determined by symbolic sartorial signals	Dress codes serve to enforce structural variables in all organizations and can also fulfil impression management functions for senior managers
You can't make a silk purse out of a sow's ear	Those attempting to dissimulate status through apparel can easily be detected by sensitive observers	It is impossible to compensate for lack of business competency by superficial cues such as dressing the part of senior management
Out of sight, out of mind	Semantic and episodic memory storage is such that retroactive interference causes person factors to be forgotten	Employees who do not keep in regular contact with headquarters through e-mails and voice-mail run the risk of being excluded from central decision-making
Absence makes the heart grow fonder	Selective memory and emotional factors associated with forgetting mean that, over time, the negative features of positively esteemed people are repressed	Judiciously timed, non-excessive communication tends to lead to better interdepartmental relations and respect for heads of department

psychologists, and are approached for their insights into all life's problems. Thus we find books about the various habits of very successful people replacing those quasi-therapeutic tomes from California.

And with the consultants and gurus have come a new jargon and a new way of speaking. Psychobabble has been replaced by organobabble. It is just as bad but uses business words rather than inter- or intrapsychic phrases. Indeed, it is possible to take good old-fashioned idioms to show how they can be translated into psycho- and organobabble. Thus 'look before you leap' in psychobabble could be 'Consider the behavioural and interpersonal consequences of your deep-seated needs and motives before confronting significant others.' In organobabble it reads 'Construct an action-oriented flow chart before embarking on the crucial implementation phase.'

To consider another example, 'When in Rome do as the Romans do'. Psychobabblers would translate this something like: 'Be particularly sensitive to implicit, functional, national-cultural norms and rituals when dealing with ethnic or linguistic minorities – and value their diversity.' Organobabblers translate this rather differently. They might say: 'Consultants should take care to observe signs of corporate culture and climate so as to act congruently with those constraints and, by so doing, maximizing efficient and effective communication.' Further examples will be found in Table 1.

It has long been pointed out that idioms and adages are often antinomous – indeed, directly contradictory. Thus 'look before you leap' is contrasted with 'he who hesitates is lost'. Indeed, it is this factor, combined with the fact that commonsense language does not tell you when (that is, under what circumstances) they may be appropriate, that renders idioms amusing but little more.

However, from the very way in which babble of either kind worked, it is almost impossible to see the contradictions in the ideas presented.

Outsourcing in HR

Outsourcing is still fashionable. It is often the fantasy of a general manager to get all the problem people in the organization together, transfer them to one single department – say stores – and then sell it off, while outsourcing the whole operation to a reasonable outfit.

Thirty years ago in his book *Up the Organization (How to stop the company stifling people and strangling profits)* Robert Townsend wrote:

> Fire the whole personnel department. Unless your company is too large (in which case break it up into autonomous parts), have a one-girl people department (not a personnel department). Records can be kept in the payroll section of the accounting department (she answers her own phone and does her own typing) acts as personnel (sorry – people) assistant to anybody who is recruiting. She lines up applicants, checks references, and keeps your pay ranges competitive by checking other companies' (Pan, 1994).

This view is a mixture of outsourcing, making redundant and transferring HR functions to other departments.

Outsourcing is a serious option. Of course, it has both advantages and disadvantages and these need to be considered carefully. But does HR take the idea seriously? Big HR departments often have relatively large subdepartments – law, training, benefits and compensation, even data processing. Could any of these be beneficially or profitably outsourced?

Take training, for instance: can one really justify in-house trainers? Are they actually training enough of the time to justify being kept on? How much time do they spend 'in the classroom'; and what are they doing the rest of the time?

Trainers *burn out easily*. Training must be exhausting – as any good trainer will tell you. They need to be entertainers, monitors, enthusiasts and educationalists, all at the same time. They have to coerce the unwilling, amuse the sense-of-humour failures and render the charisma-bypass manager charming. They need constant refreshing.

Trainers are notoriously *difficult to manage*. This is partly due to the sort of people that drift into training. Am-dram enthusiasts, intellectuals manqués, failed preachers ... all are attracted to training. They like to do their own thing, tell their own stories, go their own way.

Most trainers are not interested in, and do not understand, *business issues*. Yet, employee training must be integrated with the business plan. It has to be responsive to current organizational issues. Training suffers as a result.

Many trainers become *organo-centric*. Although it may be a huge advantage that they have a full understanding and knowledge of their particular organization, they tend to know less and less about other organizations. Despite talk of benchmarking, best practice and so on, they take their eye off others and become obsessed by internal issues and politics.

Of course, many of these problems are equally liable to be faced in outsourcing. Outside trainers may be difficult to manage and they too may not know the business well. But then all these things are a trade-off.

It is easy to see how some specialist activities can be outsourced. Indeed, the further one is away from the particular department the easier it is to see why outsourcing is a good thing. Why not outsource the canteen or the cleaning/gardening department? These are often and relatively easily done.

Take the sort of function that HR needs to do: the legal aspect of compliance. This may very profitably and successfully be outsourced because although lawyers are fearsomely expensive, one does not need much of their time in a year. Benefit and compensation specialists such as lawyers can easily be found to do specialist benchmarking or actuarial tasks.

But why not go further? Why not outsource marketing? Some organizations have done just this, arguing that it is altogether more sensible and efficient to outsource. So, and here is the crunch, why not outsource the HR function, retaining perhaps one or two senior managers to run the outsourced unit?

Surely a good HR manager could run a reasonably sized department given that they can buy in specialist help when required? They themselves need to be tough and multi-talented. They need to know enough about all the salient areas of HR to know what needs doing and when. They have to understand enough about employment law, benefits and compensation, IT systems for capturing personal data, strategic planning and training issues. But most of all they need to know where to get and how to manage the consultants and specialists they buy in on a temporary basis.

Naturally they need sufficient budget for this, and need to be rewarded for good management with share options. To get such a manager is not easy. They need real head-hunting and a decent package.

Pile them high and sell them cheap

Management by technique is both a cause and a consequence of gurus' business books. To be a successful guru you need to christen, personalize and proselytize a magic-bullet technique. Without an eponymous technique the guru is nothing. But because they have a short shelf-life and almost predictable sell-by date, one has to invent, reinvent, rename – or somehow come up with a new technique every couple of years to stay in the public view and make lots of money.

So much for supply. There is also a voracious appetite on the part of confused, perplexed and desperate managers who want a quick, successful solution to their intractable problems. Most managers are desperate for the magic bullet. Hence the demand.

The whole thing is a bit like the diet industry. Miracle diets come and go. They are invented by gurus of that world ... doctors, dieters, second-rate actors, sports stars past their best. And they are consumed at great expense but to little long-term effect by hopeful fatties who know this technique, like all the others, is probably an example of the triumph of desperate hope over experience.

Management techniques of all sorts fail for a variety of reasons:

- they are not relevant, appropriate or salient to the particular situation in which they are applied
- they need to be customized to the particular situation but no one knows how to do this
- the technique needs many years, not months, to have a measurable and meaningful effect
- one may need different techniques used at the same time, not just one technique, to achieve the desired outcome.

There is nothing wrong with using these techniques per se. But they can be dangerous if they limit thinking and flexibility. The techniques that have tended to be well known over the past couple of years include benchmarking, business process re-engineering, and total quality management. They are indeed a mysterious trinity.

Benchmarking (sometimes called best practice) is a very simple idea – find out what the world's best performers are doing and copy them. The problem for the managers is manifold. How do you define the best company? What if you are the leading company? But more importantly, how do you know there is not a better way to do the job?

To follow benchmarking is to be a follower not a leader; to replicate not innovate. The real, and ignored, question is how the best practice affects outcome. This is a process question. Indeed, analysis may reveal that the most successful company's results occur *despite*, not *because* of, best practice.

Really successful companies innovate, not copy. They seek first to understand the problems and business process and overcome the former by changing the latter. Benchmarking can involve a massive but misguided research process which always, perhaps rightly, leaves one feeling second best.

Re-engineering, also called core process redesign or process innovation, took the world by storm more than a decade ago. The idea, like all magic bullets, is deceptively simple. Most companies – manufacturing and service – are arranged around specialization not process. Thus, one follows how people or forms get processed by one department (accounts, stores, transport, HR and so on) and then redesigns the process radically.

Perhaps the reason why this idea was so popular was that it justified laying off large numbers of people. Yet a decade or so after this enthusiastic slash and burn fervour of the gurus, they recanted, and became very critical of the idea that re-engineering really was much help.

Why did it, like many other super-fix ideas, fail? First, it nearly always suggested massive reconstruction and radical restructuring. Whence this claim that there was a massive incompetence and inefficiency everywhere? If it is true, then surely the company would have gone under earlier? The more radical the re-engineering, the more the gurus got paid and the higher the expectations of success.

Re-engineering is another word for rationalization. But it has remained true since Adam Smith and Max Weber pointed out that specialization is a major key to efficiency. The difference lies in specializing around a natural business process.

If re-engineering encouraged one to have a renewed and thoughtful reconsideration of the business structure and process, it did a good job. But it led too many to make radical changes that never bore fruit.

Total Quality Management sets out to acquire quality products and services (defined by customers) by getting employees to do a systematic analysis and improvement of business processes. The idea came from a statistically minded engineer – an unlikely guru. Again, the magic bullet was forming TQM groups and employing their recommendations.

But are groups of employees able to understand the full aspects of technical efficiency? It helps to cut waste but rarely offers an overall company strategy for change. Real questions like how, when and where it should be applied remain unanswered.

Beware the snake-oil salesman guru. Companies, like individuals, are both complex and unique. Many of the techniques advocated are good ideas. But to be successful they need to be applied carefully, continuously and in a customized way that suits the needs of that particular organization. Just as diets don't work unless the dieter changes his or her whole lifestyle, nor do management techniques unless the whole business process undergoes a serious shake-up.

The primacy and recency effect

How often has one been told by one of those super-confident image consultants that 'first impressions count most'? They may even come up with some pseudo-scientific statement such as what you say in the first 30 seconds counts more than anything you might say subsequently.

However, others will say with equal confidence that it is the impression you leave people with that has most impact. That is, interviewers pay attention to, process, or weight the information they receive last the most. It is the closing statements that have most sway, not the answers to those bland, anodyne questions about the nature of the journey to the interview. But which of these two is correct?

In the jargon of the trade, do we have a primary or a recency effect? In 1925, more than 70 years ago, the law of primacy was formulated by Frederick Lund, a US psychologist, whose work showed that the side of an argument presented last changed attitudes less than the side of the argument presented first.

It was assumed that this occurred because later information is integrated into earlier information. Thus, if a person is described as 'undecided', it could mean that they are open-minded and disinterested, or wishy-washy and insecure. If it was said earlier that the person was bright, the former interpretation may be made, but if they were said to be shy, the latter would probably apply. We also have an attention decrement over time. Another reason for a primacy effect is the discounting principle – the idea that people give reduced importance to things that do not fit in with an original impression. Thus, each successive piece of data an observer receives has less information.

At least the opposing camps are right about one thing. The information acquired in the middle of an interview is least well remembered and least effective. But which of the two experts is correct? After all, it is a fairly easy hypothesis to test. The following is a straightforward description of the classic study. Make a video of an actual interview. Then splice the tape into two or more sections so that you now have a tape where the same information is presented either first or last. Of course, it's better to have opposite types of information to see the power of the effect. Thus the candidate may be extroverted in the first section, but introverted in the second. Garrulous, fidgeting, laughing, confident, followed by quiet, reserved, shy and so on. Or one could have the candidate answering difficult questions cleverly in the first half, but even simple questions badly or wrongly in the second half.

So one has two types, AB and BA. Two groups of people with similar backgrounds and motivation watch both tapes then make judgements (ratings) about the person. Thus, if the group that saw the extrovert first and introvert last rated the person as more extroverted, we have evidence of primacy, but if they rated him/her as more introverted, we have evidence of recency. So what does the research say? Alas, as in so much in life, the answer to simple questions is rather more complex. There can be both primacy and recency effects. What reviews tend to show is that where the issue is controversial and interesting, or highly familiar, we tend to get primacy effects. Where it is important, moderately uninteresting, and unfamiliar, we get recency effects. All barristers know the importance of the recency effect – the final summing up of the evidence (just before judgment) is most salient in forming an impression.

Ultimately, much depends on how serious the interviewers are about the interview, how much homework they have done beforehand, and whether they are familiar with the whole process. In fact, at really serious interviews, there seems to be more evidence of recency than primacy effects.

This has serious implications for both interviewers and interviewees. Traditionally, interviewers end with a 'your turn to ask questions' question. This is an ideal opportunity for impression management and the maximization of the recency effect. Ask cleverly disguised rhetorical questions and you may do yourself an enormous favour.

For interviewers, it may help to rate a candidate independently before the meeting, after a while, as well as at the end. Good interviewers plan what questions they are going to ask and understand what the individual's answers' particular yield or purpose is. Further, good interviewers structure the whole interview, determining who asks what, when and how. If there is reason to believe that answers to certain questions somehow count disproportionately more than others, then it may be best to keep the 'hot' ones until the end of the interview.

Professional types: The four worlds of the professional

Dealing with business professionals – accountants, computer specialists, lawyers, doctors – can be a trying business. Some are technically sophisticated problem-solvers who have no idea or notion of a client/customer and their needs. Others believe their expertise is primarily dependent on the understanding and appropriate application of complex rules and procedures.

In some large businesses and consultancies, one finds that these professionals may be crudely divided into client-facing versus backroom boys (or girls). Somehow, one gravitates to a comfortable niche that reflects personal preferences and predilections. Indeed, it may be possible to classify them into four broad groups:

1. *The adviser.* The word has a rather hollow ring now, because of the proliferation of independent financial advisers who are far from independent. The adviser is client-centred. They are genuinely interested in, care about, and listen to clients. They see themselves as specialist professionals, not academic experts. They know that problems are not standard and tend to be flexible in how to apply the rules and policies. Clients like these professionals. They tend to 'think aloud' for clients, giving them various options to choose from. They believe that the client should choose/decide based on the best advice they give. Advisers are usually extrovert, curious, and a bit maverick. Many are distrusted because they get on so well with clients. Often colleagues are jealous of them as they are asked for by name more than others.

2. *The technical specialist:* These are not your techies in the artisan sense, but those who pride themselves on knowing their area well. They have a mental library of odd cases, interesting exceptions and unique problems, yet still believe most problems are of a particular type. They are good at diagnosis, but once done, attempt to apply rule-bound standard solutions. They solve many problems well – quickly, efficiently and correctly. Although odd cases amaze them, they can be a little inflexible in applying unique solutions. They certainly come across as able, workmanlike and efficient. Crisp, down-to-earth types, they may be a little insensitive to client needs. They are not always tolerant of clients who cannot explain or describe what they want to know.

3. *The counsellor:* This description is deliberately and deliciously ambiguous. The dictionary has counsellors as those who give professional guidance and advice, often diplomats or lawyers. The word has been hijacked by the therapist johnnies who dispense all

sorts of magical cures. The counsellor enjoys client work and tries to see problems from their point of view. They tend to understand that problems are not neatly the province of one professional or another; accountancy issues have legal implications. They know the rules and procedures, but are not unduly hampered by them. They get involved and can read people well. They are different from the adviser, predominantly in their ability to think outside the box, offering unusual rule-bending solutions. They are good judges of others' characters and have a very loyal following.

4. *The expert.* Experts are academic: they know a lot, think clearly, have independent ideas. Client problems for them are an intellectual challenge. Once the client has explained the problem to the best of their ability, the expert gets to work, creating new frameworks, ever on the lookout for loopholes. The client's problem becomes their problem, but the client's feelings, anxieties and so on are soon forgotten. Expertise comes from the depth of knowledge and knowing how to apply it. They can become intrigued by problems that completely obsess them. People are not their thing – problem-solving excites them most.

To a large extent, these four types are derived from two factors. The first is whether the professional is client- or problem-centred. The client-centred adviser and counsellor enjoy client contact, build strong relationships and measure their success by client happiness. The problem-centred are more interpersonal, happy when they solve the problem elegantly. The specialist and the expert sell their expertise and their ability to come up with a clever answer.

The other dimension is about creativity, rule breaking and dependency. The adviser and the specialist work within their professional expertise. They concentrate on getting the information salient to their framework. They try to apply their knowledge to the problem. Counsellors and experts tend to be more lateral and less ego- and ergocentric. They are curious, observant and like to look for patterns. They are not scared to go beyond their remit.

The advice for the client is this. Advisers and counsellors will be easier to deal with. They will take more care and interest in you than the specialist and the expert. Counsellors and experts will probably come up with more novel (possibly complex) solutions than advisers and specialists. So, if you want a client-centred traditionalist, seek out the adviser; if you are seeking the problem-centred independent, call for the expert. If you like the technical specialist, you will prefer the standard problem-solving approach, but if you are attracted to counsellors, you appreciate the client-centred independent. Often, it is your – the client's – needs as much as the problem itself that should dictate who you choose among your professional types.

The psychology of absenteeism

It is almost impossible to come up with really accurate national or business figures on absenteeism. There are essentially three reasons for this. The first is that companies do not collect absenteeism data – they have no systems to do it, or the issue is too sensitive and hot from both a management and union perspective. The second reason is that although an organization may indeed collect these data regularly and accurately, it is, quite simply, too ashamed to publish or publicize it. The third reason is that there are too many definitions in the accident literature to be able to agree on how to collect the data. We have authorized/certified versus unauthorized/uncertified absence; contractual versus non-contractual absence, sickness (injury)/medical versus non-sickness, non-injury/personal absence and so on. In other words, simple aggregated statistics are deeply misleading because they include different types of absenteeism.

There is abundant data on the sort of factors known to be related to levels of absenteeism. At the level of the *individual* worker obvious factors include general health and resistance to illness, work-induced fatigue and shiftwork, but also non-work-induced fatigue (such as child care) and preferred hobbies (that sap energy or are dangerous).

Inevitably, *environmental* factors have an impact on absenteeism. Ambient flu and viruses are important, as are fluctuations in atmospheric conditions. Jobs with well-known stresses like uncontrollable and excessive noise, powerful unpleasant odours and bright lights also affect illness behaviour.

Certainly, *administrative* factors relate closely to all aspects of absenteeism, particularly the index of absence used, the administrative categories used for the attribution of absence and the level of aggregation of absence data – particularly whether it is by the day, the week, the work group, the shift, the plant and so on.

But we do not know – despite various scare stories – that absenteeism still has a relatively low base rate. It is not that common a problem except in very specific sectors at particular periods of time. We also know that people underestimate their own absentee records but tend to inflate views about the absence of others. Self-evidently, managers and employees hold different standards about how much absenteeism is acceptable. Indeed, the very meaning of absence varies considerably among different groups. For some people it is a form of legitimate extra pay to compensate for perceived poor pay, extra stress or reduced holidays. For others it is a way of getting even with colleagues who seem to take excessive time off work.

Certainly, supervisors' behaviours, values and modelling are crucial in shaping the attendance patterns of individual workers. Organizations themselves differ in how they measure and react to absenteeism.

It is difficult to assess the real cost of absence from work. But to use old-fashioned terminology, it is true to say that there are various *stakeholders* in company absenteeism. For the *individual* worker, absenteeism can affect income and job security, as well as reputation, which is related to job security. Equally, failing to go absent (with legitimate sick leave) may have both acute and chronic effects on employees' personal health.

The *work group* itself has a considerable stake in absenteeism, particularly with respect to morale. People in work groups are very sensitive to equity – the ratio of inputs to outputs. If a group member takes excessive and perceived inappropriate absences without some equitable cost to the person (reduced wages, increased workload when present, reduced holidays), other group members are often affected. They may take revenge by going absent themselves, so lowering the productivity of the group as a whole.

Inevitably the *organization* as a whole has a serious stake in absenteeism. It is not difficult to see how both acute and chronic levels of absenteeism affect profit, staffing, customer relations and company reputation, which affects the share price. How organizations plan for dealing with unforeseen absences is indeed a fascinating index of their adaptability.

The *unions* are stakeholders in absenteeism. They negotiate over the causes and cures of problems and often have it as a major topic of dispute.

Every *worker's family* has a stake in absenteeism. Pressures at work, particularly with regard to retaining the job in times of poor job security, could lead to ill-health that affects the whole family. Equally, pressures in the home can be a direct cause of absenteeism. Parental absenteeism patterns also provide a powerful model for young children and may influence either their readiness or reluctance to go absent. It has even been suggested that school truancy and phobia are clearly related to parental absence from work figures.

Of course the *society as a whole* has a stake in absenteeism. Social values determine the value of work and leisure, illness and health, loyalty to family and employer. Albeit a crude measure of a society's health and happiness, absenteeism figures in the former Eastern bloc countries, though rarely reported, were certainly an amazing index of the inefficiency of socialism.

So, what causes absenteeism? There are a bewildering number of explanations and theories. They are not contradictory but complementary, each emphasizing a different cause. But perhaps they indicate best of all the complexity of the whole issue:

1. *Process and decision models.* This approach suggests that absence is the result of many factors, especially personal attitudes to attendance, perceptions of company norms favouring attendance, perceived control over personal behaviour and personal moral obligation to the organization. This approach stresses that individuals make calculated and rational decisions to go absent.
2. *Withdrawal models.* The argument here is that job satisfaction is the best predictor of absenteeism but more related to frequency than overall days lost. Commitment is less important but includes the extent to which people believe the organization is committed to them. People go absent or withdraw as a reaction to job unhappiness with their work.
3. *Demographic models.* These list all related factors that predict frequent absenteeism. Age is important but may not be linear (U-shaped) in that older and younger people are absent more. Gender is important but the results are equivocal. Women are usually more often absent, due primarily to child care, but gender is confounded by many other factors (status, income). There is evidence of gender-absence cultures such that when stressed men go on strike and women go absent.

4. *Medical models.* Sickness is the major cause of illness and is usually linked to smoking and drinking (quantity and chronicity), psychological illness (particularly neurosis) and pain. The extent to which lifestyle that is modifiable causes illness which leads to absence is most often debated.

5. *Stress models.* Stress causes absence and comes from many sources – the job (intrinsic and extrinsic factors), the home life, the personality of the individual. But it could be that those who are more absent exhibit less stress due to recuperative activities. In other words, absence relieves stress – the question is what is the optimum amount.

6. *Social and cultural models.* Departmental unit climate or 'cultural' factors influence absenteeism powerfully. Normative perceptions are very important – thus the simple rating of peer absence (how much absence colleagues take) is the best predictor of own frequency of illness. People are sensitive to levels of acceptable absence and culturally acceptable explanations/excuses for their absence.

7. *Conflict models.* These suggest that absenteeism is the manifestation of the unorganized conflict between management and labour (as opposed to strikes, which are usually organized). Absence is an index or a metric of industrial relations.

8. *Deviance models.* Absenteeism is deviant because of the negative consequences for organizational effectiveness and the violation of legal and psychological contracts. It can also be seen as a product of negative traits: malingering, disloyalty and laziness. Those who take this perspective maintain that (all) job absence is a sign of wickedness.

9. *Economic models.* These are rational economic explanations for absenteeism. Absenteeism and attendance are products of labour supply. As wage rates increase it is more attractive to sell leisure for work, but as income increases people need time for consumatory purposes. Absenteeism is prone in cash-rich, time-poor workers.

Absenteeism is a complex problem with multiple, interlinked causes that are only partly controllable by managers in companies. Like a lot of business problems, there remains no simple solution to cure it. But a good start is to begin to measure it reliably to get a better idea of the precise nature of the problem in one's own organization.

Queuing at airports

The British, it is said, are natural, if not happy queuers. Johnny Foreigner, particularly the Southern European genus, finds it quaintly ridiculous, not to say very nearly impossible. But the queue, or waiting in line, as our transatlantic cousins say, is a fair and orderly way to 'process' people.

Airports are a queuer's dream. The following is a true experience – only the names and identity of the guilty have been withheld. It is a personal, not untypical episode, but it does suggest a good case study for a bit of serious and immediate re-engineering.

Having found the right terminal and check-in area, one is first faced by the pre-check-in security queue (Q1), where the ticket is glanced at and the tedious (for both parties) questions about packing the bag asked. This first queue leads often to the longest and possibly most anxiety-provoking queue (Q2) for the actual check-in desk. The anxiety is often about having to negotiate or plead for a favoured seat. Inevitably, this process lengthens the queue, as people try to sneak in more than their baggage allowance, or claim special reasons (backache, club membership) for favoured treatment. We have all seen these queues stretching for 20–30 metres as the tired, bored and anxious traveller shuffles miserably forward at the speed of a snail with gout.

Acquiring the boarding pass in the second queue might seem like a major achievement, but you have only just begun. The next queue (Q3) occurs as one goes into the departure area. Here, one must queue to have the recently acquired boarding pass and passport checked. This queue can be quick, but immediately after it, one hits the fourth, but second major queue (Q4). This is the luggage X-ray and body-frisking queue. For many, there are mixed feelings here. Because the process is so potentially intrusive (one's personal belongings are peered into and one is touched, rather intimately, by a complete stranger), it is not a particularly enjoyable experience. When crowded, there may be two very slow-moving queues in one – the first to surrender any remaining luggage to the omnivorous maw of the conveyor belt (Q4a) and the second to pass through the X-ray gate (Q5).

Five queues later, one finally reaches passport control. Often swift, as one flashes either the magnificent navy blue or flimsy burgundy passport to appropriate people, this queue can be held up by the bewildered, the forgetful, or the dubious fellow traveller.

At last, one emerges by the twinkling lights of the duty-free shops. They may be duty-free, but often the mark-up makes them a cash cow for owners. Here, one may be trapped in yet another queue, this time for the check-out (Q6).

For the fortunate air miles locked-in business traveller, there is the lounge to look forward to. Papers, a glass of wine or mineral water, perhaps even a tasty canapé, all beckon the eager traveller. But at a busy time, one may even have to queue to have the boarding card inspected again (Q7). This may or may not be the seventh queue one has endured in the past 20–30 minutes.

Three queues to go before the weary traveller even steps on to the plane. The announcement in the lounge summons one to the gate, where the business and first class passengers have to mix with the little people at the back of the bus. Passport and boarding card have to be shown to get into the boarding gate lounge (Q8). Sometimes, there are security people before the desk to engage the traveller in another pre-queue queue (Q8a).

The lounges are pretty barren and functional, and unpleasant places in which to spend any time. A PA announcement sets off the penultimate queue for the last barrier before the aeroplane, where one's stub of a boarding pass gets passed through a computer (Q9).

The final queue (which we shall call Q10) is unpleasant, and nearly always occurs on the plane itself. This is always caused by the egocentric, heavily laden passenger struggling to overstuff the over-head lockers. They block the aisles which causes a back-up of unhappy and fatigued passengers on the airbridge.

So, from entering the terminal to finally sitting down on the plane, you have to stand in 10 queues. Your ticket was examined three times, your passport five, and your boarding pass six. Granted, it was a busy time, but you stood in line for 39 minutes. You were bored and frustrated; emotions clearly shared by your fellow travellers.

Your return was from America. There, you stood in queues for only 7 minutes.

No doubt the procedures-driven, security-conscious bureaucrat could give good reasons why you had to queue 10 times for 39 minutes. Words, like safety and security, would recur again and again to rationalize and bully the customers. But the cynic may see it as no more than a job creation scheme.

Rating companies

So, you liked the product so much you thought of buying the company? The standard of service was so exemplary you wondered how the company was run to achieve that standard?

You don't have to buy and sell companies to take an interest in whether they are successful or not. It could be that you are interested in the long-term health of the company that employs you. Or that you want to do an audit on the company that has just offered you a job. Most likely you are interested in determining whether to buy shares in the company.

What should you look for? What criteria seem to mark out the chosen from the doomed; the successful from the failures? Is the evaluation of companies an art or a science? Are there really subtle yet powerful predictors of company success?

If you read, and believe, the business-school researchers, highly successful companies seem characterized by various features. Using these as a checklist may be helpful: (a) if you believe they are true; (b) if you can get enough information to make an informed judgement; (c) if the long-term, as opposed to short-term, interests of the company are important to you. The list tends to look like this:

1. *The vision thing:* A clear idea of what the company believes in and is trying to achieve. Not to be confused with meaningless mission statements. Is it sure where it is going; why and how to get there? Does it know the route as well as the destination?
2. *Cross-functional, matrix structures:* Where specialists in traditional areas regularly work in 'mixed' teams, sharing their insights and expertise. Are they aware of problems of intra-company fighting, poor communication and wasted effort of specialists who don't communicate? Does the way people work foster co-operation and reduce waste?
3. *Flat and non-hierarchical:* Where people are accountable and responsible for what they do at various levels. Does the structure look lean and mean with the right 'chief-to-Indian ratio'?
4. *A global perspective:* Is the company attempting buying and selling to the whole world as a hedge against regional downturns? Is the company aware of markets and trends outside its little area? Does

it realize the importance of expanding markets into profitable areas? Has it moved from a national, through international, to a really global perspective?

5. *Appropriately networked and outsourced*: Does the company show an understanding of the importance of partnering with other organizations? Has the company seriously thought about the benefits of outsourcing certain functions? Does it think regularly about mergers and acquisitions?

6. *IT positive and wired*: Is it an organization which realizes what IT can do and uses it appropriately? Is it using IT sensibly to save costs, store records and execute tasks? Does it update its systems? Is it a slave or master of the new technology?

7. *Stakeholder focused*: This means being aware of what the stake is and who the shareholders are. Does the company know who its stakeholders are and can it educate their expectations appropriately? Is it able to balance the different needs of different stakeholders over time?

8. *Flexible and open to ideas*: Is the company pro-development but not change for its own sake? Is it able to walk the tightrope between being a change-phile and change-phobe? Does it appreciate natural growth or regular but unplanned slashers and burners?

9. *Hungry and eager*: Not complacent; eager to win; competitive at all levels and eager to stretch itself. Does the company really want to be the best? Is there enough energy and ability to succeed?

10. *Talented committed staff*: More easily said than done, but a function of selection and training. Does the HR function really put enough in to make sure the company attracts and retains the best staff?

The problem with the above list is not that it is incomplete or inconsistent, though that may well be true, but rather that it is extremely difficult to obtain this information other than by working for the company itself at a fairly senior level or else snooping about in it in the role of consultant.

And what of looking at specialist departments and functions such as HR? What sort of criteria would one want of an HR department?

A number of criteria seem apparent. First, *numeracy* and *computer literacy*. Are there sufficient people able to, as well as active in, gathering people-relevant data (absenteeism, appraisal, productivity, morale). And are those data used regularly in decision-making?

Second, does the HR department understand the *corporate strategy* and does it have its own strategy which is integrated into it? Do members of the HR department really understand the business they are in and feel part of it? Does the HR director deservedly sit on the board? Third, is there any evidence of *entrepreneurship* in the department, or is it only a spender rather than a saver or even creator of money? Has the department seriously thought through the possibility of *outsourcing* certain functions such as training or law? Is there a real effort to be *up to date* rather than prone to fashion and folderol? Most importantly, are there people with real knowledge-based expertise such as in employment law, psychometrics, occupational health, and is that knowledge base updated?

Quite a tough task certainly, but then business is about survival of the fittest.

Reactions to training

In some organizations, being sent on a training course is a reward. A few days off work at a plush country hotel with the company even picking up the bar bill is a wonderful tonic for the weary executive. Serendipitously, of course, one might even learn something! In other businesses, to be asked to attend a training course is a punishment. It implies that you can't do your job and that you have to really demonstrate your improved performance when back in the workplace. Worst of all in the latter organization is being sent on an interpersonal skills course, as you apparently have to change your whole personality.

Employees may thus be training-phobic or training-addicted. Much depends on the type of training, however. Technical skills training (that is, computers, balance sheets) tends to be rather different from social skills courses (assertiveness, interviewing). And both are often quite different from experiential courses, which may be amazingly instructive or embarrassing. Thus, one may be at the same time a technophobe but social skills course junkie.

Trainers begin very early to get a feel for delegates' attitudes to training. Last-minute cancellations, late arrivals, perpetually ringing mobile phones, are meant to give a sense of importance. But it is in the non-verbals in the first 5 minutes that one can glean useful clues as to how anxious or enthusiastic the attendees may be.

It is not difficult to recognize at least six types:

1. *Prisoners*: they feel sentenced to the course. They don't want to be there, but have to serve their time. Most have been justly sentenced, but as we know, prison doesn't work. Often hostile and aggressive, they can easily poison things for others.
2. *Escapees*: they feel imprisoned in their office and are more than happy to be entertained, fed and watered at the company's expense.
3. *Retirees*: they really enjoy courses because they have an eye to new skills being needed for their post-early retirement career. They can be too eager or demanding on the trainers.
4. *Academics*: they are the Open University types of the training world. Bright, but undisciplined, they have learned that the seminar is a wonderful place for showing off newly acquired words like Zeitgeist, epistemological and intrapreneurial.
5. *Developmentalists*: they come from the old human potential school of ever-upward-and-onward personal development. Life is a long learning exercise and the seminar offers an ideal way to develop oneself.
6. *Thieves*: there are those at seminars whose primary aim is to steal ideas and techniques from the trainers. They may be trainers themselves and find it easier to plagiarize than create.

Public training courses are an excellent forum for networking. They also allow one to do a bit of social comparison because one can evaluate the ability of competitors or those indifferent sectors. These comparison processes can be disastrous, as people may easily find out how badly paid they are (comparatively), or more often, badly managed. So, rather than return with enthusiasms and skills, they come back to the office seething with jealousy and resentment. Perhaps that is why some companies discourage their employees from going on public courses, preferring to do everything in-house!

Traditionally, training is measured by one of four criteria: participants' reaction to the course; evidence of learning; some behavioural change; and some bottom-line change in the department, section or, ideally, company overall. The last (and best) criterion is too difficult. The first is too easy and may have nothing at all to do with the efficacy of the training. Looking at the 'happy sheets' as an indicator of the success of the training can be misleading.

Learning a real skill is often not easy. It takes effort, practice, concentration and a modicum of intelligence. Higher-order skills require that one learn many micro-skills which are later combined. It can be frustrating – as most of us can recall when we learned to drive or master the PC. And it is too easy to take out this frustration on the presenter/trainer. By contrast, it may well be that if the training course did not ruffle a few feathers, require sustained and exhausting effort, and cause a little self-doubt, it may be rated as poor. Some poor happy sheets – courses that are not particularly well rated by participants – may in fact mean that they have been challenged intellectually. Equally, glowing responses may well simply indicate an amusing 'entertrainer' has kept course participants stimulated for its duration, having in the meantime taught them nothing.

Revenue up and cost down: two management styles

It is only when times are bad that one often notices most clearly the management optimist and the management pessimist. Profitability and growth are achieved by either increasing revenue or reducing costs: preferably both. But given that one may have to put one's faith and energy into one more than the other, which to choose? Optimists seem to opt for revenue up; pessimists for costs down.

The *revenue up* strategy usually relies on three things: *increasing volume* through new products, better marketing, better sales incentives; *increasing margins* through different pricing or discount structures; and *minimizing tax* while *maximizing interest* or recovery from specific bodies.

The *reducing costs* strategy has two tough targets: *reducing direct costs* to improve labour efficiency and reduce material waste or prices; and *reducing overheads* by staff changes (relocation, firing, using temporary labour), cutting advertising, PR, outside marketing research services and other perceived inessentials, looking for smaller premises, reviewing all distribution and handling costs and minimizing borrowing costs.

The *revenue up* optimists nearly always come from the world of marketing. They tend to be extroverts who are personally more motivated by promise of reward than threat of punishment. They are expansionists, even imperialists, whose whole aim is to improve market share and make more sales. They understand about setbacks, tough competitors and bear markets but see these as a challenge. They understand that one has to spend to earn, but focus on the latter not the former.

Revenue up extroverts tend to be people-oriented. They know how to sell and motivate both staff and customers. Many are little interested in accounting or processes or technical monitoring. They like face-to-face encounters and 'closing the sale'. They are, at least superficially, charming. They certainly have a vision, a mission and all those other forward-looking things that gurus talk about, although it is not certain whether they have a strategic plan at any detailed level.

Revenue people see the glass as half-full not half-empty, and dedicate themselves to filling it up. Indeed, in times of recession they may well be at their best, doubling their personal commitment and work schedule while motivating their staff. They shun defeatist talk and are sensitive to all or any positive signs in the market. They can be inspiring to their staff, though at times naïve to their bosses.

The *costs down pessimists* are often accountants and engineers. They tend to be more introverted and sensitive to threat of punishment. They understand systems to monitor and to control and are eager to get standard processes into place. They often don't like or trust things that can't be measured – hence their reluctance to spend on advertising, PR, even market research.

They see people as their greatest cost, not as an asset, and are dedicated to cutting out waste. Most of them are not good with their people – or their customers. They e-mail rather talk to staff. They may be 'swift to chide, and slow to bless' rather than the other way around.

Cost down people are natural pessimists. They see customers as capricious, staff as unreliable and markets as nervous and whimsical. And in their eagerness to measure process they soon see opportunities to save money; particularly on the people side. Hence ideas like downsizing, outsourcing, telecottaging, and quality groups have enormous appeal because their aim is more about cost-reduction than sales. They tend not to understand the psychological processes at work as much as the material ones.

Extroverts and introverts have very different preference and styles. The former become impatient and bored when work is slow and unchanging; the latter when work is interrupted and rushed. The former welcome phone calls as a diversion; the latter find them intrusive. The former prefer to develop ideas through discussion (committee, task force, focus group); the latter through personal reflection. The former often use outside resources to complete tasks whereas the latter use themselves.

Extroverts respond quickly to requests and spring into action without much advanced thinking. Introverts think through requests before responding, even to the point of delaying action.

No wonder introverts and extroverts don't like, trust or choose to mix with one another. Extroverted, optimistic, revenue up managers see their opposites as stuffy, gloomy inadequates whose pessimism is self-fulfilling. Introverted, cautious, cost-reducers see their opposites as shallow, unreliable, risk-seekers whose wacky ideas can lead to not only their and their department's downfall, but also that of the whole organization.

It is a relief to find that most managers are neither extroverted revenue-up proponents nor obsessively introverted cost-cutters. Hurrah for the bell curve with just a slight leaning one way or the other.

Seminal experiences: a really good seminar

Good lecturers are rare in colleges and universities. The primary reason for this is that academics are not selected for their ability to teach, but on the basis of their research and writing skills. Lecturing, in fact, is a minor branch of the performing arts which attracts natural extroverts. The researcher who spends long, lonely stretches of time in libraries and laboratories is usually an introvert, who is exhausted and drained by a long lecture. But both can be good lecturers when communicating their passions to students.

A truly good lecturer can entice, enthral and excite. The paradox can be clarified and the sophistry exposed; the big picture painted and the minutiae described. One criterion of a good lecture or seminar is that students are not only encouraged to read more, but that they actually do so.

Management seminars are now big business. It is not unusual to have to pay £300-400 for a 9.45am–4.15pm day! And they can be awful – vacuously evangelical, all style and no content, or tediously dry, given by a recently redundant middle manager who should stick to the gardening.

For feedback, most business seminars require or request that one completes a 'happy sheet' to evaluate the course. There are often ratings on venue, luncheon and so on, but not always that many on the content and delivery of the lectures. The question is, what criteria should one consider? What are the hallmarks of a really excellent business seminar?

Sometimes it is difficult to separate content from style of lecturing. Some trainers and seminar leaders have learnt that thin content can be boosted by stories, jokes, parables and slides (hence the emergence of the flamboyant Captain Anecdote). The entertainer relies more on technique and technology than syllabus content. The profound lecturer has a good command of both content and style, attributes that have factors salient for any good lecture:

1. *Breadth*: There is nothing as interesting and impressive as genuine 'Renaissance Man'. The lecturer with breadth of knowledge and vision, with no disciplinary boundaries, with competence in multiple fields, is a true teacher. The expert knows more about less. Experts are fascinating on their topic, but often lost when forced to leave the security of their narrow, often esoteric, research area.

2. *Structure*: Good speakers adhere to the adage: 'Tell 'em what you are going to tell 'em; tell 'em; tell 'em what you told 'em.' To follow, remember and comprehend the lecture, the structure needs to be made clear. There is no reason why one should not tell the audience what they can expect to hear.

3. *Pace*: The successful lecturer takes his audience along at a comfortable pace, allowing time for questions and discussion, while ensuring that no one person takes up an inordinate amount of time. Seminars where a succession of facts and figures are rattled off at top speed leave the audience confused and afraid to ask for guidance. Similarly, those conducted at snail's pace, with too much detail and repetition, have a soporific effect. A really good lecturer builds in time for questions and for lively and appropriate group discussion.

4. *Variety*: A long, uninterrupted and monotonous discourse on a subject should be avoided when lecturing. Audiences stay awake

much longer when the tone and pitch of the lecturer's voice is modulated rather than monotonous, and when occasional anecdotes and jokes are sprinkled along the way.

5. *Audience participation*: A successful lecturer welcomes input from the audience, weaving it into the fabric of the talk. The lofty expert may discourage comments from his listeners, dismissing them as insignificant or uninformed. Others may like the sound of their own voice more than those of their audience. Audience comments are a valuable source of feedback and should be encouraged.

6. *Time*: The wittiest, most erudite lecturer in the world can send his or her audience to sleep if he or she disregards one of the most important tools in the lecture theatre: the clock. Good lecturers know roughly how long their talk will take, and try not to overrun. It is better to send one's audience away alert, and with at least some knowledge, than to bombard them with facts and send them to sleep.

What should one expect to leave the seminar with? Copies of the slides; a few memorable stories; business cards from other delegates? Perhaps the seminar criteria are that one knows what the big questions are in the area and where to find the answers. Also, that one has a genuine enthusiasm and interest in doing so!

It is sometimes difficult to combine a flair for lecturing with a passion for research. But the lecturer who successfully merges these two skills will be richly rewarded in the response to his or her talks.

Sour feedback

Hands up those who have recently received a 360-degree *feedback* form. And what about those who have got annual appraisal *feedback*? Who here has at one time received *feedback* from selectors after completing a personality test or an assessment centre exercise?

Giving people feedback is really *in* at the moment – in a big way. Indeed, people seem to believe in its miraculous powers to inspire, correct deviant behaviour and be rewarding in, and of, itself. It certainly is true that working in a feedback-less world is miserable.

But to be at all useful, feedback needs to be reliable, valid, differential and useful. Bland, overall ratings may be interesting, but are not really useful. Good feedback, essentially, needs to be *honest* and *specific*. And that is where the problem lies, because if it is really honest and specific, it usually has to include the negative. Calling specific negative feedback 'developmental opportunities' does not really overcome the problem. One way of giving feedback is to do it 'without interpretation'. Enter the video camera. The camera, we are told, never lies. That *may* be true, but neither does it interpret. Watching oneself do a skilled task on film still needs the expert's tutelage, not only to understand which minutiae to focus on but also how to do things differently. One needs the commentary and the interpretation along with the pictures to make video feedback really useful.

Giving negative feedback that can be heard and acted on is really a skill. Tough, no-nonsense managers often turn out to be pusillanimous when it comes to giving individuals negative feedback. Consider the ways in which messengers of bad news attempt to defend themselves. After an interview, the successful candidate is phoned; but the unsuccessful candidates are sent a letter of rejection. Appraisal systems often fail because bosses refuse to show their reports with their ratings on them; or even more feebly, rate everybody and everything as average.

There is no problem about giving positive feedback. Indeed, it is a joy. Awarding the prizes is easy. Apart from the possible envy of the less successful, it is very pleasant to give praise and rewards when they are due.

But the skilful positive reinforcer (to use the jargon of the rat psychologist) needs to use his/her feedback skilfully to maintain good performance. Any receiver of positive feedback needs to know precisely what they did – when, how and why – so that they can do it again. To be told that the talk was interesting, the essay was good, the work was rated as 'above average', really does not tell the person how to repeat the exercise and get even better. Talks are interesting because of their structure, style, wit, stories, slides and so on, and lecturers need to be told so.

The real problem lies in giving negative feedback. Take the typical scenario. The unwilling boss, goaded by the department, has to show his/her reports their completed annual appraisal form. Naturally, the employee's eyes focus not on the 7 or 8 out of 8 ratings, called excellent or exemplary performance, but on the 1 or 2 out of 8 ratings, called unsatisfactory, below standard and poor. The assumption is that the poor scores will, not unnaturally, affect any overall performance score, which, in turn, affects any performance-related pay. So, the employee first demands justification for the marks. At this point, the boss tries to describe a typical incident where this behaviour occurred (or did not when it should have). The employee then disputes the interpretation of events, blaming the customer, colleagues, equipment. This then turns into an argument about the past.

Much better to say to each employee: 'I have tried my best to give you accurate, honest and helpful feedback. The ratings represent what I believe to be true. What I will do is describe what I want to be done *differently in the future* so that your changed/improved behaviour would merit a higher score.' The focus is on the behaviour and the future, not on the personality and the past.

Some bosses, full of enthusiasm for giving feedback, do more harm than good. Armed with surprisingly few data (observations) on someone's behaviour, they can wade in with some rather gauche stuff. Their negative feedback seems to imply personality defects that are impossible to change, rather than behavioural issues which are quite often easy to fix. Receivers of feedback all wait for the 'but' words. So they ignore the stuff about 'happy with overall performance', 'particularly impressed by' and wait for the negative feedback.

And, by definition, it is the neurotically sensitive who prove the most difficult to talk to. This is because their neuroses (anxiety, hypochondria, obsessionality) lead both to poor performance, but also to incredible sensitivity to any sort of criticism. So, paradoxically, those who most need criticism least often get it because managers are frightened about making them worse – or in some instances, actually making them worse.

It is possible to counsel the neurotic. It is possible to rejuvenate the tired, and energize the indolent through feedback. But it takes preparation. Get your facts right. Give clear, specific feedback that is descriptive, not evaluative. Focus on the work-related behaviour of the employee, not their personality, their peers, or the system. And most importantly, tell them precisely what you want done differently. In fact, feedforward, not back.

Span of control

Re-engineering for a flatter organizational structure is still all the rage.

Middle managers, it is said, are expensive, red-tape bureaucrats and unnecessary. They distort and slow down communication. Hierarchies therefore lead to poorer customer service and poor quality inspection. Old ideas about a logical and restricted span of control are 'outdated'. In the new brave millennium a good manager may be able to manage effectively up to 50 staff. The popular business gurus have long been crying: 'Give up the pyramid model and adopt the *orchestra model* where a single conductor can synchronize and lead a hundred experts to produce (literally) perfect harmony.'

Supposedly, productivity, morale, quality and profits are better in the flatter organization. Or are they? Getting rid of levels of middle-aged, middle-brow middle managers has considerable appeal to many people. Shareholders see smaller wage bills; techies see an opportunity to replace people electronically; junior staff see freedom from observation and inspection – and faster promotion to senior levels. What, after all, did the middle manager do? Who will care or notice if they are not there?

Delayering, downsizing, rightsizing and capsizing gurus are agreed that flatter is better. But they are not clear on how flat or why; or indeed of the necessity of any structures in the first place. They are also extremely uncritical of the mounting evidence which suggests that various alternative models to the traditional span-of-control structure do not work. Take, for instance, the conductor model in the 'organization as orchestra'. The idea is that the CEO communicates directly with employees via monthly meetings or an in-house TV channel. Employees have to crowd into the canteen to watch Big Brother's monthly pep-talk, nicely rehearsed and scripted and with all the benefits of PR and media consultants. Attempts at this approach fail badly because the language of the CEO is either too general or too full of jargon. It is certainly too distant. One wants to shake hands with, and 'shoot the breeze' with, the CEO; to find out if he or she is human, vulnerable, honest – even likeable.

People listen to advice, help and feedback from their immediate boss – their supervisor who can monitor their behaviour directly. And they need two-way communication, which the orchestra model does not allow for. Orchestras are made up of experts who follow strict rules – hardly the model for the modern company. People need to get regular, immediate personalized feedback on how they are doing to correct errors or 'carry on with the good work'.

In fact, too flat an organization leads to many worse communication and decision-making problems. The remaining managers in flat organizations are often flooded with duties, reports and so on. Because their span of control is impossibly high, they become slow and uncommunicative – the precise problem the flattened organization was supposed to solve! E-mails and voice mail do not compensate for the increased workload.

The idea that tall, hierarchical organizations have 'too many chiefs but not enough Indians' seems particularly good reason to cull a few middle managers. It was shown recently that there were more admirals than ships in the Royal Navy due to a hierarchy getting out of hand. But the data show no evidence of the growth of managerial/ administration staff as organizations grow in size. This is because the span of control usually increases as organizations increase in size. Big, successful organizations tend to standardize procedures and systems, which saves on management time, so enabling them to supervise more people. Further, procedural administrative work can be specialized and delegated to particular support staff. Again, the research shows the precise opposite of what the downsizers claim: as firms grow, hierarchies become more efficient and proportionally smaller. The size of the HR department in a firm of 200 may be about the same size as that in a firm of 800. The middle managers who keep systems running can be encouraged to be extremely efficient – if, of course, the systems are well designed, useful and maximize the use of new technology.

Another particularly 1980s idea is that the further managers are from their customer, the less they understand them and monitor their needs. Hence hierarchies are thought to be more insensitive to customer needs. The popular idea is that bureaucrats sit in head office surrounded by support staff whose job it is to prevent internal or external customers ever getting near them. Spending some time with actual customers is a good idea – it's not a new idea but it is not really anything to do with hierarchies. The worry is that managers spend all their time with ever-demanding customers and take their eye off the ball of strategy, pricing and so on. Managers at all levels have numerous planning, negotiation and scheduling activities that have to be done by someone. Middle managers have to be concerned with internal customers, or whatever the preferred term is. This is not to say that they ignore the external customers: far from it. However, organizations need someone to think about innovation strategy as well as simple maintenance.

The most recent calls for downlayers come from software companies who believe that automation, computerization and Internet technology will allow middle-management jobs to be done faster, better and at a fraction of the cost by computers. All technology is rule-following and it is quite possible that routine work or calculative tasks may be done more efficiently with computers. Further, the experience of replacing even telephone operators with mechanical devices has radically increased customer dissatisfaction. People hate talking to machines whatever the pre-recorded message. Again the paradox: the solution exacerbates, rather than solves, the problem.

But management is emotional labour. It is also inevitably political. It is as much about risk and courage as it is about analytic calculations. Machines cannot do this sort of work. Technologies deal with standard problems presented in a format they can understand. Imagine a 'complaints desk' run by a computer. People get frightened, cross and bewildered at work. They need the emotional and informational support of peers and bosses. They need praise and to be pulled up short. These are not machine-based tasks – and probably never will be.

The outward-bound trainers say management is about courage. It is more about the heart than the head. It is as much an affective task as an analytic one. Sometimes that is true. And machines can be extremely helpful in analytic tasks but much less so with affective (emotional) ones.

So, what did the downsized manager do before being flattened out? Why have hierarchies existed for so long if they are so inefficient? And why have firms that for one reason or another have not been hierarchical often failed? The post-war miracle countries, particularly Germany and Japan, have been clearly, triumphantly and very happily hierarchical. They are almost a celebration of the genre. The salaryman has been the backbone of many Japanese companies. There is the world of difference between overmanning and optimal manning.

In short, a hierarchy is a rather good way to control work processes. It defines who is responsible to whom for what. It encourages specializations so that people with different skills, perspectives and time frames can explore their native talents. Depending on the task people are doing, problem-solving is quite different. The quality control manager and the strategic planner have very different frames and very different needs. They have different skills and different objectives. It is possible, but unusual, to find all these skills in one individual.

Middle managers attempt to spot trends, look for new opportunities and alliances and develop new processes. Planning, developing, implementing and maintaining particular strategic initiatives is the kind of thing managers in hierarchical organizations do well. They may *not* do it well of course, but that is an issue of bad selection not necessarily of bad corporate structure.

Outsourcing, team-based working and employee stakeholders are ideas that don't replace the necessity of the concept of hierarchies, but they do complement them.

The tallness of any hierarchy is determined primarily by the size of the organization and the complexity of the work done. In essence, it depends on how closely work needs to be supervised. Where work is not or can't be routinized or where people are physically distanced from one another, more, rather than less, supervision is needed. The guru of re-engineering recanted a few years ago after thousands of companies 're-engineered' their middle managers. The gain was short-lived and the pain too much to bear. Often the good middle managers were happily recalled as consultants at twice the pay and half the responsibility. In many instances the experiment failed. It is span of control that should determine the tallness of the hierarchy not the evangelical exhortations of gurus who have themselves often failed in these organizations.

The sweet smell of success : ambient scent and consumer reactions

Are estate agents right about baking bread and fresh-ground coffee smells helping to sell houses? Are supermarkets wise to have loss-making bakeries on the premises just to benefit from the effect the smell has on shoppers? Are your chances of selection for a job in part a function of your perfume or aftershave?

The topic of odour is not a particularly polite one in our society, unless we are discussing fragrant smells, perfumes or scents that are deeply evocative of past experience. But consumer researchers have long been interested in 'ambient environmental motivators of consumer behaviour', or the effect of smell on shopping if you prefer. Even if the effect is small, the product manufacturers and store designers are fascinated by the potentially subliminal effects scents may have on purchasing behaviour.

Equally, there is an industry for hiding smells – such as the smell of cigarettes. Hospitals and dentists try to hide or mask smells associated with those places because of the extent to which they are associated with pain and anxiety. In fact, it seems that more effort goes into disguising 'natural' smells by overlaying a 'carpet' of more acceptable scents.

We live in a highly scented world. We douse ourselves in scents every day, often disguising our distinctive and often attractive to the opposite sex natural odour. For many people, every morning the day begins with the use of scented soap, peppermint toothpaste, mouthwash, scented shampoo, deodorant, cologne or perfume. Why all shampoos have to be fruit- or vegetable-scented is unclear. But there do seem to be clear conventions about scent. Washing-up liquid needs to be lemony, tissues floral and so on.

Our language, in part, emphasizes the importance of odour. Thus we talk about the 'sweet smell of success' or of the slippery but lucky person always 'coming up smelling of roses'. Some people have a 'nose for where money is' while others are 'always sticking their nose into other people's business'. I 'smell success' and 'scent danger' but she 'reeks of authenticity'.

To demonstrate the power of odour, one study required men on a selection skills course to evaluate the merits of a particular woman. She differed between the different interviews only in the perfume she was wearing. Surprisingly, she was evaluated as more able and technically skilled when wearing a noticeably popular perfume. In this sense the scent gave her a halo effect – smells nice, is nice; smells good, is good.

We know that animals can detect human pheromones. There is increasing evidence that we can too. Chairs sprayed with particular pheromones were more likely to be chosen or avoided. This sense, unlike sight, hearing or touch, seems to be rather under-researched.

It seems that the human odour communication system is primitive, and operates for most of us at the level of unconscious awareness. Few people are able to send or detect complex messages or signals by the choice of chemical they spray on themselves, and are not in a position to alter the central nervous system voluntarily to induce particular scents. Most of us operate on the pleasant–unpleasant dimension and are utterly reliant on the erratic feedback of others to determine reaction. Equally, the social problem of telling somebody about 'bad breath' or 'unpleasant odour' is fraught with embarrassment. All this amounts to the fact that most of us have very little idea of the effect of our natural and unnatural smell on others we meet.

What data are there on the effects of scent on consumer behaviour? Products with the 'appropriate scent' are evaluated more positively; hence manufacturers being interested in learnt scent–product pairings. Most work that has been done on 'ambient scent' suggests that smell has positive effects in that sales go up modestly, but very cost effectively.

But people do show scent preferences. There are age differences – pine, hay, grass and horses are particularly evocative for those born prior to 1930, while sweet tarts and baking bread work for all those born up to 1970. Past experiences and associations are most important and may be unique. Some people can even be phobic about certain smells – peppermint, coffee, rubber.

Heat, noise and pollution affect behaviour at work (and play), and so does smell. The idea of the environmental modifier is to determine effective responses in the consumer. That is market-babble for 'smells change moods and moods affect buying'.

In the past decade companies have designed equipment to create pleasant fragrances in work environments, through the heating-ventilation-air-conditioning systems of large buildings. Some fragrances are designed to encourage alertness and arousal; and others the precise opposite, namely calmness. There is evidence, for instance, that lily of the valley and peppermint increase arousal and make staff work better on a vigilant task. In a whole range of studies olfactory and environmental psychologists have demonstrated that in pleasant-, as opposed to unpleasant- or neutral-smelling settings, workers are more alert, co-operative and helpful.

There is a whiff of fun about those studies but they produce fairly consistent results. Pleasant fragrances tend to lead to positive moods, which affect interpersonal behaviour in staff and customers. That is, smell affects behaviour through mood change and regulation. Scents aim to evoke memories or associations, which induce a particular mood state – and which in turn influence behaviour. There is clearly something in all this aromatherapy stuff!

Removing air pollutants and introducing pleasant smells is not particularly expensive and clearly beneficial. However, the ghost of Vance Packard and 'the hidden persuaders' is never far from public concern with environmental modifiers. Possibly fears about introduced fragrances stimulate fears about the gas attacks of the First World War. The idea that manufacturers are somehow altering (or attempting to alter) our behaviour (and succeeding) without us being fully aware still frightens people. Others are concerned about possible carcinogens in the process. In other words, they smell a rat.

But given the offer of clean, pleasantly scented air in which to shop, or stale, polluted air, it does not seem too difficult a choice. I scent a sure-fire winner.

Time-filling strategies of the underemployed

All employees have a vested interest in pointing out how overstretched and overstressed they are. Most professionals believe they have unique, chronic and acute work stress. They usually hope that acknowledgement of this fact will lead to more money, more staff (possibly both), and less work. And perhaps sympathy from spouse, peers, colleagues and friends. However, this dissimulation can lead to another rarely discussed source of stress at work: boredom stress, or the tedium of underemployment.

The underemployed can be both a nuisance and a serious problem for people working at capacity. They are found in all sectors and may not even realize their status. Particularly at management level, the underemployed boss can seriously threaten the profitability of the organization. They call pointless meetings, send long and tedious e-mails, trap hapless colleagues by the photocopier, invent peculiar rituals; and by these strategies, harass the hard-working people in the organization. They love new faddish ideas and, quite naturally, attend lots of training courses. In fact, they are often out of the office because, quite frankly, it makes little difference to their work output.

The worst possible personality combination is the relatively dim, neurotic attention-seeker in the role of an underemployed manager. While doing little themselves, they can seriously distract an office of hard-working individuals. Having fought so long for promotion to a managerial job, it can come as a surprise to the new incumbent that there is relatively little to do. Previous underemployed managers have been able to secure what many suspect – the higher you go, the less you actually do! However, a manager must be seen to be busy, hence the scenario of the bored bureaucrat bewildering the busy.

Boredom through underemployment rather than adolescent ennui arises from a number of sources. Some jobs are inherently tedious. Consider two examples: attendants at museums and security guards. The first group has to keep an eye on the public, try to spot lunatics before they start slashing works of art, and ensure that school parties don't make off with the collection of Roman coins. The second group has to watch out for intruders, to try to stay awake while slumped behind a desk in a warm room, and ensure that people don't break into the building and steal all the computers while they (the guards) are asleep. The coping strategy in both cases seems to be self-hypnosis into a state of glassy-eyed semi-wakefulness.

Another source of boredom is repetition. This comes from having to perform the same simple task over and over again. A favoured technique of bored workers is to break or sabotage the machine that they operate. Modern Luddism is as much to do with varying the monotony of jobs as the original form was to do with saving them.

Other jobs are dull because they are essentially all about monitoring. Pilots are required to monitor computers; so are security camera or X-ray staff, but because they have to be alert, their jobs are regularly rotated. Some monitor machines, others monitor people. The favourite trick of the bored people-monitor is to stop and frustrate the public. However, stopping someone who is driving a large, expensive car is far more amusing, since a little ritual humiliation makes the minutes fly by. Security people have to be past masters in the art of spotting important people in a hurry and demanding to be shown their identification. It is the revenge of the underemployed on the overemployed.

It can be argued that a psychological cause of boredom is being ignored. Hence the manifold use of 'attention-seeking' strategies by those who feel they are overlooked, marginalized, or sidelined. Security and safety guards may feel undervalued, but they know that by randomly locking doors, changing entry codes, and inspecting private spaces in the name of safety, they can underline their importance within the organization.

But what about the underemployed people manager? Yes, they do still exist. But how do they cope? It is meetings that remain the favourite forum of the bored and underemployed manager. Shadowing studies of real managers show that many spend as much as two-thirds of their time in meetings. Some of these gatherings are genuinely used to canvass and share opinions, others to make decisions. But all too often, they are called to diffuse responsibility by making collective decisions on risky topics.

Re-engaging the underemployed is not easy. Often their jobs need a severe dose of re-engineering, which could be a polite synonym for removing such jobs. One might even call in consultants like Hay or Wyatt, who have expert and comparative systems for job evaluation: they will certainly be able to offer impartial advice on what the job is worth, or even whether it should exist at all. But if this is too difficult, less drastic measures may be used. The number of meetings called or attended should be limited to three a week and requirements for the outcome documented. The underemployed need their goals and targets to be re-evaluated and 'ratched up' in the performance appraisal system. Feedback from the work-stressed colleagues, subordinates or clients may help to provide evidence to the underemployed of how people actually see them.

Beware the underemployed. They are frequently well dug in and difficult to move. They squeal loudly when challenged and usually have a history of resistance to change. Paradoxically, it is they who have often survived previous restructuring efforts aimed at removing them.

Below is a guide to recognizing the seven deadly sins of the underemployed manager:

1. *Meeting addicts*: They attend, call and participate in two to three times as many meetings as properly employed peers.
2. *Too eager to manage by walking about*: This is really an excuse to stroll around and interrupt others in the so-called guise of employing a particular management style.
3. *Involved with union or related affairs (welfare, health and so on)*: The fact that they don't work any harder than others, but can do all that other stuff is the key to their underemployment.
4. *Excessive communicating by the chosen medium – e-mails, circulars, faxes and so on*: Remember, they are bored and lonely and want others to talk to them.

5.   *Course enthusiasts*: Eager to go on a range of courses that get them out of the office. Frequently absent, but not through illness.
6.   *Slow to respond*: Paradoxically, they are slow to respond to requests (for example, providing data) and always complaining about the effort involved. Remember that they have to keep up the appearance of being overworked.
7.   *Interested in development and planning*: Possibly interested in the past (archive-obsessed), but more likely to love strategic planning. Always better to plan than to do.

Five out of seven is a good indicator of serious underemployment.

TIPS: a form of performance-related pay?

Tipping started, so the myth goes, when gratuities were dropped into a box marked TIPS – To Insure Prompt Service. However, much confusion and resentment surrounds this quaint habit. In the United States, tipping is institutionalized, organized and codified to a forbidding extent, and heaven help the naïve person who breaks the unwritten rules. You may easily receive abuse from a waiter or taxi-driver if you 'forget' to tip or simply do not give enough.

There are three rational explanations for tipping. Tips buy social approval and save embarrassment; tips buy a more equitable (and comfortable) relationship with servers; tips buy better service in future.

We know a few facts about tips based on research in the restaurant business: most tips are around 15% in the United States and 10% in the UK; the percentage of the tip to total cost is an inverse power function of the number of people at the table; physically attractive and/or attractively dressed waitresses receive greater tips than less attractive waitresses; tips are bigger when paid by credit cards, relative to cash payers; tips are not related to whether alcohol is consumed; tips increase with the number of non-task-oriented 'visits' by waiter and waitress, but unrelated to the customers' ratings of service; often, but not always, men tip more than women.

In the United States (possibly) alone, tip size is positively related to various other factors: whether the server touched the diner; whether the server initially squatted in their interaction with the diner as opposed to stood; the size of their initial smile; whether the server

introduced himself/herself by their first name; the number of inciden-
tal (non-task-oriented) visits to the table.

Economists argue that tipping has a rational economic explanation.
A tip is a payment for something extra (extra services or extra effort)
beyond those specified as normal. Most people we tip provide services
that are fairly difficult to measure, so their obligations and performance cannot be fully controlled. Hence the tip is the mechanism which
complements the fixed market price where the sole commodity (that is,
service) contains non-standard or immeasurable components.

But if this were true there would be a direct relationship between
the size of the tip and the degree to which the performed service
extended beyond normal duties in terms of speed, politeness and so
on. Although this may occasionally be the case, any waiter will tell you
that the size of the tip will vary according to the size of the dining party,
size of the bill, need for the host to impress his friends, and so on.

And economists cannot explain why we often tip one group (hairdressers, cab drivers) but not another (dentists, dustmen and so on).

Sociologists see the tip as a gift. Because the recipients of a service
feel gratitude or indebtedness to the provider, they leave a tip as a gift
supplementary to the bill, and maintaining social status and power
over the service provider. If customers tip more than the provider
deserves, this superiority is established beyond any doubt. If they do
not reward the 'extra' service with a tip, they will be under pressure to
repay with social approval or subordination. Tipping is thus a form of
social control and it is significant that in several different languages the
word 'gift' means 'poison'.

Is tipping always an expression of dominance and superiority? In
some languages the word tip contains a derogatory element, implying
that the money will be used for drink or some other improper purpose.
Further, tipping is not performed publicly as a display of rank and
power. Rather, it is characterized by privacy and discretion.

Finally, *psychologists* explain the phenomenon of tipping as a form
of ego massage calculated to enhance the self-image of the tipper. The
tip can sometimes be seen as a result of the customer's insecurity or
anxiety. Service providers who operate within our personal space or
touch us in intimate places, such as maids and hairdressers, are particularly threatening because their access to our private belongings or
bodies could affect our public face. Most of us do not resort to 'gagging
orders' for our server's silence by buying their loyalty or indebtedness.

Psychologists stress that tipping is intrinsically motivated rather than performed for the sake of external material or social rewards.

It is comforting to think, as the rational economist might, that tipping is just a form of performance-related pay for service staff. If that *were* the case there would be a clear relationship between satisfaction with service and tip – which there isn't.

Indeed, there remains a great deal of confusion and frustration about tipping, both for the tipper and tippee. Organizations don't like it because it creates competitiveness and jealousy among staff – those who are eligible (waiters) and those who are not (cooks). Further it can cause conflict as tip-hungry waiters hassle organizational senior cooks to provide faster, bigger, better meals. Hence organizations prefer the standardized service charge distributed equitably to all staff.

And the service charge idea is diametrically opposed to the discretionary tip, which frustrates the tipper. Whether one believes in performance-related pay or not, the idea of rewarding good performance equitably and uniquely is at the heart of the tip. Hence the unusual or expensive sight of people adding a tip to a restaurant bill that has service charge, cover charge and corkage charge.

Is the reverse therefore true? Should we look on performance pay as sort of tip? Hardly, because tips are paid out whimsically, as earlier research has shown. But the performance pay is, as the economists say, certainly payment for something extra.

Trainability: what you see is what you get

Most people have very few ideas about what to look for in selecting others. Sir James Blyth of Plessey looked for raw intellect, forthright honesty, determination and physical durability. He also suggested that the selector ask themselves: 'Is the candidate a shit?' and noted that if the answer was yes, they should be rejected. 'Why work with too many people you don't like?' was his reasoning. 'As it is, you are likely to inherit more than enough, so why hire more?'

What should selectors look for? Three things seem vital:

1. *Intelligence or ability*: sometimes called capacity, cognitive potential, educational attainability. Since the turn of the twentieth century, we have known about what psychologists call g- (it stands for general intelligence). Despite the hype concerning *idiots savants*,

bright people are pretty good at most things; and dim people are pretty bad. On average, bright people learn faster and adapt more quickly – when they want to. Selectors and assessors are scared of giving IQ tests, but they do use specific ability tests. School marks and university grades are only weak indicators of intelligence. Intelligence is a must and it can't be taught or trained. In fact, it predicts speed and retention of learning.

2. *Emotional stability*: neuroticism, or 'negative affectivity', is a power-ful predictor of job failure. The emotionally unstable are poor at customer relations, become capricious and irascible managers, and are prone to high levels of absenteeism, even accidents. Neuroticism is a powerful warning sign. There is a mountain of evidence that suggests both that neuroticism does not change much over the years (even with psychotherapy), and is related to long- and short-term career failure. Thus one selects for its oppos-ite – the stable; the phlegmatic; the emotionally adjusted.

3. *Conscientiousness*: the work ethic is a powerful indictor of success. Often developed in childhood by ambitious, future-oriented, middle-class parents, the conscientious are, by definition, diligent, responsible, punctilious and dutiful. They can be counted on, and their conscience is a powerful controller of their work style. Some may be a little risk-averse, others a little too self-deprecating, but they can always be relied on.

Selecting the right people is fundamentally important for one simple, single and basic reason: *people do not change much over time*. Yes, we grow older, fatter, greyer, slower, more bombastic and wrinkly. But our personality, intelligence, and many of the attitudes and beliefs that flow from them, do not change. Of course, most of us believe that we are wiser, more perspicacious and insightful than we were 20 years ago. But all you have to do is go to a school reunion to find out the curious paradox – your chums have not changed psychologically, so why have you?

The belief that we have changed is really a trick of the light. It is an incorrect attribution. People assume that their behaviour is situ-ationally determined; others are determined by their traits or make-up. Are you an introvert or extrovert? Well, it depends. Is your partner, brother or boss an introvert or extrovert? That is much clearer. They are either one or the other. We believe we are variable and change from situation to situation and over time, but that others don't. And we are wrong in this belief. All the evidence is against us.

Once one has become an adult, very little changes. Intelligence levels decline modestly, but change little over the working life. The same is true of abilities, be they with language, numbers, music or lateral thinking. Most people like to think that personality can change, particularly the more negative features such as anxiety, low self-esteem, impulsiveness or a lack of emotional warmth. But data collected 50 years apart give the clear message: still stable after all these years. Extroverts become marginally less extroverted; the acutely shy seem a little less so, but the fundamentals remain much the same.

Personal crises can affect the way we cope with things: we might take up or drop drink, drugs, religion or relaxation techniques, which can have pretty dramatic effects. But, *Deo volente*, most people do not have too many major traumas in their life, so continue much as before. The moral, then, when looking at a 21-year-old is 'What you see is what you get.' Fundamentally, they will not change much.

But what about training? Doesn't that give people new skills, ideas, attitudes? It can do, but at what cost? In fact, the assessment literature tends, if anything, to show that training doesn't work; that what is learnt is all too soon forgotten; that old habits are slipped back into; and that there is little improvement (or deterioration).

People can be groomed for a job. Just as politicians are carefully repackaged through dress, hairstyle and speech therapy, so people can be sent on training courses, diplomas or experimental weekends. But there is a cost to this which may be more than the price of a course. Better to select for what you actually see than attempt to change it. Acquiring and retaining skills is an expensive and difficult business. The cost may simply not be worth it.

Psychotherapists say people change only if they want to. Listen to those who do and have, say, given up drink, or conquered depression – and it is a state of tears, woe and massive determination over time. Training at work is not like that.

People change surprisingly little over time, even if thoroughly trained. No wonder selection is important. Don't fool yourself that you can change someone – once they are an adult – to fit your ideal. Too many marriages are wrecked on the rocks of the fantastical belief that

'I'll alter him'. Selection is fundamentally important because despite the efforts of spouses, psychotherapists and trainers, *people do not change.*

Unacceptable behaviour

It is self-evident that certain 'people characteristics' go together. People who are sociable, outgoing and talkative tend also to be fairly easy-going, lively and carefree. They have been called *sanguine*! On the other hand, those poor souls prone to being moody and anxious are often rigid, pessimistic and unsociable. They are labelled *melancholic*.

In business there is a long list of characteristics (not competencies) that the selector is usually looking for, both to *select in* and *select out*. One often hears those mid-Atlantic marketing types calling for assertiveness and aggression. Most managers want the highly motivated, achievement-oriented employee. And more and more, big business wants, seeks for, and hopefully even selects those high on creativity. Timidity, risk-aversion and poor social skills are also examined as possible select-out variables.

The problem with the wish list is two-fold. First, nearly every characteristic has pluses and minuses. Sure, the extrovert is active, cheerful and charming, but often also unreliable, easily bored and fickle about friendships. Even being a little neurotic has its benefits, particularly in the arts, where great ideas and passion may arise from powerful emotional experiences. The second problem is that these traits are often very unlikely to occur in the same individual. It is possible, but unlikely, that the reliable, even-tempered *phlegmatic* type is impulsive and optimistic.

And all this leads us to Mr Clinton's 'unacceptable behaviour'. In these politically correct days certain behaviours are very strictly taboo. The office affair, whistle-blowing company secrets to the press, and fiddling one's expenses are a great 'no-no'. But who is prone to these behaviours? Alas, some of the people with the characteristics one wants most: the assertive, creative, risk-averse manager of the future. As any advertising account manager knows, the *really* creative person is difficult to manage. Their creativity often occurs because they are unable to stop irrelevant information from entering their consciousness and as a result unrelated ideas become interconnected. This widening of associative horizons we call creativity.

We also know that creative types are oversensitive to stimuli (noise, light and so on). They have a rich fantasy life and are rarely described as compliant, straightforward or self-disciplined. Some very creative people have a clear liking for odd and unusual things, a disregard for danger and seem to enjoy humiliating other people. If very good-looking and with a reputation for genius they can be extremely dangerous to the opposite sex.

Our grandparents would call these types *cads*; our parents would call them *philanderers* and we would call them a *sexual harasser*. The sexual appetite – both in terms of quantity and quality – of the famously gifted is legendary. It is the cost of creativity. But don't assume that the office flirt is necessarily a risk-averse, creative genius dying to give up his grey M&S suit for designer flares.

Those who, like the aggressive business person who takes no nonsense from anyone and who feels free to return the fire, can be brilliant in the board meeting and TV interview but scathingly awful in the general office. The shrewd, expedient, calculating manager can also be extremely Machiavellian in his/her manipulation of others. Managers are often praised for defending their ideas vigorously and vociferously but they may equally be seen as dogmatic. And those cold, rational business people who eschew emotional displays as childish sentimentality may be unacceptably macho.

What both research and personal experience show is this: the attractive, bright, charming, creative, motivated and risk-averse manager is out there. They do exist, can be selected, hired and – with difficulty – managed. But they are prone to inappropriate behaviour of one sort or another, be it under the duvet or desk. The question is whether it is worth it to the organization.

What to do when the consultants come in

The news is out. The directors have at last decided which of the two management consultant groups to have. In the end, they favoured 'Downsize, Rightsize and Bitesize' over 'Grabitt and Runn'. This consulting group has a reputation for ruthless pruning, outsourcing and generally creating mayhem in quietly efficient companies. In fact, it prides itself on getting rid of loyal staff in the quest for the 'lean and mean' virtual organization of the next millennium. Uneasy whispers

have it that the consultants wander around companies booming
'Money talks ... bullshit walks' in mid-Atlantic accents.

So what do you do? How can you preserve your job faced with the
prying eyes of these MBA-trained consultants?

Perhaps the first reaction is to bluff: to try to look important. Tidy
your desk – look organized. Talk to others and arrange short meetings
standing up – this is teamwork. Arrive early, stay late, be at your desk
over lunch. Forget relaxed bagelfests and idle chatter. In short, employ
a bit of impression management.

But this strategy may backfire. There is probably data on you –
the HR chap will have his annual appraisals of course, whether you
like it or not, and you could have a reputation which may or may not
be accurate. Trying too hard and changing your natural pattern of
work may arouse the suspicions of managers and peers, and reveal you
as being desperate. This in turn may make you more, rather than less,
likely to be on the downsizing list.

However, there are things you can do:

1. *Observe and imitate*: watch the consultants carefully. They are bound
    to be around some time, so try to get a feel for how they work.
    Learn to speak their language and employ their work strategies. If
    they are into breakfast meetings, laptop lugging and a quick sand-
    wich at the desk, do likewise. Fit in. They try to model what they
    believe is 'good practice', so the more you are like them, the less
    likely they are to recommend your departure.
2. *Co-operate*: don't sulk, snipe or be rude. Give them the informa-
    tion they want. This does not mean that you have to become a
    crawling sycophant. In fact, you may challenge them with intel-
    ligent questions. You must sound curious and eager to learn, not
    aggressive.
3. *Get on a taskforce*: this is the best policy if available. Often consult-
    ants create a number of taskforces – a sort of committee of
    employees from all areas and levels to look at particular problems.
    Put your hand up, volunteer. This shows the right attitude. But
    more importantly, it allows you to be an insider. You find out what
    is happening before anyone else does and can take evasive action.
4. *Be modern*: make your workspace look state-of-the-art. Even if you
    don't have the first idea how to use the new technology, get it

anyway. Have one or two current books on your shelf. Buy the *FT*. Smarten up your appearance.

Expect an increased workload during this period. This is not only because of spending more time at work, but because you will no doubt be asked to search and prepare data. In doing this, be smart – in appearance and content. There are many ways of presenting data to help your case, such as looking at the accountant's presentation of the company report. Think about what the consultants want and why.

Most of all, go in with the right attitude. The whole thing is a learning experience. The worst scenario is that you learn something new, the best is that you get a career boost. There are many SOBOs about (Shoved Out, Better Off) who have been encouraged or bribed to leave companies. A surprisingly large number will tell you that it is the best thing that ever happened to them. They may have made a career switch that suited them well. Others have gone part-time or work for themselves, and would never dream of going back, even if seriously tempted.

Still others tell the familiar story of how, after a compulsory down-sizing, or even voluntary severance package with generous compensation, the company pleaded with them to come back after six months, because they did not anticipate the effects.

So when the dread cry rings out 'the consultants are coming!' don't reach for the Valium. Think more of the experience as occupational Viagra – something that may seriously pep up your whole career.

Working for monsters

What was it like working for Robert Maxwell? How does one cope with the capricious, irascible, vain bastard one may find as a boss? Is there any upside in working for charismatic, but deeply egocentric and selfish entrepreneurs? Sure, they make the workplace exciting, but that is often because they are unpredictable.

The monster boss certainly makes life more interesting. Life is a rollercoaster not a humdrum tedium. Further, they often provide excellent learning opportunities – some call them stress; others learn to call them developmental opportunities. But most of all they test your people skills and patience. Dealing with shoddy workmen, hypochondriacal staff and poor customer service seems to be a real 'doddle' once one has mastered the monster from hell.

There are a whole range of books about dealing with difficult people. Nearly all provide a supposedly valid taxonomy of types: the *sniping saboteur* who identifies your weaknesses and exploits them; the *cocky know-it-alls* who talk and never listen and can't be proved wrong; the *abominable no-men* who are doubtful, discouraging, despondent and deadly to be around; and the *whingeing whiners* who carry around with them neurotic negativism.

Some books list these types alphabetically and their titles tell it all: the *abdicator* (who zealously over-delegates) or the *meddler* (who is the opposite, namely a chorus interventionist). The opposite of the *apathetic* boss, who is passive and indifferent, is the *quarrelsome* type, who resists everything.

But those books never help one with bosses, particularly the larger-than-life characters that become well known. What is often the case is that there is a yawning gulf between the reputation of these 'super-bosses' so carefully crafted by the in-house spin-doctors and the reality one hears only from bitter, sacked employees who are happy to whistle-blow on their boss after the event.

How can you manage the boss and make your life at least tolerable if you work for an 18-carat monster? The answer is in understanding 'where they are coming from'. The secret lies in reading and responding to their moods, foibles and weaknesses; in understanding their needs and ultimately in anticipating their obnoxious behaviour before it occurs.

Consider some well-known characteristics, and consider how your particular monster fits in. For instance, take *sociability* – the extent to which your boss really likes socializing with others. The boss who scores low on this attribute is probably hard to get to know, perhaps a little shy, careful and ponderous. They may have to pretend to be outgoing but they are not. In fact, they hate it. Those bosses who are very high on sociability are easy to be with and easy to get to know, but it is unlikely that they are interested in what you are saying. They prefer talking to listening. They like being the centre of attention. They are social gadflys. Do not expect long, serious conversations with the charming, extroverted sociopaths.

Similarly, on a simple *likeability* or agreeableness dimension, bosses who score low like to argue with and challenge you. Combative, distrustful and moody, they are often the embodiment of the monster-boss. They are more honest privately than publicly. Deeply disagreeable, they like a scrap. They push, demand, cajole – and, as a result, really get things moving along. On the other hand, the manager who scores high on likeability is full of charm, agrees with everything you say but tends to progress things slowly, if at all. Conflict-averse, those high on likeability prefer people to be supported rather than challenged.

The boss who is *intellectually dim* tends to resist new ideas and innovation. These types are not really interested in data and evidence and prefer simplistic, well-rehearsed answers. Being low on IQ as well as EQ is surely being seriously short-changed. Sufficient IQ is the minimum requirement in certain jobs. Some monsters are just thick ... and know it, but most have masses of low cunning. Bright bosses accept the necessity of change and development. They are often interested in evidence and data and encourage their collection.

Similarly, the extent to which your boss is *ambitious* must dictate how he or she acts. The steady-as-you-go boss, lacking in ambition, avoids initiatives and is careful of being shown up. Security is traded off against ambition and they are neither ambitious for themselves nor for their staff. But the highly ambitious boss likes to 'run with the bull'. They may be opportunistic but it is pretty certain that their eyes are on their superior and not you, their subordinate. Your best hope is to be seen to be helpful and influential in your boss's career. Monsters are amoral and opportunistic. They lay down their friends' lives for their own.

Personal adjustment or, as politically correct US psychologists have now learned to call it, 'negative affectivity' is a very important facet of human behaviour and requires careful monitoring. This is neuroticism. It can take many forms: phobia, anxiety, depression. Many monsters are neurotic and this is obvious in their hypochondriasis and moodiness.

Those a wee bit low on adjustment need reassurance and support. In fact it may well be that a bit of role-reversal occurs, in the sense that you become the parent and the boss becomes the child. But adjustment is another word for stability and the very instability of the low-adjustment boss presents problems. Neurotic bosses need very careful handling. But psychotic bosses, particularly psychopaths, are worse. They are characterized by total lack of conscience and empathy – and brutal, uncaring, thuggish behaviour.

Stable, adjusted bosses can take feedback calmly and can deal with crisis. They are often characterized by those wonderful British characteristics of phlegmatism and stoicism. Indifferent to pain and pleasure, bulls or bears, successes or failures, the adjusted, stable boss is a much-appreciated rock in the sea of business troubles.

Finally, there is *prudence* or conscientiousness: beware the imprudent manager. They don't follow through, they don't pay their bills and they are wildly incautious about financial arrangements. Their incompetence may easily lead to financial, if not moral, bankruptcy. The over-prudent manager may, on the other hand, be too tight-fisted and short-sighted to take any kind of business risk. Most monsters are both – mean with your pay; overgenerous with their own.

Working for monsters means careful monitoring. You have to learn to read the signals – to move away from them when moody; to charm them when they are in a good mood: But following in their wake as they crash through organizations and the stock market can bring real benefits. May you live in interesting monster managerial times.

Testimonial truths

Many references and testimonials are worthless. They are written by people chosen by the candidate – obviously friends, followers and favourites who are unlikely to be honest. They may hardly know the candidate, or only in certain circumstances. Second, many referees are not honest for various reasons: to avoid litigation; to actually get rid of a poor performer or more simply because they know negative information is highly weighted relative to positive. Third, referees are seldom asked direct questions but simply required to ramble on for a page or two of bland platitudes.

Yet, in some walks of life, testimonials are brutally honest and bitingly true. Those that follow have all been culled from the military. They have been very slightly adapted to protect the innocent (and guilty) and also to be interpretable to a wider audience. Surprisingly, they are all real.

And they give a wonderful insight into managerial incompetence. If only all those called on to write assessments, references and testimonials were as honest.

Adaptability

One is tempted to suggest that he ought to get married. However, ...is already married and his charming young wife must think that she has three children rather than two.

My deputy is always down on everything that he is not up on.

A dithering and indecisive person,...............tends to wear the impression of the last person who sat on him.

...............started at the bottom and has stayed there.

The Executive tends to conclude discussion with a statement that his mind is already made up, and he does not want to be confused with the facts.

An aptitude test showed that this candidate's only real aptitude is for taking aptitude tests.

This junior executive is a carefree sort of person who does not care much – just as long as it's free.

The...............is a typical senior executive who through his career has delegated authority, shifted all the blame, but takes all the credit.

As an after-dinner speaker,...............can usually rise to the occasion, but then never knows when to sit down.

...............is like stodgy suet pudding – very difficult to digest.

This young man is about as useful as half a pair of scissors.

Alcohol

This Accounts Manager is suffering from bottle fatigue.

Life for the chief barman is a succession of burps and downs.

...............drinks like a fish, but unfortunately he does not drink what fishes drink.

When...............drinks, he tends to lose his inhibitions – and then gives exhibitions.

His favourite drink is the next one.

The............'s wife is forceful and garrulous, but well meaning. There have been occasions, however, when I have wished someone would give her a bottle of gin and a humane killer to play with.

My...............is spoiling his own health by drinking to everyone else's.

...............usually drinks doubles – and then sees the same way.

...............is struggling manfully with a drink problem; the good news is that his wife is sticking to him through thick and gin.

I have occasionally seen...............sober.

...............doesn't only drink, he also drinks between drinks.

When pink elephants get drunk, they see him.

...............never drinks more than he can stand, and as soon as he can stand, he then starts drinking again.

...............might be able to make both ends meet – if he wasn't so busy making one end drink.

If a mosquito bit...............it would probably die of alcohol poisoning.

...............magnifies his troubles by looking at them through the bottom of a glass.

As President of the...............Wine Tasting Committee, he appears rather insulted if you offer him a drink, but then manages to swallow the insult without difficulty.

...............is living proof that there is no fool like an oiled fool.

At dinner parties...............talks with more claret than clarity.

...............has the...............worried because he has too little blood in his alcohol stream.

...............is the nicest chap on two feet, if only he could stay there.

Having attended the Alcohol Rehabilitation course, he has finally succeeded in giving up giving up drinking.

It would appear the only aerobic challenge that...............accepts is when hiccuping.

It only takes one drink to make...............drunk, but it is difficult to be sure whether it is the ninth or tenth.

...............has been held up several times on his way home, but it was the only way he could get there.

...............enjoys a workout when he gets up, so he has parallel bars – one for gin and one for brandy.

Common sense

I wish...............would understand that nought is a mark.

As...............he is like a lighthouse in a desert – brilliant but useless.

...............is without doubt the most tactless person I have ever met, and we try to keep him away from senior visitors. He could be expected to ask the Prime Minister how much income tax he pays.

Socially this young...............is partial to hell-raising stag parties – but usually knows where to draw the line, or, at worst, who to apologize to the following day.

Furthermore, minor matters such as being four months overdue with library books are not the actions of a high-flying Staff Officer candidate.

In my opinion, this Sea Harrier pilot should not be authorized to fly below 250 feet.

...............is a 'pickle-jar' Officer. He can tell you the cube root of the surface area of a pickle-jar lid, and to two decimal places of that, but has absolutely no idea how to get the wretched thing off.

This pleasant...............knows he must deploy the 'laid back' approach with care. There is a time and place; falling asleep during the...............recent address was neither.

His fellow messmates have appointed him as an OSLO – Outer Space Liaison Officer.

...............has too much bone in his head and not nearly enough in his spine.

...............always stoops to concur.

............'s initiative knows no bounds – none at all, because it is common sense and judgement that he lacks.

I don't think that...............could count past 10 without taking his shoes off.

If there are any original ideas in this candidate's head, they are probably in solitary confinement.

...............is not very bright, but he can lift heavy weights.

...............has grown up a lot in the past year; and there is some optimism that his IQ will eventually catch up with his shoe size.

...............is always babbling over with enthusiasm.

The reason that...............has a stupid grin on his face is that – he is stupid.

...............is a complex fellow who always begins a mystery novel in the middle, so that not only does he not know how it ends, he also doesn't know how it began.

Courage and stamina

...............has high standards, though I have little evidence of any great infatuation with physical fitness.

He has the courage of her convictions.

She has her way when they agree, and he has her way when they disagree.

...............believes that only a certain number of heartbeats have been allotted to him, and is reluctant to use any of them up on the sports field.

...............has had a series of chest infections; he is so full of antibiotics that every time he sneezes he cures a dozen people.

It would be interesting to know whether...............has any other ambition in life apart from breathing.

This pleasant...............would appear to have a line that makes her rather popular – the line of least resistance.

With regard to hard work,...............has a notion – but very little motion.

...............is as spineless as a cream bun.

I suspect that the only exercise...............gets is when digging frozen ice trays out of the refrigerator.

Effectiveness

Even allowing for the fact that this young...............is a complete no-hoper, he has had a very poor year.

I am convinced that...............would be out of his depth in a car park puddle.

In spite of the fact that his records show to the contrary, Flying Officer B displays no sign of ever having attended Officers' Training School.

2nd Lieutenant A has given an unexceptional performance, apart from an outstanding characterization of a poof in the Unit Pantomime.

...............has fully demonstrated the ability to juggle several of his balls at any one time.

The new...............is so weak and pathetic that he couldn't pull the skin off a rice pudding.

...............is such an uncoordinated shambles that he would have difficulty fighting his way out of a wet paper bag.

The Assistant Caterer's unpolished style was typified by his walking to work with a West Ham United duffel bag slung over his uniform shoulder. His reaction to correction was to obtain an executive briefcase.

...............has the wisdom of youth, and the energy of old age.

His future looks very secure, as they will probably put him in a straitjacket.

...............needs no introduction; what he really needs is a conclusion.

He is living proof of the adage that if he couldn't take a joke, then he shouldn't have joined.

...............knows very little, but knows it very fluently.

...............often lets his mind go blank, but then forgets to turn off the sound.

...............is so smooth that his friends think they are being cultivated, whereas in fact they are being trimmed.

...............stands out among his brethren because of his size and strength, rather than his personality. The less charitable have suggested that – with the addition of a bolt through the base of his neck – he would be a natural for employment with Hammer Films.

...............is always around when he needs you.

...............can hardly wait to hear what he is going to say.

My...............has a unique talent for turning opportunities into difficulties.

Despite being appraised of his lack of effort as Combat Survival Officer, there has been no improvement in Flight Lieutenant B's conduct. He even arranged a wet dinghy drill for the day following his departure.

Probably the only thing that this...............has achieved on his own is his dandruff.

As a former SAS Troop Commander, Major S would see no reason for a mailed fist ever to be delivered inside a velvet glove, except to deaden the sound.

Although...............has only had her present job for four days, she is already two weeks behind in her work.

Although Petty Officer C has played rugby for the Navy, someone should tell him the difference between pulling his weight and throwing it around.

It is a good thing that...............does not have to pay taxes on what he thinks he is worth.

I find it surprising that the boss, with his known lack of charisma, is going to instructional duties. Such an appointment would only make sense if his new station was a school for the cure of insomnia.

When this supervisor was due to depart for a new appointment, the other managers in his department got together to give him a little momentum.

This...............cannot be paid what he is worth, because it would be below the statutory minimum wage.

...............does at least three push-ups every day, from a big leather chair and into the...............for his meals.

My...............thinks he is a thing of beauty and a boy for ever.

Now that he has reached...............he believes that he is as good at attracting women as he never was.

My young lady Doctor is a physiological contradiction. She knows perfectly well that tight clothing stops circulation, yet in her case, the tighter the clothing the more she is in circulation.

In encouraging a woman to tell him about her past,...............ensures that before she has finished – he has become part of it.

Lots of women may not recall............'s name, but his hands are familiar.

...............is the sort of chap who, if he fell on his back, would probably cut his chin.

Rather like most of the Peerage, the only thing that this man has ever done for a living was to inherit.

...............is something of a snob, but he should be less concerned with who he is descended from – and more worried where he is descending to.

...............is something of a character actor in that when he shows any character he is probably acting.

This...............does not demand high standards from himself or his men. He would probably accept an Afghan hound as a guidedog.

Integrity

Candidate Number Three thinks he can push himself forward by patting himself on the back.

Without doubting his motives I was forced to note that this pilot's dislike for a ground tour manifested itself in a stiff neck which required extensive medical attention. The pain has now gone from his neck, but it remains in mine.

...............is something of a contact man – all 'con' and no tact.

...............has an interesting financial philosophy. When he borrows money, it is against his principles either to pay interest, or to repay the principal.

If...............had to have his conscience surgically removed, it would be a very minor operation.

The...............is a rather small, lithe man who slides about the place in a rather oily fashion.

This potential...............is a man of several convictions; he has served time for each one.

Lt Col K has been baptized by fire in the past, but has now been scorched in the Ministry of Defence.

Our...............has got about as much conscience as a fox in a chicken coop.

This man is a phoney; even the wool he tries to pull over your eyes is 50% polyester.

This Padre prays on his knees on Sunday, and preys on everyone else for the rest of the week.

...............has straight hair that never lays down properly, small eyes set close together and the startled appearance of a schoolboy caught raiding the tuckshop.

The more that...............protests his honesty, the more firmly you have to hang on to your wallet.

Should...............ever offer to lay his cards on the table, it would be a good idea to count them first.

...............has a flat which I understand he shares with an unmarried lady. He intends to buy the flat, but I am unsure of his intentions towards the lady.

...............has a reputation among the wives for being an advanced member of the Wandering Hands society.

The less you have to do with him, the less you will be worse off.

...............seems too good to be true – and he isn't.

...............is the kind of friend who, if you give him a free hand, will stick it straight in your pocket.

As a 'Married Unaccompanied' Officer, Squadron Leader T's social life has been inconsistent with his declared marital status.

...............very much believes in free speech – especially long-distance telephone calls from other people's houses.

............'s wife belongs to the meddling classes.

............'s reputation as a flagrant rule breaker is not really justified, but he does spend a considerable amount of time exploring the borders of legality.

...............could give failure a bad name.

I have had to put...............on Special Report because he is too busy learning the tricks of the trade to learn the trade itself.

Few people like him, a friend who isn't in need is his friend indeed.

You can always depend on...............to depend on you.

...............has two major faults – nearly everything he says, and nearly everything he does.

The science of heredity is what makes parents of children like him wonder about each other.

Four major publishers of fiction are bidding for the rights to this ....'s Travel Expense claim.

When............'s conscience bothers him about something that he's done, he will come forward in a very open way and then lie about the whole thing.

You can always tell when.............. is lying; if his lips are moving, he is.

...............tries to whitewash himself by blackening others.

It would be interesting to know on what experience...............biases his opinions.

You can often see...............smiling when things go wrong – mainly because he's just thought of someone he can blame it on.

This ambitious...............is a man of firm convictions, just as soon as he knows what everyone above him thinks about the subject.

...............needs to construct a partition between her vivid imagination and the actual facts.

...............is the sort of person who would not hit a man when he is down, but would kick him hard instead.

...............always thinks twice before speaking, so that he can come out with something really nasty.

I would advise...............to buy fire insurance instead of a life policy, because there is no doubt where he is ultimately going.

A suitable motto for this young...............'to err is human, but it feels divine...'.

The first candidate stated that he was careful about his health, and that he now only smokes filter-tipped marijuana.

You cannot believe............... even when he swears that he is lying.

The only thing that keeps...............from being described as a barefaced liar is his beard.

I get the impression that...............would steal a dead fly from a blind spider.

Look at this Candidate and then at his shoes; you will see three heels.

...............has a sunny disposition but a shady past.

...............is so mean that he would throw a drowning man both ends of a rope.

...............apparently studied Meteorology so that he could look in a woman's eyes and tell whether.

...............is the sort of man who, if he murdered his parents, would ask for mercy on the grounds that he had recently become an orphan.

...............is part of the modern generation who are willing to do an honest day's work, but then want a week's pay for it.

Intelligence

As long as his backside points downwards, this young man will never make it as aircrew in the Fleet Air Arm.

This...............gives the distinct impression that he has not got both oars in the water.

As an Oxford graduate,...............has a tendency to be condescending to less clever colleagues. I have myself found this trait to be rather irritating.

...............is basically a large collection of recessive genes.

...............is not very smart. In fact, he is depriving a police dog of a promising career.

If............'s brains were dynamite, he would not have enough to blow his cap off.

...............is a short, thick-set person with practically no neck. His assessments are very much those one would expect from a person of his build.

It is a wonder of neuroscience how such a big head can hold such a tiny mind.

The only reason that...............manages to keep his head above water in this appointment is that softwood floats.

There is no doubt that the Postie is a man of rare intelligence, because it's pretty rare for him to show any.

...............has a mind which is always on the tip of his tongue.

The Interview Board's opinion was that if Candidate E had just a little more sense, he could be described as a half-wit.

By retaining this young man in the Company, we will be depriving an English village of its idiot.

...............has a mind like concrete – all mixed up and permanently set.

The only bone of contention in my............'s argument is the bone that lies between his ears.

The reason why...............has a chip on his shoulder is that it is sourced from the wood higher up.

The...............has an open mind that should now be closed for repairs.

Intellectually, he is such a lightweight that he could tap-dance on a chocolate eclair.

...............is recovering from an unusual accident which occurred at sea when a thought suddenly struck him.

It is stretching the imagination enormously to picture...............as the end product of billions of years of evolution.

It would appear that...............is listening to his psychiatric adviser and then drawing his own confusions.

This...............must be the one person to have a sixth sense, because there is no evidence of the other five.

If ignorance really is bliss, then...............is the world's happiest person.

I have come to the conclusion that...............is even smarter than Professor Stephen Hawking, because only a dozen people understand Hawking and no one can understand...............

To be fair, he has demonstrated an admirable coolness and calm when faced with danger, although I would attribute this to a lack of intelligence and imagination.

We have tried very hard, but have now come to the conclusion that it would take a surgical operation to get an idea into............'s head.

I often wonder whether...............is smoking something unusual, because he has that certain nothing when it comes to creative thought.

...............is not just an ordinary moron, he is the moron's moron.

I understand from the psychiatrists that he is totally psycho-ceramic – a genuine crackpot.

One always senses that there are a few cogs missing from............'s intellectual gearbox.

The final candidate, Mr WOODHEAD, was most aptly named.

Leadership

...............will not set the world on fire and if by chance he did, he certainly would not be able to put it out.

His men would follow him anywhere, but only out of curiosity.

You cannot help admiring the..............., because if you don't, he'll sack you.

...............has many of the attributes of a natural leader combined with a vigorous personality. However, his followers tend to reduce in numbers as they realize the rather erratic nature of the course on which they are set.

Flight Lieutenant W confuses aircraft captaincy with the incantation of meaningless phraseology.

...............always tells his staff that even if it is only a suggestion, they should never forget who is actually making it.

...............usually talks of principle, but tends to act entirely on self-interest.

Should the boss pat you on the back, he is probably working out just where to stick the knife in.

This Head of Department is the sort of chap who would like to eat his cake and have yours too.

...............is a strong supporter of law and order, but only if he can lay down the law – and then give orders.

If the...............wants your opinion he will most certainly give it to you.

...............is leading his staff on such a rat race that they are on strike for more cheese.

...............has a difficulty for every solution.

Our...............is so insignificant that he could get lost in a crowd of two.

This person serves one most useful purpose in life, in that he is a horrible example to everyone else.

I can recall............'s father as being a remote, mean bastard; his son is a chip off the old glacier.

If...............was a little more laid back, he would be supine.

I have to report that Squadron Leader H is the last sort of chap we should have involved in the training of our young men, even Navigators.

As............... he has a perfect way of ending meetings; he tells all those opposed to his plan that they can resign.

There are so many 'yes men' on his staff that the Headquarters has been nicknamed 'The Land of Nod'.

...............is as spineless as a length of wet spaghetti.

Success has not changed this...............one bit; he is still the same stinker that he always was.

As far as...............is concerned, a friend in need is a friend to stay away from.

You can be certain that...............will never get dizzy from doing a good turn.

...............is the sort of person who considers himself too good to be true.

...............is so controlled, and so tight, that he is unable to perspire freely.

With a little more effort on this person's part, he could become a total nonentity.

Flying Officer A possesses all the qualities one would expect in a Captain – of a pirate ship.

Although highly competent in submarine matters, he is a rather lazy Executive Officer. With his excellent powers of delegation, he would be far better suited for Command.

When put under pressure, her voice rises to a pitch that can only be understood by bats.

Having heard so much about him, I had hoped that...............would not live up to his reputation, but sadly, I have been disappointed.

Organization/management ability

...............was once a farmhand; he should return to an agricultural career as soon as possible.

Our...............is somewhat disorganized and has three pairs of spectacles. One is for near sight, the second for far sight, and the third to look for either of the other two.

...............is really not so much of a has-been, but more of a definitely won't-be.

As..............., he has carried out each and every one of his duties to his entire satisfaction.

Her interests have been broadened since she married a Phantom pilot.

If hedonism was a religion, my Medical Officer would be its high priest.

Since my last report...............has reached rock bottom, and has now started to dig.

The...............is somewhat wrapped up in himself, but it makes for a pretty small parcel.

Not given to displays of enthusiasm nor an energetic man,............... ponders at length over problems. I suspect that if he discovered a fire, by the time he had called the Fire Brigade, the blaze would have burned out.

People and things are here today and gone tomorrow, but the ....is always here today – and here tomorrow.

It is uncertain what this Navigator's future will be, mainly because this will involve the Medical Branch having to make a decision.

My...............is always ready to help you get what is coming to him.

...............is running a large-scale operation, but with a small-scale mind.

I agree that..............., when faced with a problem, usually stops to think, but unfortunately he then forgets to start again.

...............has not got many faults, but he certainly makes the most of the ones he has.

The only time that my............is absolutely certain of where he is going is shortly after he has taken a laxative.

They say that the...............'s deputy kisses the boss's feet every day. This is not actually true, because his boss doesn't come to work every day.

The only job that this young trainee has any interest in, and is highly qualified for, is a tester in a mattress factory.

...............appears to think that he is indispensable to the organization, but a pair of shoe trees could do a better job at filling the appointment than he does.

As a child it would appear that this manager wanted to be a marketing specialist badly. He has now achieved his ambition, because he is a bad marketeer.

The...............candidate will never be interested in teamwork; it appears that all his life he has followed the path of least assistance.

...............is the sort of person who considers himself too good to be true.

The new...............has been accurately described as a 'big thinker', but by someone who lisps.

There is so much unhappiness in his Department that it is frequently closed for alterations.

My............... is the sort of pessimist who always turns out the light to see how dark it is.

During her Naval career, she moved in the best triangles.

It would appear that before he joined the Navy, this young stoker paid his taxes with a smile; the Inland Revenue are now after him for the money.

When unsure of himself, this young man mumbles; when in trouble, he delegates. In a stable organization, he will probably go all the way to the top.

Personal qualities

As the sole Brit working in Headquarters, he bore the shame of not being American with dignity and patience, while the monosyllabic Forrest Gump lookalikes jockeyed for position and influence around him.

Even though he comes from a long line of Dullards, I would not breed from this Officer.

At all times the...............is ably assisted by his wife, although I do wish she would acquire the art of selecting the correct dress for an occasion.

...............needs to have his corners rounded off.

This..............is technically sound, but socially impossible.

He is a Northumbrian with a very open personality and no hint of affect-ation or guile. He is therefore not a natural candidate for..............duties.

My Assistant Secretary sets low personal standards, and then consistently fails to achieve them.

Personal hygiene is not this............'s strongest suit, in fact he smells like a Zoo-keeper's boot.

This..............has turned out to be more elegant than useful.

There is reason to be sorry for those who have to work with this man. In general, life is what you make it, but then..............comes along and makes it worse.

Physically weak, she is rather like warm beer – and is similarly flat.

..............is so fond of chaps that her legs are putting in for Separation Pay.

The..............has a dark and almost swarthy appearance, and when he lets his hair get out of control he resembles a Mexican bandit.

..............is a tall, thin, bearded and very smart officer with the culti-vated aura of a rather dangerous gangster.

The only disturbing character trait is his affection for a tarantula spider that he keeps in his office.

I am told that our..............is something of a flower that grows wild in the woods.

This student's flying was interrupted for two months by a car accident which very much confirmed that he is a 'middle-of-the-road' character.

The............'s primary interest means that he can only count up to sex.

There is nothing that..............would not do for a friend, and he intends to keep it that way.

..............is eccentric; he does not wear socks, and also dresses like Lawrence of Arabia.

..............has gone the way of all flash.

..............is so conceited that he ordered his ID card photograph to be retouched.

..............has a large moustache, a large waistline and a matching opinion of himself.

The............'s armpits have been compared less favourably to the interior of a Sumo wrestler's jockstrap.

I think that............'s inflated ego is Mother Nature's compensation for her mediocrity.

He considers himself to be a self-made man, but he:
 would have done better if he had let out the contract,
 adores his maker,
 left the job unfinished,
 makes you wonder whether he is boasting or apologizing.

How this chap ever gained a Queen's Commission will remain one of life's great mysteries. If it were not for his uniform, I would judge him to be of Junior NCO rank in both manner and appearance.

............'s financial problems seem to stem from the fact that he was once a prolific sower of wild oats. He is now finding the harvesting fees rather expensive.

The..............tends to deprive you of privacy without providing any sort of company.

My..............is a lively officer with style, and has matured well over the past year – even though he does wear some terrible bow ties.

............'s swollen head is merely Mother Nature's attempt to fill a vacuum.

For what it's worth, my wife also reports well on his qualities.

As............'s host, you wish he would leave and let live.

It is amazing how the..............manages to enter a room voice first.

...............speaks eight languages, but cannot hold his tongue in one.

The............'s usual comment is a guffaw, and his proclivity for social solecisms like nose-picking and hair-combing are unrestrained by any sense of occasion. Even in an increasingly permissive society, I cannot see him being promoted.

...............has a superiority complex for no good reason.

The...............is oilier than the Sea Empress.

............'s cheerful demeanour overrides hardship, and he is caring without being patronizing. It is therefore surprising that he is also well liked and supported by his superiors.

It is a source of wonderment that – while exercise is supposed to eliminate fat – Miss S still has a double chin.

In fairness, our...............is doing his best and does not look obese – rather he appears to be about a foot short in stature.

The...............has an attractive, vivacious, trouble-making wife.

This...............should become a Socialist politician. He doesn't just sit on the fence – he changes sides more often than a windscreen wiper.

Should the...............ever pat you on the back, he is probably trying to get you to cough something up.

When...............was growing up, his main ambition was to be a pirate, and it's not everyone that can realize their ambition in the way that he has.

...............very much believes in the greatest good for the greatest number, but his idea of the greatest number is 'Number One'.

The...............never forgets a favour, just as long as he did it.

Every morning the............'s wife carries out two vital actions – she brushes her teeth and then sharpens her tongue.

I have advised...............that, if they ever put a price on his head, he would be well advised to take it.

When she took a lead part in the Station play, the Air Staff Officer's performance had a very happy ending when the curtain finally came down.

..............has risen from obscurity – and is headed for oblivion.

..............has only three failings in his drive for the top, namely a gross shortage of talent, a complete lack of ambition, and a total absence of initiative.

My initial impressions of..............were not favourable; he is over-weight and gives the impression that 'manana' is far too urgent a concept for him.

..............will always remember what he gives – but then forgets what he receives.

...........'s only saving grace is that he does not mean to be an oaf – he just is one.

I understand that Ms G's present difficulties result from an incident when someone offered her a couple of drinks in his flat – and she reclined.

..............sent his picture to the Lonely Hearts Club, but they replied that they weren't that lonely.

The..............has all the dynamic personality of the side wall of a deserted squash court.

Although unmarried an Old Harrovian, he is not a contender for a senior appointment. He is much too big, is not very good at writing letters – and he would be very expensive to feed.

The..............is unhappily unmarried.

Even if his intellect was a tenth of his body strength, which it isn't, this..............would still be a stupid officer.

..............has, like everyone else, the right to have some faults. Sadly, he totally abuses that privilege.

Our..............is something of a manic depressive – easy glum, easy glow.

The..............is so narrow-minded that he has to stack his ideas vertically.

There is no middle ground where this..............is concerned; you either hate him or detest him.

In evolutionary terms,..............is on the return trip.

The only person who drinks more beer in the Mess than this officer is his wife.

It is likely that if he dies, most people would attend the Director's funeral to be absolutely sure that he was dead.

Our...............is the sort of person who reads the obituary notices to cheer himself up.

The............'s new glasses have helped his vision, but without changing his point of view.

This.............. has not been himself lately, and everyone hopes he will stay that way.

At ship's cocktail parties the manager has a surefire way of handling temptation – he yields to it.

In social terms the...............is still embarrassed at having been born in a bed – with a woman.

There is no point in telling this young Trainee a joke with a double meaning, because he won't get either of them.

This..............is so lazy that he won't even exercise discretion.

..............is a very personable officer who could charm the warts off a frog.

This..............candidate's style of soft sell would be more successful if he was given the right vehicle for his talents, namely an ice-cream van.

At the ship's Sods Opera, his talents as an entertainer could best be described as half-comedian, and half-wit.

This..............claims that he is self-made, but it's a pity that he left out the working parts.

She has little willpower, and even less won't power.

This young man has had to give up one bad habit on joining the Royal Marines, and he no longer smokes pot while playing poker.

One young recruit was so tough that he was awarded a scholarship to Borstal.

There is nothing complex about this retired...............Officer, since anyone can grasp her.

This...............can always be counted on to do the right thing too late, or the wrong thing too soon.

...............table manners need improvement; when he is taking soup, the noise is similar to an elephant seal dragging himself up on to the beach.

I understand that...............was bitten by an adder, and that it was a terrible sight watching the poor creature curl up and die.

There must be a lot of good left in this retired manager, but none of it ever comes out.

A chunky individual, the...............is an ardent sportsman, though modest in both manoeuvrability and stopping distance.

If............... were to swim through shark-infested waters he would survive, thanks to professional courtesy.

This young MOD Desk Officer appears to be frank and earnest with women. I understand that in London he is Frank, while in Portsmouth he is Ernest.

Although this...............is hoping to settle down eventually, his social behaviour indicates little life expectancy.

This young woman is a lover of the outdoors, but doesn't do too badly indoors either. Her taste in the opposite sex has a very uniform quality – sailors and Royal Marines.

Candidates like Mr X do not grow on trees, they swing from them.

...............is the sort of chap who cannot be ordered around, unless it is a round of drinks.

If the...............ever took a £5 note out of his pocket, the figurehead of the Queen would start blinking in the light.

The...............is so cold-blooded that if a mosquito bit him it would die from pneumonia.

Every organization is supposed to cherish its eccentrics, but I find this difficult in the case of...............; his moustache is too long, and his hair too short.

It is quite difficult to know what makes this experienced...............tick, but nearly impossible to understand what also makes him chime on the hour.

As a dedicated fisherman, he has the kind of temperament that goes with a person who finds a night on a cold and windy beach to be a stimulating experience.

A suitable finishing touch to this Officer's report would have been a Swan Vesta match.

The members of this new Young Officer intake are alike in many disrespects.

The only thing...............will share with you willingly is a communicable disease.

...............is the sort of man who would knife you in the back – and then promptly report you for carrying concealed weapons.

As I write this, spring is very much in the air, but not in Warrant Officer J.

Give...............an inch – and he will measure it.

This young lady manager recently met a man in the strangest way – they were introduced.

My driver should learn some other four-letter words like can't, won't, stop and don't.

...........'s private life is a bed of ruses.

The...............has not let a woman pin anything on him since he was a baby.

The...............has dirty fingernails, and a mind to match.

...............is never troubled by improper thoughts; in fact he enjoys them very much.

This...............appears to think that the world owes him a giving.

Although the...............always tries to get something for nothing, he is quite happy to complain about the quality of service.

Should...............ever pay you a compliment, he will then ask for a receipt.

His appearance indicates many years on hard stations but good rations.

...............never gets the 'flu because no self-respecting virus could stand him.

She is so unpleasant that the chap who took her out recently got a certificate from the Royal Humane Society.

If Moses had actually met the..............., I'm sure there would have been another Commandment.

My impression is that the less he knows, the more stubbornly he knows it.

This............'s son failed to impress the Board; he is so conceited as to be almost useless.

Uneducated, ungrateful, unforgettable – and unfortunately mine.

I had many doubts about the principle of reincarnation until I encountered this young man; his alter ego is Walter Mitty.

Power of expression

...............adopts a rather tangential approach to problems, deftly sidestepping the main issues to arrive at a conclusion which bears little or no relation to the original problem.

The Canteen manager regularly appears in theatrical productions – both on the stage and off.

...............speaks no foreign languages and even has difficulty with English; he tends to communicate in grunts.

The............'s wife loves wordy causes.

As a decision maker,...............is a master of the 'definite maybe' and of the 'positive perhaps'.

When...............opens her mouth, it seems that this is only to change whichever foot was previously in there.

In speech the...............tends to be rather long-winded, and insists on continuing his involved arguments even when his subject agrees with him;...............will not take 'yes' for an answer.

My...............must learn to resist the temptation to produce the right answer instantly; most of the time he cannot wait to hear what he is going to say next.

When there is nothing more to be said,...............is still saying it.

...............has both a diarrhoea of words and a constipation of ideas.

Miss Q never opens her mouth unless she has nothing to say.

When all is said and done,...............just keeps on talking.

This............'s vocabulary is rather small, but the turnover is terrific.

...............would be much better off if his mind could work as fast as his mouth.

The...............has an oily tongue to go with his slick mind.

In conversation, this...............would do well to follow the example of his skull shape and come to the point early.

...............is the sort of person whose word is never done.

If...............ever said what he thought, he would suddenly become speechless.

...............can talk 50% faster than anyone can listen.

This talkative...............should be on an allowance of 250 words a day.

The smaller............'s ideas are, the more words he uses to express them.

Any attempts at insight into............'s religious beliefs have foundered on the rock of incoherence.

...............is the sort of chap who would take two hours to tell you that he is a man of few words.

I cannot understand how this Intelligence Corps Officer has reached the SO2 grade; my Chief of Staff confirms that he holds the record for 'I don't knows' this year.

No one is the............'s equal to using more words to say less about nothing.

..............can be relied upon to contribute more heat than light to a discussion.

The claim that new technology has developed a fog which can be made to order is no news to this young man.

The............'s stories tend to have a happy ending, mainly because his listeners are delighted when they finally end.

This..............is a young man of few words; the trouble is that he keeps repeating them.

If the room falls silent, you can safely conclude that..............has told a joke.

The..............is such a motormouth that he could talk a glass eye to sleep.

..............is a Grandmaster of the inappropriate remark.

The..............always speaks straight from the shoulder; most unfortunately, some of his comments do not appear to start from higher up.

You like..............a lot when you first meet him, but he will soon talk you out of that.

This..............teaching technique is described as akin to a bicycle wheel; the longer the spoke, the greater the tyre.

He can be highly lucid and creative on paper, but verbal exchange is lethal for anyone seeking a straightforward and useful answer.

This Staff College student shows great potential. Ask him what the time is, and he will tell you how his watch works, in extraordinary detail.

..............communication skills are something of a lottery; he is usually on a different planet to those around him, and one can never be certain that he has understood a given task.

Professional knowledge

Some eight months ago I forecast an improvement in this Aircrew Officer's performance, once he became operational. Regrettably, he then crashed his aircraft into the sea.

When this pilot lifts into the hover, he initiates a sequence of events over which he appears to have very little subsequent control.

...............is a big gun of small calibre and immense bore.

My Principal Medical Officer claims to be a GP, but he is so full of himself that he is regarded by his staff as something of an 'I' specialist.

It's not so much that the accountant lacks presence of mind when conducting his financial duties; the problem lies more with a total absence of thought.

On a recent progress test this...............candidate not only got every answer wrong, but he also misspelled his name.

Flying Officer E is now just safe enough to be entrusted with the aircraft while the captain attends to the call of nature. We try not to crew him with captains with weak bladders.

When asked what she thought about Red China, this potential Officer said that it was acceptable as long as it did not clash with the tablecloth.

The...............is the sort of diplomat who can speak for an hour without notes – and without a point.

To paraphrase Charles Dickens, the............'s expenditure of words is far too great for his income of ideas.

This young...............handles the nurses to good effect.

He has decided to learn the trombone, I think, because it is an instrument with which you can succeed by letting things slide.

............'s conceit is in an inverse relationship to his lack of ability.

My...............could talk the hind leg off a donkey, and is in no way embarrassed by knowing nothing about the subject he is discussing.

My secretary appears to have been hired on the basis of glamour, rather than grammar.

We were disturbed to find that this student............... was intending to leave in the near future, because we had hoped that he would be leaving by the end of this week.

This..............intends to become an author and has just finished something which was accepted by a writer's magazine – the application form for a year's subscription.

In the matter of seduction our..............is always ready, villain and able.

This student's overall performance has confirmed that he ceased to develop intellectually at a relatively early age, and that he will always remain oblivious to the consequences of his invariably crass and stupid behaviour. He was formally counselled by me regarding his specific shortcomings and low assessments; his reaction was that he thought he had better join the Royal Australian Air Force.

The..............thinks he knows it all, and then keeps proving he doesn't.

This young man has been born for watchkeeping duties; his family may be listed in Who's Who, but he certainly doesn't know what's what.

..............remains optimistic about his career, but in this matter he stands alone.

This Dentist has been filling in.

I have yet to fly with this Pilot Officer, but having seen him pull up the aircraft steps in an outward display of efficiency before his navigator had even climbed aboard, I am not exactly looking forward to the experience.

Reliability

..............is certainly very fit, and smashes tiles and bricks with either foot or hand.

This young lady has delusions of adequacy.

............'s final exit was true to form in that he failed to appear at a farewell luncheon arranged on his behalf.

As a work colleague,..............is long on promises but short on memory.

Real talent – and Cambridge-educated too!

When..............wishes you 'good morning', it would be a wise precaution to check this with the Met Office.

This...............is very highly strung; unfortunately, he has not been strung up high enough.

There are many who consider that the programme runs a lot better on............'s day off.

...............will only face the music if he can call the tune.

His Department clubbed together to buy him an appropriate gift. It was both timely and striking – a carriage clock.

There is a lot less to this Officer than meets the eye.

I must admit to liking Captain E, particularly as he has the good taste to be the only other officer in the Brigade who supports Queen's Park Rangers.

It would not be possible to describe this Administrative Officer as a quitter, because he has been sacked from every appointment that he has ever had.

This former actor is something of a dandy who has long been waiting for something to turn up............... should have started with his own shirt sleeves.

I have been asked to write...............a satisfactory letter of reference. ....worked for us for a year, but is no longer working for us. We are very satisfied.

...............is a most dependable person, because you can always depend on him to get it completely wrong.

As a ship's officer in my frigate, Lieutenant A has been almost invisible.

He remains overweight, scruffy and very noisy. These faults might not be so bad if he was a member of the Stoker fraternity, but in a Leading Steward such failings are unacceptable.

Fat, untidy and cantankerous,...............maintains a wide range of interests outside the organization. He is a man of narrow views and limited reliability, and on current form he just about deserves to remain employed until the end of the week.

Delightful, delinquent but potentially disastrous; he should not be allowed anywhere near real soldiers and live ammunition.

Tact and cooperation

This...............should go far – and the sooner the better.

His wife, who is antisocial and ill-mannered, fortunately refuses to take part in any.............. functions.

...............regards free speech not as a right, but as a continuous obligation.

When the war starts, this young man will end up with a chest full of silver. If captured, he will make the life of the prison camp commandant Hell; until then, he continues to practise on me.

As guests go, you wish he would.

The Padre can stay longer for an hour than most people do for a week.

...............has a wide circle of nodding acquaintances.

...............not only encroaches on your time, he trespasses on eternity.

...............leaves little to your imagination, and even less to your patience.

...............is a character. He has a lively Cockney turn of phrase, a well-developed sense of the ridiculous, and is much liked by everyone. His suitability for an exchange tour is very much a matter of taste; the Australians would like him, but I am not sure about the Americans.

My...............can talk for hours about the value of silence.

...............stands for everything that he thinks I will fall for.

Supervising this Officer is like serving on a bomb disposal unit – one is never sure when he is going to go off.

The only time this young woman will listen to an argument is when her colleagues are having a go at each other.

This...............has been described as a 'grumpy bear'; he is more like a consumptive porcupine with ingrowing quills.

This...............thinks the world is against him, and what's more – he is right.

He joined my ship as something of a blue-eyed boy. I have found him to be so full of bullshit that the eye colour on his ID card should be changed to 'brown'.

The.............. is the sort of chap who will roll out the carpet for you one day, and then pull it from under you the next.

...............is a genius, because he not only takes infinite pains in what he is doing, he also gives the same.

Is this candidate a direct descendant of Attila the Hun?

He is an unpleasant, irritating, offensive and obnoxious individual – and these are his good points.

It is hoped that one day...............may come forth with a few brilliant flashes of silence.

The...............is ably supported by his wife, who is a great exponent of the appealing art of décolletage.

Since his last report,............'s personal situation has improved, from his own point of view, in two basic ways; he has ditched his wife, and acquired a desirable car.

...............closely resembles a Teenage Mutant Ninja Turtle.

...............is the sort of man who makes you wish that you had a hearing aid – so that you could turn it off and shut him out.

The Assistant is so unpleasant that the last time he was in Hospital, he even got 'Get Well' cards from the nurses.

I hope that Flight Lieutenant B sorts himself out; there is potential in there somewhere. I would not see him as an AdC, other than to an Air Officer who has a low blood pressure problem.

Flight Lieutenant K has requested an exchange tour in the USA; posting this officer to America would be akin to restoring tax on tea.

I dislike this............'s attitude to his superiors; it would appear that his motto for success is that it isn't who you know that matters, but who you 'yes'.

We will probably have difficulties with this young...............; when he was at school he made his teacher stay in after work.

...............is the sort of chap who will tell a woman that her tights are wrinkled, even when she is not wearing any.
If getting up people's noses was a prerequisite for promotion, he would be CEO by now.

If this young...............lives long enough to become an adult, it will be a remarkable tribute to his instructor's self-control.

Everyone has a good word for the..............., but they tend to whisper it.

You can rely on...............to tell a woman that she is a sight instead of a vision.

The sparks certainly fly when this young lady uses a knife and fork.

The...............continues to be a reliable social chameleon; he is able to blend into the current mood, no matter how raucous the occasion.

The Finance Director is only dull and uninteresting until you get to know him; then he is just plain boring.

...............is good for people's health, because when they see him coming they tend to go for long walks.

Socially this...............is temperate and, on first acquaintance, quite like-able. However, he soon becomes a bore and is unpopular with his subordinates, his colleagues – and me.

This impertinent youth not only explains everything, but he also then explains his explanations.

...............is a good man, even if there are still some dinosaur genes lurking.

I could not warm to...............even if we were cremated together.

When...............slaps you on the back, it is to make sure that you swallow what he has just told you.

Some people are born great, some become great;...............just grates.

In short, he is one step ahead of notoriety and two steps astern of fame.

The...............should be kept away from cocktail parties; she is the human equivalent of a social hand grenade.

Zeal and initiative

.... reminds me very much of a gyroscope; he is always spinning around at a frantic pace, but not really going anywhere at all.

When he joined my organization, this.............. was something of a granny, but since then he has aged considerably.

.... is the type of person who approaches every subject with an open mouth.

Sergeant L is a real trier – who nearly knocks his cap off every time he salutes.

A long-standing middle-of-the-road executive, ... is now grinding to a halt at the kerbside, and has taken the cul-de-sac of voluntary redundancy.

.... is a highly polished chap, but in a slippery sort of way.

In both attitude and commitment, ... resembles a slug on an ice rink.

.... reminds one of a slightly unruly colt that needs schooling to bring out the best.

.... rarely sets the common room on fire, and not just because he has given up smoking.

As Deputy Manager he is the personification of keenness without actually being very useful.

I have interviewed the applicant. There is definitely an opening in my Headquarters for this passed-over young man, but please make sure that he does not slam the door on the way out.

.... tends to follow the path of least persistence.

.... is very much like a puppy which wants to be loved, but only succeeds in upsetting dishes and ruining the furniture.

.... is the sort of chap whose journey through life is characterized by pushing on doors marked 'Pull'.

This Assistant Secretary (Personnel) was fired, with some enthusiasm, because he wasn't fired with much enthusiasm at all.

This teacher is such a total drongo that his idea of an exciting night is to turn up the heat on his electric blanket.

This trainee works eight hours and sleeps eight hours a day; the only problem is that they are all the same hours.

No one is.............. equal at hitting the nail squarely on the thumb.

The.............. has strong views; he holds that Vlad the Impaler was something of a limp-wristed social worker.

It is amazing what this secretary can get away with, and still keep her amateur status.

The only thing that.............. grows in his garden is – tired.

The Deputy Chief Instructor has stopped drinking coffee in the morning because it keeps him awake for the rest of the day.

.... is rusting on his laurels.

This accountant does most of his work sitting down and that is where he shines.

.... never puts off until tomorrow what he can put off indefinitely.

For.............., the process of getting up in the morning is a major conflict between his mind and his mattress.

This potential recruit does not know how long he has been out of work, mainly because he cannot find his birth certificate.

.... reminds me of my old Labrador; he will never learn any new tricks nor will he move any faster.

My Correspondence Officer is almost dyslexic, but I am told that the dogged determination with which he tackles 'Patience' and 'Minesweeper' on the Ship's Office PC displays the kind of intellectual edge and computer skill desirable in today's Navy.

This young trainee has become so lazy that even loafing appears to have become hard work.

............'s greatest pleasure in life is having lots to do, and then not doing it.

.... will, if you are not careful, have the time of your wife at a party.

Unfortunately, when the wages of sin are paid, ... is likely to get time-and-a-half.

The only regular exercise that the CEO gets is when jumping to conclusions.

This young Cadet spends a lot of time shining up to the Head of Department, and very little effort on polishing off the work.

Not only does.............. expect to get something for nothing, he also wants it gift-wrapped.

Quizzes, questionnaires and quandaries

It is no accident that all sorts of popular magazines and newspapers have self-assessment questionnaires. 'Are you a demon or a dodo under the duvet' quizzes in women's magazines; 'Can you delegate' on the business pages; and 'A pet for your personality' in the lifestyle magazines. Most of these questionnaires are not psychometrically validated but simply a form of harmless fun.

But they can be useful. They can guide one into thinking about certain issues. They often offer interesting memorable typologies for understanding self and others. They are a safe means of evaluation – done privately without having to show anyone.

They can of course be misleading if taken very seriously. They are never rocket science but give approximate answers. One should never change one's life on the basis of them. But if they raise an issue, further investigation may be necessary. If so, good, reliable, validated tests should be sought.

The bogus quiz

Below are the results of *your* 360-degree feedback. They represent a summary of the comments of your boss, some of your close colleagues who know you, and your direct reports. The most critical dozen points have been listed. For our records, we would be interested in how accurate you think each is. Put a percentage (where 100% is totally accurate) next to each:

Per cent
accurate

A. You have a fairly strong need for other people to like and admire you.

B. You have a tendency to be critical of yourself.

C. You have a great deal of unused intellectual capacity which you have not turned to your advantage.

D. While you have some personal weaknesses, you are usually able to compensate for them.

E. Disciplined and self-controlled outside, you tend to be a bit of a worrier inside.

F. At times, you have serious doubts as to whether you have made the right decision or done the right thing.

G. You prefer a certain amount of change and variety and become dissatisfied when hemmed in by restriction and limitation.

H. You pride yourself as an independent thinker and do not accept others' statements without satisfactory proof.

I. You have found it unwise to be frank in revealing yourself to others.

J. At times, you are extroverted, affable, sociable, whereas, at other times, you are introverted, wary, reserved.

K. Most of your aspirations tend to be pretty realistic.

L. Security is one of your major goals in life.

For nearly 40 years, psychologists have been investigating the Barnum Effect. It was the famous circus-act producer Phineas T. Barnum who said: 'There's a sucker born every minute' and had as his formula for success 'A little something for everybody'. The Barnum Effect refers to the phenomenon whereby people accept as true feedback about themselves because it is supposedly derived from valid measures. In other words, people fall victim to the fallacy of personality validation, which means that people accept the generalizations, the trite bogus descriptions which are true of nearly everybody, to be specifically true of themselves.

Fifty years ago, a US psychologist called Ross Stagner gave a group of personnel managers a well-established personality test. But instead of scoring it and giving them the actual results, he gave each of them bogus feedback in the form of 13 statements derived from horoscopes, graphological analyses and so on. Each manager was then asked to read over the feedback (supposedly derived for him/herself from the 'scientific' test) and decide how accurate the assessment was by marking each sentence on a scale: (a) amazingly accurate; (b) rather good; (c) about half and half; (d) more wrong than right; (e) almost entirely wrong. The statements you have just completed are based on these. More than half felt that their profile was an amazingly accurate description of them, while 40% thought it was rather good. Almost none believed it to be very wrong.

Many researchers have replicated this result. A French psychologist advertised himself as an astrologer in various newspapers and received hundreds of requests for his services. He replied to each letter by sending out mimeographed identical copies of a single, ambiguous 'horoscope'. More than 200 clearly gullible clients wrote back praising his accuracy and perceptiveness. An Australian professor regularly asks his first-year students to write down in frank detail their dreams, or to describe in detail what they see in an inkblot – the more mystical the task, the better. A week later, he gives them various bland statements shown in the table for rating as before. Only after they have publicly declared their belief in the test are they encouraged to swap feedback. The humiliation of being so easily fooled is a powerful learning experience.

Research on the Barnum Effect has, however, shown that belief in this bogus feedback is influenced by a number of important factors, some to do with the client and the consultant (their personality, *naïveté* and so on), and some to do with the nature of the test and the feedback situation itself. Women, contrary to popular belief, are not more susceptible than men, though of course generally naïve or gullible people are (tautologically!) more susceptible to this effect.

Believing in 'bogus' feedback is really dependent on two things: whether it is pretty general (and true of everyone), and overall, pretty positive. One of the most important factors in giving believable bogus feedback is the perceived specificity of the information required to do the reading in contrast to the bland lack of specificity in the answer. The more detailed the personal data gathering, the better – so you have to specify exact time, date and place of birth to astrologers. In one study, a US researcher gave all his subjects the same horoscope and found that those who were told that the interpretation was based on the year, month and day of birth judged it to be more accurate than those who were led to believe that it was based only on the year and month. And, of course, all the paraphernalia attached to the 360-degree feedback is a good example where, after people receive general statements they think pertain just to them, their faith in the procedure and in the diagnostician increases. A client's satisfaction is no measure of how well the diagnostician has differentiated him or her from others, but it is utterly dependent on the extent to which they believe it is *specific to them*.

The second factor belies the truth that we are all hungry for compliments, but sceptical of criticism. Feedback must be favourable and, on the whole, positive, with the occasional mildly negative comment (that in itself may be a compliment) so that people will believe it. This confirms another principle in personality measurement – the 'Pollyanna Principle', which suggests that there is a universal human tendency to use or accept positive words or feedback more frequently, diversely and facilely than negative words and feedback. It has been shown that, according to the evaluation of two judges, there were five times as many favourable as unfavourable statements in highly acceptable interpretations, and twice as many unfavourable statements in rarely accepted interpretations.

Hence the popularity of astrology and graphology – feedback is based on specific information (time and place of birth for astrology; slant and size of writing, correctness of letters, dotting of i's and crossing of t's, use of loops and so on, in graphology). It is nearly always favourable. It is often the anxious (worried, depressed, insecure) who visit astrologers, graphologists, fortune-tellers. They are particularly sensitive to objective positive information about themselves and the future. Therefore, the very type of feedback and the predisposition of clients make acceptance highly probable. Thus, if the general description seems true (and it probably is), people frequently conclude that it must be even more true when even more information is given. Furthermore, this process is enhanced over time for two reasons.

Since Freud, it has been known that people selectively remember more positive events about themselves than negative, and are thus likely to remember more feedback that coincides with their own views of themselves than information that is less relevant or contradictory. Second, of course, people have to pay for the consultation. There is one other reason why people validate graphology and astrology: the self-fulfilling prophecy. It is quite possible that if one is told 'As a Virgo, you are particularly honest' then this may lead one to notice and subsequently selectively recall all, or any, albeit trivial, instances of behavioural confirmation (pointing out that a person has dropped a bus ticket, or giving back excess change). The self-fulfilling prophecy may work on both a conceptual and a behavioural basis. Thus Virgos come to include the trait of honesty in their self-concept, but also they may become slightly or occasionally more honest. In this way, graphology and astrology predictions may come true because accepting the predictions partly dictates that our behaviour will change appropriately!

Feedback needs to be specific and valid. That often means negative. Of course, in the mumbo-jumbo of training courses, it is not called negative feedback but *developmental opportunities*. Good, honest feedback may be hurtful and surprising – and, by definition, not always believable. If your annual appraisal or 360-degree feedback is warm and vague, beware – it may be bogus.

Brainstorms

Are you a trendy leftie or happily right on? There are essentially two sorts of people in the world: those who believe there are two sorts and those who don't. Psychologists and management scientists have long delighted in distinguishing people, types or categories, naming different types of individuals and the way they go about work and play.

New developments in brain scanning and computer analysis led various consultants to differentiate the way in which *people process information*. In the wonderful world of brain mapping, real as well as hopeful scientists have distinguished between right and left hemispheres, which control the left-hand side and right-hand side of the body respectively. This is their personal thinking style – not how bright they are (capacity), but how they think and solve problems. The metaphors they used were easily borrowed from the sexy cognitive neurosciences. So, *left* hemisphere processing styles are analytic, reflective, logical, deliberative, single-track, convergent and academic; whereas *right* hemisphere processing styles are impulsive, intuitive, global, liberative, multi-track and divergent. Lefties like language and unstructured images. Lefties like details, facts, logic, linear, reality-based, sequential and structured ideas: they are planned and organized types. Righties like the overview and the big picture, fantasy-orientated, holistic, analogical patterns: they are touchy-feely types.

Before we get any more involved, test yourself. Read each of the following statements and give yourself a score out of 10 for each. 10 means totally true of me; 5-ish sort of, sometimes; and 0 never true of me.

1. I like to keep my work activities scheduled and structured.
2. I prefer things to be generally stated and seldom worry about specific facts.
3. I believe I base work decisions on facts, not feelings.
4. I like using images in remembering and thinking.
5. I like things to be concrete and seldom make errors.
6. I have vivid dreams.
7. I can easily think of synonyms for words.
8. I prefer a playful approach to problem-solving.
9. I appreciate standard ways to solve problems and reach solutions.
10. I follow my intuition regardless of the facts.

Total up the odd numbered-statements, which give you your left-brain score (out of 50). Then total the even, right-brain items. Subtract even from odd. If your score is greater than 20, you are very left-brained; if it is between 5 and 20, you are moderately left-brained; between −5 and 5 a bit of both; between −5 and −20 moderately right-brained; and if more than −20 you are very right-brained.

'Left-brain skills', it seems, limit one to being a manager, whereas 'right-brain skills' mean one can be a leader. Poor old lefties like to administer (not innovate); they like to get involved with systems and structures (not people); they have a short-range, bottom-line obsessed view (not long-term, horizon-orientated); and they tend to imitate their bosses, happily accepting the status quo (not originate and challenge things as they are).

One argument goes that most businesses have enough analytic, rational, left-brained managers and need more holistic, intuitive, right-brained creatives. Lefties, it seems, are dull, obsessive and totally uncreative. Or is it creatives who come up with all this? The trouble is, these desirable chappies don't fit in because:

- They are rather *disorganized* and find traditional time management strategies confining and unstimulating.
- They are *non-conforming*, breaking and even openly resenting rules and regulations.
- They are *chaotic, inconsistent* and have trouble following through.
- They eschew logical calculations and data for those mysterious concepts called *intuition* and *imagination*.

- They are *easily bored* and seek out novelty.
- They can be overly *sensitive* (perhaps neurotic), basing their arguments (such as they are) on personal values rather than data analysis.

Is it true that most businesses have selected out right-hemisphere holistics? Or is it that they either don't need them or don't like them?

Any account manager at an advertising or PR company will tell you the problems of managing their right-brained, right-on creatives. Managing creatives is like herding cats. Many have minds of their own and are well known for being unreliable, unsocialized and (almost) unemployable.

One of the great problems for organizations genuinely interested in using the services of right-brained creatives is selecting them.

Many talentless frauds and impostors hide behind the intuitive left-brain label. It is clearly easier to select and test lefties – you can or cannot do calculations, follow instructions and so on. But creative solutions are not like that – except from a long-term, retrospective point of view. Charlatans know this and hence favour the creative positive; even challenging the established business practice of measurement and analysis.

The actual left/right brain description is, of course, a metaphor, not a physiological reality. In fact, real brain scientists are deeply disparaging about all this phoney anatomical talk. Further, many of the simple-minded left/right brain distinctions cloud and confuse many issues such as preferences, skills, aptitudes and emotions. It may be a form of shorthand, but it is barely legible.

All businesses need original thinkers and visionaries. They also need people managers and charismatic, transformational leaders. What they don't need are vacuous airheads (who might be termed no-brainers), who threaten their business success with hare-brained schemes which are bound to fail. The trick is to know the difference.

Common sense in management

The so-called 'discipline' of management science often has low status in business schools, partly because the hard men of science (accountants, actuaries, economists) despise the 'soft waffle' of organizational behaviour and management psychology. Management science is thought to be a trivial, expensive and pointless exercise in describing or proving what we already know. All of its findings are intuitive, unsurprising and uninformative; worse, it is packed with esoteric, mid-Atlantic jargon which clouds common sense in the pretence of clarifying it. In short, organizational psychology, seen as part of management science, is simply dismissed as nothing more than common sense.

But there are problems with the common sense argument. First, common sense is frequently contradictory. 'Clothes make the man' is at odds with 'You can't make a silk purse out of a sow's ear'. 'Out of sight, out of mind' and 'absence makes the heart grow fonder' also seem contradictory. Although it is possible that both are true under different circumstances, common sense does not tell you which. Equally, the equivocal nature of various research findings may be explained by psychological processes operating quite differently in different circumstances.

Second, if all management is common sense, nothing can be counter-intuitive, or the result of faulty reasoning. Research in the sciences is full of such examples and it would not be surprising if some aspects of management science were the same; that is, the opposite of common sense. Thus we know that people commonsensically use brainstorming to generate the maximal quality and quantity of ideas for a creative problem when the literature quite clearly specifies that it works less well than the individuals working alone. Here we have an example of common sense being proven wrong.

It could be argued that current management knowledge is in fact absorbed from management science, as it is frequently popularized in newspapers and magazines. Thus, ironically, common sense could be the *result* of the ideas of management science being commented on in the popular press. A frequently discussed finding from research cannot remain non-obvious to managers, any more than a joke can remain funny to people who hear it over and over again. As all organizational psychologists will tell you, the media are very interested in organizational research findings on issues such as job motivation, productivity, stress and satisfaction. Indeed, it is this very popularizing of ideas and findings which at first may be mysterious or even counter-intuitive, but with constant exposure end up looking very drab.

Further, if all organizational psychology is common sense and most people supposedly have this curious trait, why is there so much disagreement on management issues, processes and procedures?

Albert Einstein defined common sense as the collection of prejudices people have accrued by the age of 18, and Victor Hugo maintained that common sense was acquired in spite of, rather than because of, education. It must be a desirable thing to possess in the world of selection and development.

Writers of textbooks in clinical, organizational and social psychology are sensitive to common sense objections and attempt to quash them early in the text. A favourite way of doing this is to devise a quiz to test knowledge. The following two quizzes have been derived from a variety of sources.

1. In most cases, leaders should stick to their decisions once they have   T   F
    made them, even if it seems they are wrong.
2. When people work together in groups and know their individual   T   F
    contributions can't be observed, each tends to put in less effort than
    when they work on the same task alone.
3. Even skilled interviewers are sometimes unable to avoid being influ-   T   F
    enced in their judgement by factors other than an applicant's qualifi-
    cations.
4. Most managers are highly democratic in the way that they supervise   T   F
    their people.
5. Most people who work for the government are low risk-takers.   T   F
6. The best way to stop a malicious rumour at work is to present covering   T   F
    evidence against it.
7. As morale or satisfaction among employees increases in any organiza-   T   F
    tion, overall performance almost always rises.
8. Providing employees with specific goals often interferes with their   T   F
    performance; they resist being told what to do.
9. In most organizations the struggle for limited resources is a far more   T   F
    important cause of conflict than other factors such as interpersonal
    relations.
10. In bargaining, the best strategy for maximizing long-term gains is   T   F
    seeking to defeat one's opponent.
11. In general, groups make more accurate and less extreme decisions   T   F
    than individuals.
12. Most individuals do their best work under conditions of high stress.   T   F
13. Smokers take more days' sick leave than non-smokers.   T   F
14. If you reprimand a worker for a misdeed, it is better to do so immedi-   T   F
    ately after the mistake occurs.
15. Highly cohesive groups are also highly productive.   T   F

Quiz 1   True   False

Answers: 1–5 True, 6–12 False, 13–14 True, 15 False.

If you scored 5 or less, why not try early retirement? Scorers of 6 to 10 should perhaps consider an MBA. A score of 11 or above – yes, indeed, you do have that most elusive of

1. Relatively few top executives are highly competitive, aggressive and   T   F
    show 'time urgency'.
2. In general, women managers show higher self-confidence than men   T   F
    and expect greater success in their careers.
3. Slow readers remember more of what they read than fast readers.   T   F
4. To change people's behaviour towards new technology, we must first   T   F
    change their atttudes.
5. The more motivated you are, the better you will be at solving a   T   F
    complex problem.
6. The best way to ensure that high-quality work will persist after training T   F
    is to reward behaviour every time, rather than intermittently, when it
    occurs during training.
7. An English-speaking person with German ancestors/relations finds it   T   F
    easier to learn German than an English-speaking person with French
    ancestors.
8. People who graduate in the upper third of the A-levels table tend to   T   F
    make more money in their careers than average students.
9. After you learn something, you forget more of it in the next few hours   T   F
    than in the next several days.
10. People who do poorly in academic work are usually superior in   T   F
    mechanical ability.
11. Most high-achieving managers tend to be high risk-takers.   T   F
12. When people are frustrated at work, they frequently become aggres-   T   F
    sive.
13. Successful top managers have a greater need for money than for   T   F
    power.
14. Women are more intuitive than men.   T   F
15. Effective leaders are more concerned about people than the task.   T   F
16. Bureaucracies are inefficient and represent a bad way of running   T   F
    organizations.
17. Unpleasant working conditions (crowding, loud noise, high or very   T   F
    low temperature) produce dramatic reduction in performance on
    many tasks.
18. Talking to workers usually enhances co-operation between them.   T   F
19. Women are more conforming and open to influence than men.   T   F
20. Because workers resent being told what to do, giving employees   T   F
    specific goals interferes with their performance.

                                                                       all   qualities:
common sense.

Quiz 2   True   False

Answers: 1=True, 2–7 False, 8–9 True, 10–11 False, 12=True, 13–20 False.

Score 1–5: Oh dear! Pretty naïve about behavioural science!

Score 6–10: Too long at the school of hard knocks, we fear.
Score 11–25: Yes, experience has helped.
Score 16–20: Clearly a veteran of the management school of life.

Critics of these tests are quite legitimately entitled to ask whether the topics are representative of organizational psychology or whether the authors scoured the literature in the desperate hope of finding more counter-intuitive evidence. There is some evidence of this. Further, many sceptics would, no doubt, like 'chapter and verse' references to back up these statements, believing that the results remain equivocal in this area at the very least, or that many of the statements really require qualification.

More importantly perhaps, anyone with a psychometric background would ask for some evidence of validity for these tests. Do MBAs and experienced and successful managers score more highly than housewives or students? This research has not been done; nor would it be very easy to do. To decide on 'known groups', the method is to distinguish those conspicuously knowledgeable in terms of selection, development and other areas of occupational psychology from the group who have little knowledge or experience, but this is not simple.

But these questions should not deter the researcher. There will always be those who reject, dismiss and pooh-pooh organizational psychology issues, because they believe they are 'merely' common sense. To have a well-validated test to prove them wrong would certainly be an attractive idea to many.

Decision-making styles

Suffering, say the existentialists, is about choice. But then so is practically everything else. Not to decide is to decide. As Napoleon Bonapart correctly noted: 'Nothing is more difficult, and therefore precious, than to be able to decide.'

According to the oldest (live) business guru Peter Drucker, decision-making is the unique and specific 'executive task'. A real executive is one who makes a quick, clear and hopefully judicious decision and then gets someone else to do the work. One cannot govern by ifs and buts. The inability to make judicious and timely decisions is probably the principal reason for executive failure.

Many successful business people have reflected on the decision-making process. A trade union boss, used to the old school management, once said after a decision had been announced: 'never explain and never apologize'. Another boss, who came from the diametrically opposed world of PR, said the best thing any person can do is to try to make the major decision-makers believe that the outcome you want is their original idea.

The gurus of empowerment stress that decisions should be made as low down as possible in the organization. The entrepreneurs, on the other hand, are impressed by the speed of the decision rather than who does the deciding.

As always, the proverbial wisdom is deeply contradictory. Some argue that the only person who can change their mind is the person who has one; it is a sign of prudence not arrogance. Others insist that chopping and changing is a bad sign. Yet all are agreed on the frustrations associated with indecision. We all know of the committee that concludes that the decision is maybe, and that that is final. Sam Goldwyn is celebrated for saying: 'I'll give you a definite maybe.' It is probably true that the percentage of error multiplies the longer people deliberate. It is better to err on the side of daring than caution and yet the sin of procrastination is perhaps the most common in the boardroom.

Of course, in theory, it is not difficult. All you need to do is define the issue in the clearest jargon-free language. Then gather all salient facts about the issue (cause, consequence, interested parties, costs) and list all the possible decisions and their probable outcome. Then, and only then, decide on the basis of the facts and the values you believe in.

Decision-making presents problems in every organization. Indeed, one has to make decisions about how to make decisions: *who* is invested with the authority and responsibility for decision-making about *what*; is it a *group* (meeting) or *individual* activity; and what are the *roles*, *rights* and *responsibilities* for those making and following decisions. Decisions can be debated and decided openly – even on the Web, or more commonly made by small power-wielding cabals in dark (but smoke-free) rooms.

Decisions are often made in groups not to ensure democratic principles but to diffuse responsibility. And yet individuals are occasionally encouraged to make decisions. The desire to remain popular or appease all parties is often the downfall of otherwise good executives. There will always be a person or a faction opposed to the decisions made.

Psychologists who wrote about 'group think' described it as a collective pattern of defensive decision avoidance. It is, in short, a way in which fairly tightly knit groups, usually under pressure, avoid confronting the serious problems that face them. It may well be that exactly the same preferences occur within individuals who find decision-making difficult.

Consider your own style:

		SA	A	D	SD
1.	I like to evaluate all alternatives	4	3	2	1
2.	To be honest, I don't make decisions until I have to.	4	3	2	1
3.	I admit to wasting time on trivialities before making a decision.	4	3	2	1
4.	I feel pessimistic about ever making good business decisions.	4	3	2	1
5.	I collect considerable data before decision-making.	4	3	2	1
6.	I prefer leaving most business decisions to others.	4	3	2	1
7.	I often delay acting on decisions after I have made them.	4	3	2	1
8.	I always feel immensely pressured when making important decisions.	4	3	2	1
9.	I must be clear about my objectives before choosing what to decide.	4	3	2	1
10.	I often fear the responsibility that goes with decision-making.	4	3	2	1
11.	I put off thinking about deciding as long as I can.	4	3	2	1
12.	I constantly worry about what can go wrong when decision-making.	4	3	2	1
13.	I like weighing evidence for and against extensively.	4	3	2	1
14.	I prefer that experts rather than I make most business decisions.	4	3	2	1
15.	I have been known to miss many decision-making deadlines.	4	3	2	1
16.	I spend much effort after a decision trying to convince myself that I was right.	4	3	2	1

A = Agree; D = Disagree; SA = Strongly Agree; SD = Strongly Disagree

Painstaking: add together	1, 5, 9, 13
Buckpassing: add together	2, 6, 10, 14
Procrastinating: add together	3, 7, 11, 15
Hypervigilant: add together	4, 8, 12, 16

Score above 9 in any category and you need help.

The painstaking style is that of the obsessional prone to analysis paralysis. Gathering the facts and being clear about their implications is a good thing but can easily go too far. The painstaking decision-maker has problems with uncertainty. They have low tolerance for ambiguity, which is pretty tough given how ambiguous and unclear the world is.

The buckpassing style means that, fearful of the consequences, and in particular the possibility that one may have to be accountable and responsible for bad decisions, it is easier to leave it up to someone else – select committee, experts, consultants, even politicians whom one can blame if anything goes wrong.

Procrastinating is perhaps the most common of all the sins in decision-making. The hypervigilant are the most neurotic of the decision-making world. They are the victims of irritable bowel syndrome, migraine and other side effects of business decision-making.

Ethics at work

Business ethics used to be a relatively simple issue. For most people, the concept of *caveat emptor* (let the buyer beware) was enough. It was, so most believed, the duty of companies primarily to serve their share-holders, employees and customers by maximizing profits and staying within the law. But over the past decade or so, business people have been considering in more detail the relationship and responsibility between companies and society. As a result, the discipline of business ethics has arisen, with its own journals and professors and the bric-a-brac of academic respectability. Its questions include:

- Should a company place the interests of its shareholders before those of its employees or of the environment?
- Should a company be responsible for all the social consequences of its operations?
- When is regulation necessary, and when is it excessive and counter-productive?
- What does a corporation 'owe' its employees?
- To what extent should an organization be accountable for its products?
- Is there an ethical difference between tax avoidance and evasion?
- Is the only social responsibility of business to maximize profits?
- Is being seen to be green (environmentally aware) good?

The idea of corporate social responsibility goes back a long way. At the end of the 19th century, Carnegie in the United States, and Rowntree and Cadbury in the UK, took the idea of paternalistic responsibility for workers and the immediate neighbourhood very seriously. To a large extent their ideas were based on two principles:

- The *charity* principle, which was to assist the less fortunate, such as people who were elderly, handicapped, sick and unemployed (the deserving poor).
- The *stewardship* principle, which required business organizations to act as caretakers of the land and people and to hold these in trust for the benefit of society.

This really constituted no more than the application of the old *noblesse oblige* maxim. By the middle of the 20th century, these 'ethical' principles were under attack by many critics of various persuasions, who argued that the principles:

- are simply a capitalist smokescreen, hiding owners' profit and greed
- simply reduce market efficiency
- have only marginal impact and should be facilitated by other means
- are quite simply too impractical, costly and ultimately unworkable
- neither indicate the appropriate magnitude of social concern nor have to weigh social against other responsibilities.

In the United States criticisms of the ethics of social responsibility led to the development of ideas of corporate responsiveness. It was argued that if companies learn of a salient social problem, they should act on it, proactively. However, it was argued that this approach did not explain which values social responsiveness should try to encourage. This 'new' principle did not specify how to manage a conflict of values effectively. Hence, the interest in business ethics, which is the study of people's rights and duties at work and of the rules that are applied in business decisions.

Business ethics questions apply at very different levels:

- At the *societal* level, questions concern the ethics of dealing with certain countries, the desirability of capitalism versus socialism,

the role of government in the marketplace. At this level the
discourse is about societies and principles.

- At the *stakeholder* level, questions concern the employees, suppliers,
  customers, shareholders and those related to them. Ethical questions here are about the company's obligation to these various
  groups.
- At the *company policy* level, the questions concern all the company's
  rules and regulations, the ethical implications of lay-offs, perks,
  work rules, motivation, leadership, payment schemes, and so on.
- At the *personal* level, the ethical questions are about how people in
  the organization should and do behave with one another.

Business ethics is for the interfering, underemployed busybody. Those
who can, do; those who can't or won't, form or join business ethics
committees.

The primary responsibility of managers is organizational effectiveness. However, their decisions and actions inevitably have an
impact on society as a whole and therefore, argue some, they have the
social responsibility to engage in activities that protect and contribute
to the welfare of the community.

But an organization's social responsibility is a matter of intense
debate. At one extreme are those who believe that organizations are in
business exclusively to produce for profit those goods and services that
society wants (be it atomic weapons or live-saving drugs). For them,
social responsibility is a lot of irrelevant, politically correct nonsense.
At the other extreme are those individuals who want to regulate organizations so that they can do business only if they help to solve social
problems, do no environmental harm and put back some of their profits into society. For them managerial ethics is an obsession.

In the 19th century, social responsibility was expressed in the principle of charity – a paternalistic *noblesse oblige*. This was replaced by the
principle of stewardship, which suggests that organizations become
stewards or trustees of society because they have an obligation to see
that public interests are served.

However, we are now in a new era. No longer are companies
reminded of their legal and moral obligations but they are encouraged
to be proactively socially responsive. Not only are organizations seen
to have economic and legal responsibilities (to be profitable and operate legally) but to have ethical responsibilities to meet society's expect-

ations for conscientious and proper behaviour, even when these expectations are not reflected in the letter of laws and regulations. Some even stress discretionary responsibility to carry out voluntary acts, even though failing to do so would not be judged unethical. Acting as a good 'corporate citizen' is an item on every large company's agenda.

Where do you stand? Consider the following:

1. *I believe ...*
   a. What's good for me is good for my country.   1
   b. What's good for my company is good for our country.   2
   c. What is good for society is good for our company.   3

2. *In business ...*
   a. Money and wealth are most important.   1
   b. Money is important, but so are people.   2
   c. People are more important than money.   3

3. *I believe ...*
   a. Let the buyer beware (*caveat emptor*).   1
   b. Let us not cheat the customer.   2
   c. Let the seller beware (*caveat vendor*).   3

4. *I believe ...*
   a. Labour is a commodity to be bought and sold.   1
   b. Labour has certain rights, which must be recognized.   2
   c. Employee dignity has to be satisfied.   3

5. *Ultimately ...*
   a. Accountability of management is to the owners/shareholders.   1
   b. Accountability of management is to the owners, customers, employees, suppliers *and* other contributors.   2
   c. Accountability of management is to the owners, contributors and society.   3

6. *I feel ...*
   a. Technology in business is very important.   1
   b. Technology is important but so are people.   2
   c. People are more important than technology.   3

7. *I believe ...*
   a. Employee personal problems must be left at home.   1
   b. We recognize that employees have needs beyond their economic needs.   2
   c. We hire the whole person.   3

8. *I feel ...*
   a. That government is best which governs least.   1
   b. Government is a necessary evil.   2

c. Business and government must co-operate to solve society's problems.   3
9. *I think ...*
a. The natural environment controls the destiny of humankind.   1
b. Human beings can control and manipulate the environment.   2
c. We must preserve the environment in order to lead a quality life.   3

10. *Business ethics are ...*
a. Bunk.   1
b. Worth considering.   2
c. Essential.   3

Score: 10–13 – Profit-maximizing management: You feel that managers have one primary responsibility to society, that is to underwrite the country's economic growth and oversee the accumulation of wealth. Business managers should pursue, almost single-mindedly, the objective of maximizing profits. Neither the principle of charity nor the principle of stewardship should play an influential role in shaping corporate social responsibility because what is good for business is good for the country.

14–22 – Trusteeship management: You feel organizations have to respond to the demands of both internal and external groups, such as shareholders, customers, suppliers and creditors. Consequently, organizations should shift their orientation to trusteeship management, in which it is the job of corporate managers to maintain an equitable balance among the competing interests of all groups with a stake in the organization.

23–30 – Quality-of-life management: You believe that the pressure on managers to behave in socially responsible ways should be intensified. Issues such as poverty, pollution and deteriorating inner cities raise widespread concern about the quality of life. Managers have to do more than achieve narrow growth economic goals. They need to manage the quality of life by helping to develop solutions for society's ills.

EQ

Is emotional intelligence (EI) a crafty oxymoronic book title aimed at the naïve manager, or a genuine intellectual breakthrough? Is EI (like MI – military intelligence), like any of those other funny, sweet-and-sour observations: business ethics, Australian culture, social science or industrial action? Do you need a bigger EQ than IQ to succeed at work, or is this merely an old, rather simple idea, dressed up in jargon?

Psychologists have argued and demonstrated that intelligence and emotionality are unrelated. They are orthogonal factors that have no influence on one another. Measures of intelligence are of *maximum* performance; those of emotionality of *typical* performance. Now, we are told that EI is a type of social intelligence that involves the ability to monitor one's own and others' emotion, to discriminate between them, and to use this information to guide one's thinking and activities. True to political correctness, the opposite of intelligent is not dim (thick, underpowered), but illiterate, the implication being that one can be taught EI.

EI, it seems, is an umbrella concept that covers six related areas: recognizing your own emotions, regulating your own emotions, using your emotions to motivate yourself, empathizing by being aware of and understanding the emotions of others, recognizing others' emotions, and managing others' emotions.

So, why has this mish-mash of psychobabble and common sense attracted so much popular attention? The answer is simple: EI explains everything, from poor performance at work to disintegrating managers. Daniel Goleman, in his book Emotional Intelligence (Bloomsbury, 1996), wrote a chapter called 'Managing with heart'. He argued that teamwork, open lines of communication, co-operation, listening and speaking one's mind are characteristics of EI and essential at work.

We are told that empathy and compassion are in, and that the manipulative jungle fighter boss is out. Leadership and being a good manager are about being attuned to the feelings of those people that managers have to deal with (up, sideways and down). Goleman argues for three basic applications of EI – being able to see grievances as helpful critiques, which is using feedback effectively; creating an atmosphere in which diversity (the really 'in' buzzword) is valued, rather than a source of friction; and networking effectively.

The real test is this: would you prefer the CEO of your company to have a high EQ or IQ? Yes, of course you want both, but they are not found too close together in nature. So do you want a cold but clever boss, who understands the business, keeps his/her eye firmly on the bottom line, reads the market signals, but is a little clumsy, shy and gauche? Or would you prefer the perceptive, empathic, socially adept boss, equally able to charm customers, employees and the media?

The former, high-IQ person, may be respected but not particularly liked, but the latter is often greatly loved if not respected for his/her business acumen. It is not usual to find a boss with both high IQ and EQ. Perhaps the best solution is to have a good mix of IQ and EQ on the board – yes, of course, but could they get on with one another? One suspects that the bright might despise the warm, who are in turn offended by what they perceive to be intellectual arrogance.

But the good news is that whereas IQ can't be learnt, EQ can. You can learn various intellectual tricks, but it is really not likely that you can raise your (adult) IQ much. On the other hand, it is easy to acquire EQ skills. There are plenty of courses that teach this sort of stuff. They are variously labelled 'social skills', 'interpersonal skills', 'assertiveness', 'counselling' and 'communication skills'.

So, what one needs, in the old-fashioned terminology of one's parents, is charm and rapport. Forget the MBA, destroy the spreadsheet, and take up Dale Carnegie, whose 50-year-old books are still in print.

How about a rough and ready estimate of your own EQ? Try the following:

		True	False
1.	I often try to understand my workers by imagining how things look from their perspective.	T	F
2.	I really get involved with characters in a novel I read or a film I watch.	T	F
3.	I often have tender feelings for people at work less fortunate than me.	T	F
4.	I hate to be tense in an emotional situation.	T	F
5.	My feelings are not easily hurt at work.	T	F
6.	People tell me that I am very aware of the feelings of others.	T	F
7.	I believe that I am pretty good at making other people like me.	T	F
8.	I sometimes appear to others to be experiencing deeper emotions than I actually am.	T	F
9.	I have no trouble changing my behaviour to adapt to different people and situations.	T	F
10.	I tend to be what people expect of me.	T	F
11.	I can become fairly excitable in a major crisis.	T	F
12.	I have little difficulty in devoting myself to others fairly completely.	T	F
13.	I have a reputation for being very warm in my relations with others.	T	F
14.	I am pretty perceptive with other people.	T	F
15.	I am not afraid to show strong emotion (cry) in appropriate circumstances.	T	F
16.	I am a good conciliator with strongly antagonistic groups.	T	F
17.	I find it easy to make friends with others in the workplace.	T	F
18.	I am always very aware of the impact of what I say and how I say it on the person on the receiving end.	T	F
19.	I have no difficulty in giving colleagues and subordinates warm praise for the work they do.	T	F
20.	I have often been told by people at work that I really understand them.	T	F

Total up the 'Ts' that you gave.

Score 15–20: You either have a very high EQ or have seen through the whole thing
Score 11–14: A pretty normal, sensitive person, with sufficient EQ
Score 6–10: A bit low on EQ – fancy a social skills workshop or empathy seminar?
Score 1–5: Oh dear ... an emotional illiterate from a broken home or a minor public school

The impostor syndrome

It is said that behind every successful man there stands an astounded woman. What is less often said is that many talented, conspicuously hard-working and able people who have achieved success somehow believe that they do not deserve it. In fact, they believe that they are impostors. Those who feel they are impostors seem to have difficulty accepting and enjoying the success that they earn. Many handicap themselves by stumbling through life, setting unrealistic goals they know that they (or anyone else) can never achieve. Feeling an undeserving person can be dangerously self-fulfilling.

The feelings may develop because of particular early parental expectations, or because their teachers and peers never expected them to succeed. So when they did, they assumed it was chance and that, equally by chance, their success might go away. Or, just as frequently, they may have been led to expect moderate success in another field. Thus, if a sporty type became a successful businessman, he/she may believe he/she is an impostor because success may not be due to business acumen and knowledge, but the fact that people like and admire sporting fitness and prowess. As Oscar Wilde shrewdly noted: 'In this world, there are only two tragedies. One is not getting what we want, and the other is getting it.' Sometimes, depression follows success because people with the impostor syndrome worry: 'where do I go from here?' Some believe that because they are impostors, they cannot continue to be successful – and make sure they fail!

One of the greatest dangers of the impostor syndrome is that of self-handicapping. This is a piece of psychobabble which refers to the many self-defeating actions that successful people use to impede success or justify failure. Drink, drugs and damsels may be used to achieve the strategic goal: in excess each interferes with a person's ability to perform as well as they could were it not for the handicap. This tactic enables many a self-defined impostor to attempt to obscure the meaning of subsequent evaluations. The prototype of a career self-handicapper is the alcoholic who began his drinking after his/her career was marked by early success, a lucky break or an important act so spectacular that it seems impossible to equal, let alone surpass. Of course, chronic procrastination, depression and panic attacks will also do to justify failure in anticipation of performance evaluation.

In an empirical demonstration of self-handicapping strategies in action, two psychologists asked two groups of students to work on a problem-solving task. One group received problems that were soluble, but the other unknowingly worked on problems that had no solutions. Before proceeding to a second problem-solving session, each was given a choice of two drugs that were ostensibly of interest to the experimenter. One of these drugs was supposed to enhance performance; the other was described as impairing performance. The students who had previously worked on solvable problems generally chose the drug that would improve their performance. The other group, whose experience probably led them to believe that they might not do well on the next task either, showed a strong preference for the interfering drug. By handicapping themselves with a drug, they provided themselves with a convenient excuse in case they did poorly on the second task. What they had done was to prepare a good explanation for their possible failure.

But don't panic! One can be taught, quite easily, to avoid the success impostor syndrome and the nagging feeling that one is an impostor. A few quite specific issues need to be addressed. First, challenging the expectations of oneself and others derived from success. Next, one needs to redirect attention to the *process* of succeeding rather than the products of success. It is also important to learn to accept affection and admiration from others, without believing all are sycophants after the spoils of success. Successful people also need to avoid the tendency to withdraw from, or be passive in, developing or maintaining personal relationships. The scorn (or paranoia) that successful people develop for those who pursue them is a naturally occurring psychological response to being in a position where they never have a need to initiate social contacts.

'Success', said American poet Emily Dickinson, 'is counted sweetest by those who ne'er succeeded.' Paradoxically, real success, just like failure, may be difficult to deal with.

How comfortable are you with success?

Below are statements indicating feelings and attitudes about yourself and your abilities. Please indicate how true you feel these statements are as they apply to you, using the guidelines below: 1 represents 'not true at all' and 4 'very true'.

1.	I feel that other people tend to believe I am more competent than I am.	1	2	3	4
2.	I am certain my present level of achievement reflects my abilities.	1	2	3	4
3.	Sometimes I am afraid I will be discovered for who or what I really am.	1	2	3	4
4.	I find it easy to accept compliments about my intelligence because they are mainly true.	1	2	3	4
5.	I feel I deserve the awards, recognition and praise I regularly receive.	1	2	3	4
6.	At times, I have felt I am in my present job and salary level through some kind of mistake.	1	2	3	4
7.	I feel pretty confident that I will succeed in the future.	1	2	3	4
8.	I often tend to feel like an upstart.	1	2	3	4
9.	Fortunately, my personality often makes a strong impression on people in authority.	1	2	3	4
10.	So far, my accomplishments for my stage in life are perfectly adequate.	1	2	3	4
11.	I am not sure why I have achieved the success I have.	1	2	3	4
12.	I often achieve success on a project when I think I may have failed.	1	2	3	4
13.	I often feel I am concealing secrets about myself from others.	1	2	3	4
14.	My public and private self are precisely the same.	1	2	3	4
15.	Very few people really know how average I am.	1	2	3	4
16.	Most of my success is due to 'lucky breaks' I have exploited.	1	2	3	4

Scoring: Add together the scores on items 1, 3, 6, 8, 9, 11, 12, 13, 15, 16. Then reverse score (1=4, 2=3, 3=2, 4=1) items 2, 4, 5, 7, 10, 14 and add them to the first list.

0–20: You're fine, don't panic
21–40: Perhaps you deserve the success you have
41+: A possible, or potential, victim of the success syndrome: watch your self-handicapping strategies.

Money madness

Nearly everyone is in business to make money. But saying so, indeed, talking seriously and honestly about money at all, is pretty rare. Money matters are frequently discussed – the rate of tax, cost of living, property prices – but personal finance still remains a taboo topic. Celebrities and ordinary mortals seem happier to talk about the intimate ramifications of their sex lives and mental health than about their monetary status, salary or financial transactions. Secrets about money matters do not occur in all cultures. In the openly materialistic cultures of South-East Asia, enquiries into others' and open discussion of one's own financial affairs seem quite acceptable. In our culture, money issues are often denied, overlooked or ignored in courtship, argued about constantly in marriage, and the focus of many divorce proceedings. Contested wills between different claimants can turn mild-mannered, reasonable human beings into irrational bigots.

Many philosophers and playwrights have written about the irrational, immoral and downright bizarre things that people do with, and for, money. The media frequently focus on compulsive savers and hoarders (who live in poverty but die with millions in the bank), or compulsive spenders who recklessly run through fortunes often obtained unexpectedly. The former are compelled to save money with the same urgency that the latter seem driven to lose it. Robbery, forgery, embezzlement, kidnapping, smuggling and product-faking are all quite often simply money-motivated.

The dream to become rich is widespread. Many cultures have fairy tales, folklore and well-known stories about wealth. This dream of money has several themes. One is that money brings security, another that it brings freedom. Money can be used to show off one's success as well as to repay those who in the past slighted, rejected or humiliated one. One of the many themes in literature is that wealth renders the powerless powerful and the unloved lovable. Wealth is a great transforming agent that has the power to cure all. Hence the common desire for wealth and the extreme behaviours sometimes seen in pursuit of extreme wealth.

There are two rather different basic fairy tales associated with money. One is that money and riches are just deserts for a good life. Further, this money should be enjoyed and spent wisely for the benefit of all. The other story is of the ruthless destroyer of others who sacrifices love and happiness for money, and eventually gets it but finds it is of no use. Hence, all he or she can do is give it away with the same fanaticism with which he or she amassed it.

Money is a hot topic because it has powerful associations. It can stand for *security*. Emotional security is represented by financial security and the relationship is believed to be linear – more money, more security. Money is an emotional lifejacket, a security blanket, a method to stave off anxiety. Evidence for this is, as always, clinical reports and archival research in the biographies of rich people. Yet turning to money for security can alienate people because significant others are seen as a less powerful source of security. Building an emotional wall around themselves can lead to fear and paranoia about being hurt, rejected or deprived by others. A fear of financial loss becomes paramount because the security collector supposedly depends more and more on money for ego-satisfaction. Money bolsters feelings of safety and self-esteem.

Money, of course, also represents *power*. Because money can buy goods, services and loyalty, it can be used to acquire importance, domination and control. Money can be used to buy out or compromise enemies and clear the path for oneself. Money and the power it brings can be seen as a search to regress to infantile fantasies of omnipotence.

Money is *love*. For some, money is given as a substitute for emotion and affection. Money is used to buy loyalty and self-worth. Further, because of the reciprocity principle inherent in gift-giving, many assume that reciprocated gifts are a token of love and caring.

And for many people, money is *freedom*. This is the more acceptable and more frequently admitted attribute attached to money. It buys time to pursue one's whims and interests, and frees one from the daily routine and restrictions of a paid job.

Because of all the complicated emotions and associations of money, there are a number of pathologies surrounding money. Five are well known:

1. The *miser*, who hoards money. They tend not to admit to being niggardly, have a terrible fear of losing funds, and tend to be distrustful, yet have trouble enjoying the benefits of their own money.
2. The *spendthrift*, who tends to be compulsive and uncontrolled in his/her spending and does so particularly when depressed, feeling worthless and rejected. Spending is an instant, but short-lived gratification that frequently leads to guilt (and debt).
3. The *tycoon*, who is totally absorbed with money-making, which is seen as the best way to gain power status and approval. They argue that the more money they have, the better control they have over their world and the happier they are likely to be.
4. The *bargain-hunter*, who compulsively hunts bargains even if they do not really want them, because getting things for less makes people feel superior. They feel angry and depressed if they have to pay the asking price or cannot bring the price down significantly.
5. The *gambler*, who feels exhilarated and optimistic when taking chances. They tend to find it difficult to stop, even when losing, because of the sense of power they achieve when winning.

But perhaps there is no way to be normal with money. As Vic Oliver observed: 'If a man runs after money, he's money-mad; if he keeps it, he's a capitalist; if he spends it, he's a playboy; if he doesn't try to get it, he lacks ambition; if he gets it without working, he's a parasite; and if he accumulates it after a lifetime of hard work, people call him a fool who never got anything out of life.' So how normal or sane are you about money? Consider the following 20 questions. Circle 'y' for yes or 'n' for no.

Questions	Yes	No
1. Do you find yourself worrying about getting or spending money most of the time?	Y	N
2. Are you very inhibited about talking to others about your money (income, investments, savings)?	Y	N
3. Do you buy things you don't need because they are said to be bargains?	Y	N
4. Do you invest considerable effort in attempting to find out a way to spend less money and save more?	Y	N
5. Have you often been told that you are careful with money?	Y	N
6. Do you regularly exceed the spending limit on your credit cards?	Y	N
7. Does gambling give you an unforgettable burst of excitement?	Y	N
8. Would you happily walk a long distance to save an easily affordable bus fare?	Y	N
9. Are you constantly puzzled about where your money goes and why there seems to be none left at the end of the month?	Y	N
10. Do you sometimes use money (be honest, now!) to control or manipulate others?	Y	N
11. Do you refuse to take money seriously, believing that it is not that important?	Y	N
12. Do you resent having to pay the full price for any item when you shop?	Y	N
13. Do you regularly lavish presents on others?	Y	N
14. Do you spend a large proportion of your free time shopping?	Y	N
15. When you legitimately ask for money from others, are you overcome by guilt or anxiety?	Y	N
16. Are you increasingly anxious about whether you can pay your bills each month?	Y	N
17. Do you spend money on others but have problems spending it on yourself?	Y	N
18. Are you addicted to retail therapy – shopping when angry, depressed or upset?	Y	N
19. Are you reluctant to learn about practical money matters, like paying bills?	Y	N
20. Do you think about your finances all the time?	Y	N

A. Score five yes's or less and you're OK. You are unlikely to suffer from any major form of money madness. After all, 'it's only money'.

B. Score over 13 and you may be classed as obsessive. Others must have remarked on this pathology. You may need help – but for goodness' sake, don't go to an 'independent financial adviser'.

C. Score between 6 and 12 and you're pretty normal, but depending on which questions you answered yes to, you may have a hint of the miser or spendthrift about you.

Remember what Henry Ford said: 'There are two fools in this world. One is the millionaire who thinks that by hoarding money, he can somehow accumulate real power, and the other is the penniless reformer who thinks that if he can only take the money from one class and give it to another, all the world's ills will be cured.'

Music while you work

One of the more enduring black-and-white images of the Second World War, and its associated grim years of rationing, is of teams of young women faking pleasure by rhythmically moving to 'music while you work'. The message was that even tedious, humdrum, mundane tasks performed to 'catchy tunes' made for higher productivity and better morale.

There are reports of surgeons who like to operate to music. Presumably, one can always choose appropriate music to fit the complaint – Handel's *Water Music* for those suffering from bladder problems; the *1812 Overture* for excessive flatulence; Schubert's *'Unfinished'* for plastic surgery; Dvořák's *New World Symphony* for childbirth; and Mendelssohn's *Fingal's Cave* for stomach ulcers.

Since the turn of the 20th century, industrial psychologists have been interested in the possible benefits of music at work. They found that feelings of euphoria during periods of musical stimulation had a physiological basis (changes in blood pressure), which could help with certain types of work. It seemed that young, inexperienced employees engaged in doing simple, repetitive, monotonous tasks increased their output when stimulated by music.

But they also found that not all workers like music. About one in 10 complain, and the number increases sharply with age. Further, quality of work can be adversely affected by the use of music in the work environment.

Early studies showed that the benefits of background music depended as much on the type of music as on the task performed. Simple rather than complex, instrumental rather than vocal, quiet rather than loud was preferred and was beneficial overall. Schoolchildren who claim not only to be able, but to be better at doing their homework with television in the background are simply deluding themselves. Builders, plumbers and 'rude mechanicals' who insist on inane pop stations played loudly so as to annoy others are unlikely to be distracted from their physical labour. It may make the time pass more quickly, but it is not likely to improve communication.

Some shops play 'background music' or Muzak. Some follow research advice, which suggests that slow, quiet, repetitive, low-information music provides optimally arousing conditions. Others like to play seasonal music – carols at Christmas and Caribbean music in the summer – to focus customers' attention on certain products. Others, often shops with products aimed at young people, play pop music loudly, both as an attractant into the shop as well as a stimulant to the attention-deficit customers inside. But does it increase sales?

Music can be used to soothe, but also to excite. It is often an effective mood indicator, as all movie-goers know. But what is its effect at work? Some people have radios, tape recorders and CD players in their offices and workspaces. Many listen to the car radio, and the odd Walkman can still be seen on the odd walking man. Essentially, for most, non-routine office work, music, or indeed any background information, be it music, speech or pictures, is a distraction. And because distractions distract, they have a poor effect on performance.

Music certainly can help relieve boredom in tedious tasks like driving. But listening to a complex play on the radio while negotiating the traffic may increase rather than lessen the likelihood of accidents. The human information processor simply becomes overloaded.

Generally, extroverts like and need distraction more than introverts. Stimulus-hungry, they can be quite comfortable working in noisy environments. In fact, they may create noise if it is too quiet. Introverts, on the other hand, because they are usually cognitively overaroused, actively seek 'peace and quiet' to work in. Being chronically underaroused (like an engine cutting out), an extrovert's whole life is dedicated to finding stimulus fixes. Their impulsivity, sociability and excitability are all a function of their need for stimulus; whereas introverts, who are overaroused, seek the precise opposite. Music is just another stimulus. Extroverts concentrate for longer on mundane, mechanized tasks with music, and their performance on complex, concentration-demanding tasks is less inhibited by music than introverts'.

So, if you run an assembly plant employing extroverts, you should seriously consider the idea of introducing a good sound system. But if you have introverted workers, ban radios and keep noise levels down. Perhaps that is why the latter group is so opposed to open-plan offices.

What about your working habits?

		Agree					Disagree	
1.	I prefer to have background music at work or while I'm reading.	7	6	5	4	3	2	1
2.	I have difficulty concentrating if the room is absolutely quiet.	7	6	5	4	3	2	1
3.	I feel comfortable if the TV or radio is on while I work, or read or concentrate on something different.	7	6	5	4	3	2	1
4.	When working or concentrating I like to be in a place where other people are talking or working.	7	6	5	4	3	2	1
5.	I turn on all the lights in my work area when I am concentrating.	7	6	5	4	3	2	1
6.	I like to read or take my difficult work outdoors	7	6	5	4	3	2	1
7.	I prefer to work independently, and concentrate better when I am alone.	7	6	5	4	3	2	1
8.	I don't like working in groups.	7	6	5	4	3	2	1
9.	I am more productive at work and study better when I am by myself.	7	6	5	4	3	2	1
10.	I don't need a lot of help while working or studying.	7	6	5	4	3	2	1
11.	I work and concentrate better with another person present.	7	6	5	4	3	2	1
12.	I often need to stand up, stretch and take a short break, then come back to my work.	7	6	5	4	3	2	1
13.	It's really difficult for me to sit in one place for a long time.	7	6	5	4	3	2	1
14	Sometimes I pace around the room, office or hall when I'm working, reading or concentrating.	7	6	5	4	3	2	1
15.	I don't like interruptions or having to get up when I'm working.	7	6	5	4	3	2	1

Now add up 1–6, 11–14. Reverse scores (that is, 7=1, 6=2, 5=3, 4=4, 3=5, 2=6, 1=7) for 7–10, 15, then add to amount. Scores between 15 and 65.

50–65 An extreme extrovert whose liking for stimulation may adversely impact on complex work

41–50 You may be quite happy working in an open-plan office

26–40 A pretty normal response to stimulation: an 'ambivert' who likes a moderate amount of audio and visual stimulation

16–25 An introvert, easily distracted by others and music

0–15 An extreme noise- and stimulation-sensitive introvert, who needs a sensory deprivation room to work at their best

Personality and being pissed off at work.

What causes job satisfaction? Is job satisfaction a necessary precursor of, or a simple consequence of, productivity at work and the reward that it brings? Or is job satisfaction more a function of the individual personality and values than anything else?

Over 40 years, a group of US researchers made a startlingly obvious discovery. They found on interviewing a fairly large number of people in depth that self-reported job satisfaction depends on a particular set of characteristics/conditions, whereas job dissatisfaction is usually the result of an unrelated and different set of work-related conditions.

According to the theory, people have two major types of needs: *hygiene needs*, which are influenced by the physical and psychological conditions in which people work, and *motivator needs*. Hygiene needs were said to be satisfied by the level of certain conditions called hygiene factors or dissatisfiers, which are all concerned with the context or environment in which the job has to be done. When these factors are unfavourable, then, according to the theory, job dissatisfaction results. Conversely, when hygiene factors are positive, then barriers to job satisfaction are removed. However, the fulfilment of hygiene needs *cannot in itself* result in job satisfaction, but only in the reduction or elimination of dissatisfaction.

Unlike hygiene needs, motivation needs are fulfilled by motivator factors or satisfiers. Thus, whereas hygiene factors are related to the context of work, motivation factors are concerned with the nature of that work itself and the consequences of work. According to the theory, the factors that lead to job satisfaction are those that satisfy an individual's need for self-actualization (self-fulfilment) in their work, and it is only from the performance of the task that individuals can enjoy the rewards that will reinforce their aspirations. Compared with hygiene factors, which result in a 'neutral state' (neither satisfied nor dissatisfied) when present, positive motivator factors supposedly result in job satisfaction. When recognition, responsibility and other motivator factors are absent from a job, however, the result will not be dissatisfaction, as with the absence of hygiene factors, but rather the same neutral state associated with the presence of hygiene factors.

This theory led to the widespread enthusiasm for job enrichment (rotating, enlarging jobs), defined as an attempt by management to design tasks in such a way as to build in the opportunity for personal achievement, recognition, challenge and individual growth. It provided workers with more responsibility and autonomy in carrying out a complete task, and with timely feedback on their performance.

Two recent studies have added some interesting new insights into the job satisfaction conundrum. Behavioural geneticists working with identical twin adults separated at birth found that job satisfaction, like intelligence and personality, was substantially heritable. In other words, it is not only features of the job itself that determine satisfaction but the characteristics of the jobholder. Most of us actually know the whingeing, whining, complaining, job-dissatisfied person who wanders from job to job complaining each time about the same issues.

A second study found personality correlates of the two factors – motivation and hygiene – discussed above. The researchers found that extroverts were very sensitive to the motivator factors whereas neurotics were highly sensitive to the hygiene factors. This confirms other theoretical work, which asserts that extroverts will respond more readily to reward whereas introverts react primarily to punishment. The extrovert is motivated to gain a promised reward; the introvert is motivated to avoid a threatened punishment.

Also, the overapplication of the principle tends to lessen the intended effects, dampening the motivational qualities of reward and punishment: because the extrovert is motivated by opportunity to gain reward, too much rewarding reinforcement tends to create a sating effect on the extrovert's desire to achieve. Since the introvert is motivated by a need to avoid punishment, too many threats or actual enforcement of the negative reinforcement places the introvert in the position of being unable to avoid punishment, and so he/she becomes immobilized and the motivational effect of punishment is decreased.

The motivating effects of reward and punishment are not mutually exclusive: an extrovert does not wish to be punished, and will react to negative reinforcement; and all introverts want to be rewarded and are motivated by positive reinforcement.

Neuroticism is a powerful predictor of life and work satisfaction. Neurotics are more powerfully attracted to, and motivated by, extrinsic physical factors than stable people. Indeed, some European reviewers have found neuroticism one of the most powerful trait predictors of all aspects of job performance. Neurotics are more sensitive to hygiene factors which are likely to lead to dissatisfaction, rather than those which are related to satisfaction. This may account for the observation that it is the worker with negative affectivity (neurotics) who is most likely to express by self-report (complaints) and behaviour (absenteeism) their dissatisfaction with various extrinsic factors in the workplace.

Below are 18 characteristics many people look for in a job. Put a tick next to 9 of these only, representing those job facets you value most:

Opportunity for personal growth at work ____
Job security (permanent job) ____
Use of your ability (knowledge at work) ____
Supervisor (fair and considerate boss) ____
Recognition of doing a good job ____
Convenient hours of work ____
Responsibility (empowerment) ____
Job status ____
Achievement at work ____
Opportunity to interact with people ____
Influence in the workplace ____
Benefits (good vacation, sick leave and so on) ____
Interesting work ____
Co-workers (pleasant fellow workers) ____
Advancement (chances for promotion) ____
Pay (the amount of money that you get) ____
Meaningful, important work ____
Work conditions (comfortable and clean) ____

Scoring: Odd numbers total = Motivation factors
Even numbers total = Hygiene factors

The higher the motivational score and therefore the lower your hygiene score, the happier you are at work and the more stable you are psychologically.

Schadenfreude

Is there anything quite as sweet as seeing a loathed work colleague fall from grace after a career-limiting decision? Is it not true that one really believes there is justice in the world when a particularly nasty, vindictive and egocentric boss gets the flick in an organizational restructuring? And is it not immensely satisfying to see some cocky, computer-obsessed high-flyer have to admit that the old way of doing things is the best? Of course it is.

The British press, it seems, enjoy nothing more than placing people on sky-expanding pedestals one moment and then rejoicing in knocking them over the next. We are, it seems, deeply ambivalent about success – admiring and praising it the one moment, but being spitefully envious the next. The film star, the celebrity, the business person has always to pay the price of their success and fame. What the press giveth, the press taketh away. The tabloids seem masters of the art of *schadenfreude*. But do they mirror the society in which they dwell or somehow encourage its excesses? Are we masters of a concept – *schadenfreude* – we can't even pronounce properly?

We all like to believe that the world is just. All good films and books make sure the good guys win out in the end – the hero, dressed in white, accompanied by the beautiful and wronged damsel, gallop off together into the sunset. But alas, we all know from bitter experience that it is not a just world. The rain seems to fall on the just and unjust alike. Hence, it is especially galling when the second-rate, the dishonest, the plainly opportunistic, succeed. We long to see them fall, and rejoice at the sight of it.

But it is also true that many of us seem equally pleased with the deserving faulter. Sometimes, rather than feel sorry for the demise of the beautiful, the talented and the rich, we (somewhat guiltily) enjoy seeing their fall from grace. For every *Hello* magazine celebrity success there are dozens of *Private Eyes* rejoicing in the come-uppance of the erstwhile successful. The trouble is that they do not distinguish between the deserving and the undeserving; the good and the bad; the talented and the talentless. In fact, the pleasure experienced at seeing the mighty fall is often a direct function of the perceived genuine talent relative to our own.

A sense of humour is mostly a keen appreciation of someone else's misfortune. We are, nearly all of us, far from indifferent to the fortunes of our fellows at work. We are taught that it is appropriate and correct to be happy for the success of others, and to empathize when things go wrong. But many of us envy the success of others. Envy is painful: it means that we lack something that is important to us. The worst part of envy is the resulting sense of inferiority, which is why it is such an affecting and unwelcome emotion. It can 'eat into' one and act as a powerful negative force.

Schadenfreude – pleasure at another's suffering – is often an enjoyable emotion. It results from the readiness with which people feel pleased when an envied or disliked person suffers a minor setback or major misfortune. *Schadenfreude* may be pleasurable for different reasons. It may lead to personal and direct gain – the job of a sacked superior – but it also reduces painful envy. Equally, *schadenfreude* often helps one believe again that the world is just – because, all too often, those who give us pleasure by their fall are those who we believe attained their position by unethical means in the first place – or so we like to think.

It is really not clear whether *schadenfreude* is a politically correct emotion or not. We are supposed to approve of those whose corrupt, exploitative pursuits lead them to fall from grace – but not really enjoy the experience. Certainly, we are not supposed to relish the successful business person who makes a serious one-off error, such as Gerald Ratner's remark about his own products. After all, a temporary lapse of judgement can hardly mean that the world is a just place.

Schadenfreude is a word too difficult for Australians. They have their own – the tall poppy syndrome. This is the culturally approved act of cutting down, demolishing or severely impairing a person who has outshone or outperformed others. It is a way of dealing with envy and reducing everybody to the mediocre.

The trouble with the tall poppy syndrome is that it celebrates the average and the mediocre. It can also stifle innovation and industry. 'Tall poppies' may grow, in human terms, because they are exceptionally able, very motivated or simply positioned to understand and exploit the conditions around them. Being jealous of, and attempting to insist on conformity in the talented is, for the group as a whole, deeply short-sighted. To celebrate and learn from the success of the talented is indeed healthy.

The trick lies in distinguishing those who fully deserve their success and those who have tricked, lied or bamboozled their way to the job. If we really believe that we live in a just world then it is perfectly acceptable to experience *schadenfreude* with the latter but not with the former. Organizations can exhibit or indeed condone *schadenfreude*. This can be seen in how they deal with success and failure of top people. The usual trick is 'celebrate success' in a rather stylized spin-doctorish sort of way, while 'brushing under the carpet' or worse 'telling half truths about' those who fall from grace. The real *schadenfreude* values, however, can be spotted in how one describes and lampoons one's enemy. You can bet that if it's OK to experience *schadenfreude* about people in rival companies falling from grace, it's also OK to do the same with people in one's own organization!

To help you find out if you indulge in *schadenfreude*, complete the following questionnaire, circling either 'T' for true or 'F' for false:

		True	False
1.	People who are very successful deserve all the rewards they get from their achievements.	T	F
2.	It's really good to see very successful people fail occasionally.	T	F
3.	Very successful people often get too big for their boots.	T	F
4.	I resent the fact that some people have the money to buy all the things they want.	T	F
5.	At work, it's probably better for people to be average than at the very top of annual appraisals.	T	F
6.	People shouldn't criticize or knock the very successful in our society.	T	F
7.	Very successful people who fall from the top usually deserve their fall from grace.	T	F
8.	Those who are very successful in business ought to come down from their pedestals and be like ordinary people.	T	F
9.	The very successful person deserves public recognition for his/her accomplishments (that is, honours such as knighthoods).	T	F
10.	Arrogant, successful business people should be cut down to size.	T	F
11.	One should always respect the self-made person at the top.	T	F
12.	Generally, I feel sympathetic towards the very successful people when they experience failure and fall on hard times.	T	F
13.	Very successful people sometimes need to be brought down a peg or two, even if they have done nothing wrong.	T	F
14.	Our society needs a lot of very high achievers who we should support and not envy.	T	F
15.	People who always do a lot better than others need to learn about what it's like to fail.	T	F
16.	I admit to being intensely envious of certain work colleagues.	T	F
17.	It's very important for society to support and encourage people who are very successful.	T	F
18.	Generally, I am satisfied with my abilities compared with other people.	T	F
19.	Very successful people usually succeed at the expense of other people.	T	F
20.	Successful people who are at the top of their profession are usually fun to be with.	T	F

Give yourself 1 if you scored:
True: 2, 3, 7, 8, 10, 13, 15, 16, 19
False: 1, 4, 5, 6, 9, 11, 12, 14, 17, 18, 20

Score 0–8 You are an empathic meritocrat, quite happy with your lot.
Score 0–13 At times a little resentful and envious of the successful in our society, you suspect that many have got to the top by means other than their ability and effort.
Score 14–20 A connoisseur of the spectacle of the fallen *wunderkind*, you are the person who put the Freud in *schadenfreude*.

Teleworking

What happened to teleworking? The promise by some business gurus was that the costs and frustrations of commuting to work in business clothes just to be interrupted by underemployed meeting addicts was a thing of the past. Millennium workers will, it seems, give and receive 'nil by mouth' at work – it is screen-to-screen interaction from now on.

The data on the expansion of the electronic collage may be pretty unreliable, but everything indicates that it is rapidly expanding. A recent US study showed that 62% of companies encouraged telecommuting in 1996, up from 40% in 1994. In late 1997, more than 10 million Americans telecommuted and nearly 70% of 500 companies employed telecommuters. European data are less reliable, but a similar growth pattern indicates that the virtual workplace is a reality now. *Investors in People* commissioned a British study, which showed that 73% of companies responding had 'arrangements in place for teleworking'.

The 'seamless web of technology' seems to allow us to choose when and where to work, and who to make into a virtual team. However, seamlessness could also spell endlessness and the distinction between home and office disappears. Not surprisingly, though, the techno-gurus are wildly excited by the prospects of the networked electronic cottage organization (NECO).

The idealized picture of the home-based teleworker was the handsome (male, but more often female) executive dressed in designer tracksuit in a state-of-the-art IT office composed of blond wood, shiny chrome and sleek computers. The office would be attached to a beautiful home in a rural idyll. Reduced commuting would help the greener and cleaner environment. And the happy teleworker had ultimate flexibility. They could structure all the work around their personal commitments – children, aged parents, animals and so on. The Internet, with e-mail, the fax machine and the new generation of computers, we were told, would be the superior new medium of communication. We could all work in our preferred space, at our preferred time of day, in comfortable clothes and free from petty and trivial interruptions.

One study on telecommuters found that they reported being 40% more productive while working away from the office, mainly because they have fewer distractions. Another study conducted by telecoms giant AT&T found that telecommuters were so happy that one said they would look for another job if they were forced back into the old office.

Even more impressive, people could be virtual teams that may never meet but have total access to one another. The advantages were listed:

- teleworking eliminates lack of access to experts – everyone is on line, all the time
- intercontinental teams can be formed – proximity is not an issue
- consultants can be hired and do not need to charge travel, lodgings and downtime
- one can hire the best people in the world to join the network at negligible cost
- people can easily be part of different teams at the same time
- because everything is on line, swift responses to any event, including demands of the market, are possible.

All upside and no downside, so it seemed.

Organizations were tempted to support this strategy, which claimed to encourage work in the non-traditional workplace. They were told that teleworking led to space savings, reduced absenteeism, greater retention, and therefore increased employee satisfaction leading to increased productivity. Indeed, teleworkers may even become independent of those costly things called pension plans and so on, and essentially become self-employed.

Yet the sceptic who wanted good evidence for these claims was usually frustrated because little evidence existed to prove that teleworking was better for all involved. The cost of all the IT equipment which had to be regularly updated seemed to be forgotten in the calculations. Some managers expressed their doubts (Hewlett-Packard teleworkers have to pay for their own equipment). Tele-employees were difficult to monitor. Were they at work? Were they producing anything? All that blue-sky thinking is all very well, but 'where's the beef?', as George Bush once remarked. Some suspected that it was no more than a type of paid child care. Was company family-friendliness going too far? Surely, teleworking was really only for those who did not need close supervision, regular feedback, and who could be trusted? Telecommuting really makes sense only with the right job, the right person, the right reason and the right boss. Those are pretty tall orders. Not all employees had such a suitable alternative location for teleworking – the quiet, spacious 'spare bedroom'. In fact, surprisingly few ordinary workers have a home environment conducive to any sort of work.

Other important issues seemed to go unanswered. How frequently should boss and teleworker be in touch; who is responsible for maintaining and insuring business equipment; what are the conditions of work; what are their measurable outputs of work? What do customers think of teleworkers? And, more importantly, what are the psychological needs of certain individuals that are not satisfied in the satellite telecottage? After all, office gossip and political games in the office are (reprehensible) fun. People are a source of stimulation. 'Shooting the breeze' with co-workers in an unstructured and casual way is great fun. Getting out of the house too can, in itself, be liberating.

Many people find teleworking alienating. Electronic communication is too cold, too impersonal. We are social animals built for social interaction, skilled at reading non-verbal cues, happy to be in contact groups.

An organized job gives one a sense of identity and loyalty. One study found that teleworkers gradually lost their identification with an interest in their organization, and vice versa. Out of sight, out of mind. Teleworkers can become forgotten telecolonial people.

Somewhat paradoxically, teleworkers need to be ambitious, self-disciplined, conscientious individuals. Yet, because they are so often forgotten, those types do not want to telework. The politically astute leaders of tomorrow know that the world is run by those who turn up to face-to-face meetings, attend breakfast briefings and cocktail parties and keep their eyes open. So, the less ambitious, the near-to-retirement, and the 'quality-of-life' brigade drift into teleworking – and they are precisely the types who are not really suited to it.

In the short term, telecommuting cuts costs. But the longer-term issues may be serious because by neglecting the psychological consequences of telecommuting, the short-term gains may easily turn into long-term losses.

How well suited would you be to teleworking? Try the following quiz:

		Yes	No
1.	Do you have a quiet, airy, spacious spare room at home?	Y	N
2.	Would you describe yourself as well organized and conscientious?	Y	N
3.	Are you perfectly happy with your own company?	Y	N
4.	Can you concentrate better in a very quiet environment?	Y	N
5.	Are you made exhausted by commuting to work?	Y	N
6.	Have you always been able to achieve things unsupervised?	Y	N
7.	Are you highly computer-literate?	Y	N
8.	Do you like working odd hours (that is, late at night, very early in the morning?)	Y	N
9.	Are most of your close friends drawn from circles outside work?	Y	N
10.	Do you know other people who are happy and contented teleworkers?	Y	N

Answer more than 7 yes's and you may make a happy teleworker.
Answer less than 3 yes's, and the likelihood is that you still enjoy office work.

Teleworking is certainly not ideal for everyone. Extroverts find that they get bored because they miss out on the daily contact. The ambitious discover that they are left out of the public-corporate loop. Sometimes, the extremely conscientious feel cheated because their boss cannot observe how genuinely hard they are working. And the brightest and best leave the organization because, as teleworkers, they are seen as cheap labour – the long-term consequences could be disastrous.